D0938580

THE CHINA TRADE

Wallpaper strip from the Carrington House, Providence, Rhode Island, circa 1810. 94″ × 44″. *Rhode Island Historical Society.*

THE CHINA TRADE

Export Paintings, Furniture
Silver & Other Objects

Carl L. Crossman

With a Foreword by Ernest S. Dodge

THE PYNE PRESS
Princeton

To ALMA CLEVELAND PORTER, who first awakened
my interest in the China trade, and

to RICHARD MILLS, who expanded and deepened it

Second printing, 1973
Library of Congress Catalog Card Number 72-79149
SBN 87861-031-6
Printed in the United States of America

Contents

List of Illustrations

Full color illustrations are indicated by the use of SMALL CAPITAL letters.

Frontispiece: WALLPAPER STRIP FROM THE CARRINGTON HOUSE, PROVIDENCE

Foreword

The recent surge in interest in things Chinese has been stimulated in part by political events; especially the Presidential visit to Peking. But the interest in China trade material, particularly paintings and porcelains, goes back far beyond that.

For some years everything connected with the American China trade has been receiving increased attention from collectors, antique dealers, art connoisseurs, galleries, and museums. This enthusiasm has been accompanied by increased knowledge and sophistication in the field and by a steady rise in prices.

No small part of present awareness and knowledge of China trade imports has been due to the assiduous research of Carl Crossman, the author of this book. He first became intrigued by China trade material while on the staff of the Peabody Museum of Salem. Indeed, his last chore as a staff member was organizing, arranging for, and installing the special exhibition of Chinese Export Porcelain at the Museum for the summer of 1964, one of the most penetrating, analytical, and definitive exhibitions of its kind ever mounted. The catalogue which he wrote for the occasion is a standard reference and has been reprinted.

Six years later, in 1970, he arranged another exhibition for the Museum on paintings, furniture, lacquer, ivory, silver—in short, everything excepting porcelain. This exhibition was equally successful, and the catalogue he prepared for it is another substantial contribution to the growing literature on the subject.

He has continued his interest in the China trade at the Childs Gallery. The articles, which he has had published in *Antiques* and elsewhere, have invariably added something new to our knowledge.

This book is the culmination of a decade of profitable research, study, and familiarity with China trade material. It is a book that fills a need and opens new horizons in our knowledge of the cultural manifestations inherited from nearly a century of Sino-American commercial relationships—the by-products of the trades in tea, silk, and opium.

The new information which the author has discovered regarding artists, merchants, ivory carvers, silversmiths, and shopkeepers is very great. His identification of schools of work, as well as the work of individuals, is a tribute to his tenacious sleuthing, his quick eye, and his penetrating mind. For the first time he has made it possible to be specific on a subject which hitherto has been mostly vague and obscure. He has taken a topic filled with myth and old wives' tales and set it on the road of exact scholarship. He is a catalyst in the field. My prediction is that this will not be the last book from his pen.

Ernest S. Dodge

Preface

A new awareness of how many objects and furnishings in the late eighteenth-century American home might have been made in China has developed over the past decade. Federal and Empire furniture, Western-style portraits, paintings on glass, and silver—hitherto thought to be American—have been identified as Chinese through scholarly research and historic documentation. As new discoveries are made, it becomes apparent that any object a Westerner wished to have made could have been produced in Canton both well and inexpensively.

During this period, nearly a fourth of the decorations and furniture found in the house of an American China trade merchant might well have been of Chinese manufacture. Floor carpets, window shades, draperies and other standard household decorations were imported in massive quantities. As more of these objects have been discovered, confusion has been increasing over what was actually made in China. Cane and wood sofas and couches and chairs in the Western style, which were made in China and used on vessels in the China trade, have been thought to be either English or American. The same is true of much of the bamboo furniture in what has been called the "Brighton Pavilion" style. This subject is discussed in depth in an attempt to resolve some of the questions inherent in a subject so complex.

The problems of the identification of Chinese export silver in the Western style have been scholarly resolved through the work and perseverance of John Devereux Kernan and H. A. Crosby Forbes. Since a full-scale book on the subject will be published shortly, only a summary chapter on the silver, with some of the important marks listed, has been presented here. The gift of the Oldham Collection of China trade fans to the Peabody Museum in Salem has made scholars and the public alike aware of how extraordinary and exotic some of the early fans were. Fans were an important trade item, dealt in by the tens of thousands, and it seemed necessary to devote an entire chapter to this new subject.

Several collectors have become aware of a number of early portraits of Western merchants which were done in Canton at the end of the eighteenth and the beginning of the nineteenth century. These portraits have been variously ascribed to European, English and American painters, but are, indeed, all Chinese works in the Western style. There have been vastly erroneous statements about those China trade paintings executed in the second quarter of the nineteenth century. The confusion over the relationship of George Chinnery to the Chinese port painters has been so involved and extensive, that groups of paintings by other known China trade port painters have been ascribed and attributed to the "Chinnery School." The discussion of Chinnery and Lam Qua, his pupil, should help to reduce the overuse and misuse of the term "Chinnery School."

This book has been written and published to answer some of the basic questions of what is or is not China trade. A great deal of new material has been unearthed and presented, with period references and accounts, but a tremendous amount of research is necessary to establish more data on the early objects and painters. It is hoped that this book will stimulate both interest and further research and that more atypical objects, in the Western style, will be discovered. The undertaking was first conceived at the time of the China Trade Show at the Peabody Museum in Salem, Massachusetts, in 1970. The catalogue for that exhibition formed the basic outline for the book. At the time of the exhibition, it became apparent that the Peabody Museum would be the greatest single source of information on the China trade and the objects traded in because of the voluminous collections and the extraordinary quantities of shipping documents and accounts of the early-nineteenth century traders and merchants stored there.

The Peabody Museum is the outgrowth of the original East India Marine Society, a group organized in Salem in 1799. Many of the objects brought back by the early members were given directly to the Society's museum and are entered in the early catalogues of the collections. Thus documentation on the objects of the very earliest part of the nineteenth century, and the China trade, is unique and impeccable. The Peabody's large collection of Chinese paintings of the ports and ships made it possible to study signed and labeled works and identify the styles of several of the painters, so that paintings in other locations could be attributed. These attributions are just as plausible as those made of Western paintings by scholars in the field, since many of the painters had highly individual styles.

Discussion of export porcelain, a subject extensively explored and published over the past thirty years, has been postponed. A companion volume to this book, on the subject of export porcelain for the American market, is projected. It is hoped that readers of this book who have additional information will address the author.

C. L. C.

Introduction

1. Portrait of Benjamin Shreve of Salem, circa 1802. Miniature on ivory, American. Artist unidentified. *Peabody Museum, Salem.*

Although Europeans had been trading with the Chinese since the establishment of a permanent settlement at Macao by the Portuguese in 1557, Americans did not enter the China trade until 1785. British mercantile regulations had prevented the Colonists from trading in the Orient, but, by the time of the signing of the Treaty of Paris in 1783, seafaring men of the new nation possessed sufficient ocean-going vessels with which to extend foreign trade.

The first American vessel to depart for Canton was the *Empress of China,* with Major Samuel Shaw as supercargo, or business agent, and John Green as captain. Landing in China in 1784, the vessel returned to New York in 1785 laden with teas and silks. For her main cargo out, the *Empress* carried ginseng; the Chinese believed this root, found in the New England woods, possessed great medicinal powers. Ginseng was to become one of the basic trade commodities. Americans had difficulty finding marketable products for the Orient, since the Chinese wanted money and only a limited number of raw products such as furs, ginseng and bêches-de-mer. As the Americans learned more of Chinese needs and desires, they established trading posts such as Astoria on the Northwest coast to obtain seal skins and furs. Sandalwood was obtained from Hawaii, and bêches-de-mer, or sea slugs, which the Chinese considered to be a great delicacy for the making of soup, were gathered and dried throughout the South Pacific. Like all other items for trade and resale, prices rose and fell in Canton according to supply and demand, and the stock trade items were seldom so desirable or financially rewarding as the Americans would have liked them to be.

When dealing with the Chinese, Westerners were required to hire a pilot for the vessel at Macao, and proceed 70 miles up the Pearl River to the Whampoa Anchorage. Here the ship was left at anchor with the crew, and a *comprador,* who would supply the ship with food and other needs, was engaged. Here also was paid measurement and *cumshaw,* or taxes and bribes,

2. Figure of the Chinese merchant Yamqua, life size. Given to The East India Marine Society in 1801 by Benjamin Hodges. Head and hands of carved wood by Samuel McIntire. The robes were Yamqua's own. *Peabody Museum, Salem.*

for doing business in China. A "linguist" (the term then generally in use for "interpreter") was engaged, and a Co-Hong merchant was secured to purchase the cargo. The supercargo and the captain proceeded to Canton, 10 miles up the river, in small Chinese boats or Western cutters. The actual Western area in Canton was a small strip of land about one-quarter of a mile long that ran along the Pearl River just outside the walls of the city. The area was specifically assigned to the *Fan Kwae* or "Foreign Devils," as the traders were known to the Chinese. In 1720 the Emperor K'ang Hsi had given a group of Canton merchants licenses to conduct trade with the foreigners in this area. These merchants made up the Co-Hong, and every trader going to Canton had to secure his vessel, negotiate for the sale of his cargo and the purchase of the majority of his new cargo, with a merchant member of the Co-Hong.

On the strip of land for the foreigners were erected a number of *hongs,* which were residences and trading headquarters for the Western merchants. Each country engaged in the trade occupied a hong, which consisted of a front building facing the river and a series of other buildings behind connected by courtyards. Thus the address, #5 French, referred to the fifth building back in the French hong. Not all Americans stayed at the American hong, for often there was not sufficient room or they could get a better rental price elsewhere, from the Swedish, Dutch or French hong. The building usually contained public rooms and dining facilities, as well as rooms on the upper floors. The number of hongs was generally 13, but the number changed with fires and additions. By the 1830's, the lesser, or "outside" merchants rather than the major Hong merchants filled a considerable number of orders for the Westerners. The breakdown in restrictions had led to freer trade and more merchants were available for trade; however, most Americans still preferred to deal with those merchants, like Houqua, in whom they could trust implicitly.

Western women were strictly forbidden in Canton, and any woman staying in China before the 1830's was required to stay at Macao. The trading season at Canton usually lasted about six months, an interval based on the timing and intensity of the monsoon, an occurrence which greatly affected the flow of shipping. The season was from mid-summer to mid-winter. At the end of this time, the hongs were closed and the men retired to Macao. The Westerners were severely limited in their activities at Canton and were under constant surveillance by the Hong merchants and a Chinese police force. The gardens across the river at Honam were generally open for the Westerners to wander in during the first part of the nineteenth century, but, with an increase of trouble with Westerners over opium, that area later was also restricted. The wealthier Hong merchants maintained lavish houses and gardens at Honam, and invitations to soirées with the Chinese were greatly coveted by American traders.

The China trade and life in China had changed considerably for the Americans by the mid-nineteenth century. With the opening of the Treaty Ports of Hong Kong, Shanghai, Amoy, Foochow and Ningpo in the beginning of the 1840's, the traders went to places other than Canton to purchase teas and silks. The introduction of the great tea clippers at mid-century affected the market in both China and the West; with tremendous quantities of tea and silk being shipped in each vessel, the market rose and fell according to the number of voyages per year. The possibilities of great fortunes being amassed seriously diminished, and several of the large trading firms lost vast sums of money, coming to the point of bankruptcy, because of the competition and economic changes in the West.

The items made for Chinese export changed also; the quality lessened and the decoration became gaudier; and, on the whole, workmanship left much to be desired by the 1860's. The porcelains of the earlier period, decorated to the Western taste, were no longer in demand since the English and Continental porcelain factories could make a comparable, if not better, product for less money. By the time of the Philadelphia Centennial Exhibition of 1876, the China trade as it had been known in the eighteenth and early nineteenth century was over. Steamers and advanced transportation brought on a period of tourist travel, and the items made for this market were much inferior to those which had been so carefully produced over the previous hundred years. The objects exhibited at the Centennial of 1876, however, were made by the finest craftsmen and were the last quality objects to be made for the West.

There was an extraordinary demand for Chinese-made items in America, and although silks and teas were the basis of the trade, there was money to be made in china, ivories and other smaller commodities bought for a speculative market. The manufactures of the China trade fall into two categories; those bought for resale in the West, and those specialty items the traders and merchants bought for themselves, their families and friends for furnishing their houses. Often it is the second category that offers more interest and value to collectors. Since these objects were the finest made at the time, and the most expensive, they were not the best investments for resale, but they were moderately enough priced to attract the merchants who wished to expend money on Oriental items that presumably would not reach the commercial market at home.

Since the time when the *Empress of China* sailed to Canton, countless diaries and books of the trade have chronicled the voyages and life in Canton and Macao. Along with the romance and adventure of the voyage went peril and, often, disaster. For every man who made a fortune, another hundred men slaved away on board the vessels for months and years at a time, suffering from disease and boredom, for a sailor's pay and no share in the voyage. For the owners, the investors, the supercargos and the captains, a good voyage under ideal conditions could return a considerable amount of money, and, in many instances, a fortune, but it was a risky venture at best.

Such a large body of literature exists on the basic business aspects of the China trade and foreign life in China that, rather than reiterate these particulars, an account of a single voyage by an American merchant, typical of the thousands of voyages made between 1784 and 1840, may serve as a concise and accurate view of not only the products made by the major Chinese merchants and the conditions under which they worked, but also of the traumas, serious problems and fears that such a voyage engendered.

1 In 1819, Benjamin Shreve of Salem, Massachusetts, undertook a voyage to Canton as supercargo and captain of the newly built ship *Governor Endicott,* a vessel owned by an extraordinarily wealthy man, Pickering Dodge of Salem. Shreve had had considerable experience at sea, and had successfully traveled to China in 1815, 1816 and 1817. Born in Alexandria, Virginia, in 1780, he had sailed to South America and Europe extensively before embarking on

3. Brig *Governor Endicott,* painted at Leghorn, 1822, by Guiseppe Fedi. Watercolor on paper, 19″ × 26¼″. *Peabody Museum, Salem.*

his first trip to Canton. Shreve had proved himself an agent who kept impeccable records and a buyer who could be trusted to purchase those things which not only made money but were of fine quality.

Shreve enjoyed dealing with the same merchants repeatedly, and was very decided in his opinions of them as men and as merchants. He was fussy about his living accommodations, but rarely overspent his allotment for the voyage. He faced both tragedy and success with a healthy attitude, and although he might have had a rather high opinion of himself as a trader, he was not afraid to admit a mistake. A real "shopper," he spent days wandering around the streets of Canton to get the best possible buys. He was extremely devoted to his wife Mary (née Goodhue) and went out of his way to buy all the small things she requested. Shreve was also very generous and brought home many presents for friends and relatives. Even though he kept no diary, the Shreve Papers, now in the possession of the Peabody Museum, reveal much about the man, and his accounts give us a detailed picture of actual life in Canton.

Captain Shreve was careful to keep copies of everything he wrote, from a receipt to a ship invoice. All his letters were written in duplicate or triplicate, and he referred to them often. Requests for all purchases, both large and small, were transcribed from the letters of the investors to small notebooks bound in green Chinese silk which he always carried. In the books were notes of weights, costs, current market values, requests and orders filled. Additional information was added to the books while he was negotiating with the merchants.

As supercargo and master, Shreve was solely responsible for the business end of the voyage as well as the sailing of the ship. His investors obviously had great faith in his sailing and buying abilities, since, on the 1819 voyage, they entrusted almost a quarter of a million dollars in Spanish trade dollars and goods to him to be sold for silks, teas and nankeens. The money was shrewdly handled, and yielded a good return despite adversity.

The cargo for the trip was loaded in Boston in spring, 1819, and the barrels of silver dollars, each marked with an investor's name, were placed on board; there was approximately $152,000 in silver invested. The largest investors in specie were Pickering Dodge, Dudley L. Pickman, Jr., Daniel Parker, Joseph Tilden, William Pickman, E. and I. Breed with Ebenezer Francis, and Shreve himself. Each of these men had a minimum of $7,000 in silver in the voyage. The rest of the investors placed anywhere from $100 to an average of $4,000. Each investor also sent a letter specifying how he wished his money to be spent. Hence, Shreve had to keep extremely careful records; each man wanted different quantities and different types of silks and fabrics; few left the initial decision to Shreve. To keep the accounts of some twenty-five merchants, Shreve made charts and diagrams and recorded specific requests in his small silk books. An 8 per cent commission on silk, 10 per cent on nankeens, and 2½ per cent on teas was deducted. The investors were also charged $.50 per ton of 40 cubic feet of freight coming from China to be paid on delivery in the United States.

Not all the investments sent out to China were in the form of specie. Pickering Dodge had most of his money in trade commodities for the Chinese. Dodge shared with Nathaniel Robinson 10 cases of quicksilver, and Dodge alone possessed 113 cases of ginseng, 1,441 bales of raw cotton, 56½ bales of Bengal cotton, 14 kegs of quicksilver, and 92 mats of cotton. Samuel Parkman, Jr., shipped 93 pigs of lead and 184 kegs of quicksilver. Dodge's total investment was just under $100,000, a goodly sum for the period.

Several of the investors were encouraged by their wives to ask Mr. Shreve to do some spending for them. The smaller the order and the less the cost, the more finicky the purchaser became, it would seem from these records. On June 5, 1819, Gideon Tucker wrote that his wife wished a number of blue and white stone china plates, with gilt edge and four "turtle-shell" combs, for which he sent $34; later that afternoon, deciding it was not enough, he forwarded another $16 with additional instructions. Charles Thorndike of Salem had in mind investing in tortoise-shell combs to sell in Salem, and, in his letter of advice, he drew out the sizes and designs of the four types of combs he requested. There were to be some with plain tops, square or rounded; some with carved tops; some large, some small, and the price for each was specified. Thorndike was obviously used to Canton prices and designs for combs and found these items good commodities in Salem. Of particular interest was his request for a number of combs with small teeth for children.

Although Dudley Pickman, Jr., invested mostly in silks, he seemed more concerned with his small orders. First and foremost on his mind were two sets of lacquer "waiters" or trays, six in each set, in graduated sizes. One set was for his use, the other for a friend. "The waiters of the oval form, extended like those at your house [octagonal] the common ovals hold much less than yours." A diagram of the shape accompanied the note. For his children he wanted a small dinner set, but he wished to spend only $3 to $4—hardly enough for any quantity of good porcelain. He then qualified his order by saying that if it could not be secured, Shreve should buy a few pieces of small china, but not a tea set, since they already had one. For his silk order he enclosed a pattern card which had been brought back from

China two years earlier. He also enclosed a pattern card with the stamp of the silk merchant *Washing,* with a small sample of black Levantine, which he wished to reorder.

Joseph Tilden made a pattern card which he wanted followed *exactly.* Then he added, "The shipment would not have been made but for the confidence [I] have been induced to place in your personal respect." William Proctor wanted several lacquer boxes and any other small items that Shreve might think he would like; also 500 to 1,000 uncarved tortoise shells for the American and European markets. Most of the men, if they did not send pattern cards, which apparently had found their way to America from the Chinese silk merchants in great quantity, listed exactly which of the various kinds of silks they required. The silks Shreve bought were to be very much like those he had purchased on his previous three voyages.

After assembling his orders and cargo, Shreve set sail for China in late spring of 1819, with a crew of 19, including Samuel, a Chinese. The trip was not easy, and from the very beginning he disliked the way the new ship handled, finding her to be one of the dullest sailers he had ever known. On July 31, off the coast of central South America, Shreve sat in his cabin and sadly wrote, "Shipped a tremendous sea . . . . washed overboard every man on deck." The gale was the most awful he had ever witnessed, and the damage to the ship was crippling. The eight men washed overboard were not recovered, leaving the ship with a crew of eleven. The damage was so extensive that survival seemed doubtful. In his letter to Pickering Dodge (sent off months later), he enumerated the losses: mizzen mast, wheel, companion way, binnacle, sky light cover, capstan, boats, rail on both sides, several stanchions, almost all the ring blocks, and last, but most important, the rudder. All the sails and masts were damaged. The vessel was helplessly afloat at sea. The most troublesome loss was the tool box, since the crew was left with only one hammer and three or four saws for making repairs. A spar was placed over the stern for a temporary rudder.

Shreve faced the problem of finding another vessel to tow them north for repairs, but none was in sight. Fortunately, the weather was fair after the gale, and no further heavy seas threatened the ship. To Dudley Pickman he wrote that he hoped his wife would not worry and that he was terribly disappointed in not being able to reach China before the monsoon. In this particularly philosophical letter, attempting to straighten out his thoughts on the tragic loss of life, he wrote of the things of importance in his life in the following order: an "approving conscience," an irreproachable character, good health, a good wife, and plenty of money! The last reason was obviously the motive for his being in the China trade. He felt that he must have an irreproachable character and an "approving" conscience, because of the number of people who had placed their faith in him as supercargo and master. The letter continued, "This is an instant when probably unapprehensive of danger were 8 of 19 of us buried in the mighty deep." Sudden death was to concern him for the remainder of the voyage, for he had come to realize for the first time, after almost a quarter of a century at sea, how tenuous a hold men have on life.

After struggling at sea, Shreve wrote to Dodge on September 20; he had consulted closely with Henry Carwick, his first mate, as to where to head for help. The Cape of Good Hope was impossible to navigate because of the steering problems, and so they decided to head for St. Salvador (Bahía), in central Brazil. "I am now doing that which is for the general benefit of all parties concerned." His letter to Dodge on the twenty-sixth of September had more bad news: "I am now in sight of the Coast of Brazil. . . . Quicksilver is coming up the pump." The quicksilver had been partially destroyed when the kegs rotted from the water which had seeped into the hold during the gale.

On October 8, after reaching Bahía, he wrote to His Excellency the Count de Palma, Governor of the Province of Bahía, that he had $150,000 in specie on board, which he wanted safe until the ship was refitted. He complained that the bank charged the use of the money, plus one-half per cent commission. The customs house wanted 2 per cent for counting and for being responsible for the cash. Shreve thought both demands were unfair to one in his straits. His main concern was to keep the money in separate barrels, which were marked with the investors' names, and he did not want them opened for counting.

His letter to Dodge two days later warned of the tremendous expense and time for the necessary repairs, "I must have recourse to your dollars. . . . I shall not attempt to touch the property of the shippers but leave it to yourself to settle the business." Each shipper or investor was responsible for a certain portion of any necessary repairs, and the best way to settle the matter would be by general averaging. At this stage, after discussing procedures and prices with the firm engaged to repair the vessel, he decided to re-rig her as
3 a brig, since it would be less expensive and the vessel would sail better.

Shreve became increasingly anxious to have the repairs speeded up, but the work dragged on. In early November, he complained to Dodge, "You would be surprised how little work is done by a carpenter in this country." By this point the money had been placed in the customs house at no expense; however, the delay cost them ten days. The incompetence of the carpenters caused the rudder to be fitted three times before it would actually work. The surviving crew was well, and by December 19 he had signed on a new crew consisting of three Englishmen, three Portuguese and two Italians, since he could find no American seamen. Bills to Shreve from provisioners in Bahía indicate the ship's men were getting a good and varied diet while on shore: fowl, eggs, onions, vegetables, beef, fish, wine, sugar, turkey, rice, limes, mutton, pumpkins and oranges, etc. Several of the sailors were given advances on their pay for their extended stay in port. The repairs were all carefully itemized in a bill to Dodge: planks, labor charges, nails, cotton to mend cotton bags which had rotted, long boat rudder, brass, nails, a blockmaker, caulker, and blacksmithing. The total stay and repairs required $4,864.26 of Dodge's available silver.

By March 11, Shreve was off Anjier and wrote that the passage was tedious and he was worried about pirates at the Straits of Gasper and the lack of adequate guns aboard the *Governor Endicott.* The vessel sailed much better as a brig and he was generally pleased with the overhaul. The *Governor Endicott* arrived at Macao in early May, and Shreve made the necessary arrangements for hiring a pilot boat to take the vessel to Whampoa. The charge for the pilot was about $60. The brig was put at anchor at Whampoa after having been visited by the *hoppo,* or Chinese customs agent, and the *cumshaw* and measurement were paid. The fee for a vessel of the size of the *Governor Endicott* was probably about $4,000. Part of this was in the form of a tax, while the remaining sum involved an out-and-out bribe to do business. A "linguist" was obtained and after negotiating for a *comprador* to supply the vessel and crew while at anchor, Shreve hired a small boat and proceeded 10 miles up river to Canton.

4. Henry Carwick of Salem, first mate upon the *Governor Endicott* under Benjamin Shreve, 1819–1821. By unidentified Chinese artist, painted in Canton in 1820. Oil on canvas, $23\frac{3}{4}'' \times 18''$. *Peabody Museum, Salem.*

Shreve did a considerable amount of looking before finding a place to stay. His comments in 1815: "American Hong No. 2 and 3 rent from $800; Danish factory, #2 price $800 (per season) has a hall and sleeping rooms, with rooms below for servants, not very good." The French hong, #4, was $1,000, partly furnished, and had a hall and five sleeping rooms. "French #5, price, $1,200., furnished with chairs, table lamps & bedding has a hall and six sleeping rooms—very good if not very airy—the best of these four but is high." The Swedish hong, #3, was judged not very clean, and #4 was dismissed for not having a vault. What place Shreve decided upon on the 1819 voyage is not known.

Shreve had also noted on his earlier voyages opinions on various merchants he met, and the ones he liked to do business with in 1820. Eshing, the silk merchant, was very dependable, and one Shreve especially favored. Synchong, the porcelain dealer, he considered the "first" and "dearest" (most expensive). When Shreve had left Salem in 1815 on the *New Hazard,* Dudley Pickman had written him a memorandum about the Co-Hong merchants which was to have a great deal of influence on Shreve's future trade dealings. This letter, which has become a classic on the China trade, read in part:

> The most important thing in your voyage is in securing your ship. You had better not employ a Man of doubtful Character *at any rate.* Engage with a security merchant of the first Character even at rather higher prices for your goods and you will be sure to have a good cargo and without being delayed beyond the time stipulated for. There are generally about 12 security merchants, with one of whom you must engage of those who were in the Hong in 1805, when I was at Canton, 5 or 6 did much American Business.

Then followed a note on the individual merchants of the Hong:

> Moqua: Capt Wheatland [Salem] old friend, declined American business.
> Hooqua [*sic*] does business for Perkins house, considered very rich close [*sic*] to be depended on. . . . I should prefer him to any of those now in the Hong

> who were there when I was at Canton. [Shreve felt the same since the American trader bought so much of his cargo from Houqua.]
> Ponqua: too poor to deal with.
> Chunqua: Mr. Ingersoll thot "a big Rogue" I should have nothing to do with him.
> Conseequa—a very uncertain man I should not have perfect confidence in him. Some of the Philadelphians are very fond of him.

The list continues, but few of them were individual candidates for Shreve by 1820.

In 1820, Pacqua seems to have secured the majority of the cargo, while Namshong arranged to take most of the money on the ship in trade for silks. Restrictions were not so tight as they had been in 1805 and dealing with the "outside," or smaller, merchants was easier. The bulk of the Chinese goods was obtained through the security merchants, but the smaller orders could be arranged with the outside merchants. Pickman spoke very highly of Eshing; by the time Shreve arrived on the 1819 voyage, the firm was probably being run by Eshing's nephew. Washing, the merchant from whom Pickman had silk samples, was very highly thought of by him. Pickman felt Synchong to be the best of the porcelain merchants, and it is interesting that Shreve bought the tea set for Pickman's children in 1820 from this merchant. Pickman's advice on written contracts and business dealings was well taken by Shreve, and the entire memorandum was undoubtedly closely followed with allowance for changes that had occurred since Pickman's last voyage to Canton. On June 8 Shreve wrote that he had successfully sold the cargo and had found that 1,270 pounds of quicksilver had been pumped overboard. The ginseng had sold very well, since he was there in an off season, but he insisted that Dodge realize that this was the exception since it had been selling at very low prices. Because of the season, the prices of the old teas were too high and the teas mediocre; he, therefore, decided to wait for the new teas. "I have purchased what China ware I wanted for the bilge of the ship." The silks at this time were a poor buy, so it would be necessary to wait.

On June 5, 100 tons of sugar had been purchased from Pacqua, who had bought the ginseng and the remaining quicksilver. Dodge's ginseng, cotton and quicksilver netted a total of $82,267.36, while Parkman's salvageable quicksilver returned, less commission, etc., $10,845.99. Shreve thus had the money from the sales to invest in the Chinese goods each man wanted, in addition to other small sums.

On June 25, Pacqua consented to free Shreve from his purchase of the sugar, since the American had learned from merchants in Canton it was a very poor investment; the market for sugar had collapsed in both America and Europe. He contracted with Namshong for silks which cost more than the amount of money that the Chinese merchant had earlier agreed to take: $86,513.66. Of these silks, $18,602.50 were credited to Dodge's account and $8,298.12 to Shreve's; the remainder went to the account of the other investors. Dodge's order was to be rounded out with a great quantity of teas and nankeens, and the 100 boxes of chinaware that Shreve had bought upon his arrival. One hundred fifty *piculs* of cassia filled out the order. On September 13, he bought an additional $28,988.24 worth of silks from Namshong, on the same terms as his previous purchase, for the other investors.

On September 11, 1820, well over sixteen months since he had left home, Shreve expressed in a letter to Pickering Dodge how disheartened he was that he had not heard a word from home. Discussing the trade, he said he expected only two-thirds as many ships from America as in the previous year, and, therefore, a good profit might be turned on the proper purchases.

The teas were not contracted for until the new produce arrived in October. In September, Shreve had visited the five most prominent merchants, had carefully asked each one about tea prices for the season. The five were Consequa, Pacqua, Ponqua, Kinqua and Houqua. Consequa advised great care in selecting the new teas. On the seventh of October, Shreve bought 500 chests of tea from Houqua, and on the eighth he bought an additional 300 of Souchong tea. With every purchase, he figured out the weight closely and recorded it so he would know how much the vessel would be carrying on her return voyage. The cargo home was to weigh considerably less than the 445 tons on the way out, because of the sale of pig iron to Pacqua. Most of the cassia which he bought came from Pacqua, as did additional chests of tea.

Throughout the summer and fall of 1820, while he was waiting for the best teas and silks, Shreve roamed Canton buying the small items that he needed to fill his personal orders. Henry Carwick stayed on board the vessel at Whampoa Reach, where it was anchored for the entire stay in China, but the first mate occasionally came up the river to visit at Canton. Shreve had had a roofing or housing built over the *Governor Endicott* by a Chinese carpenter Jimmy Appoo. As the silks, teas, and other commodities arrived at Whampoa, the letters and marks for each investor, which had been stenciled on the boxes, were recorded by Carwick for shipping references. Receipts were given for each item loaded on board. Each order that was filled had to have an official bill of lading signed by the Consul at Canton for export to the United States. The paper work for this type of trade was tremendous, and all of it was handled by Carwick and Shreve.

Shreve bought small supplies for the vessel when he was at Canton, but the food and liquor were supplied, for the most part, by the *comprador* at Whampoa. Shreve reminded himself to buy "some sheep skins for sponges," and numerous supplies for the boat. An American acquaintance, William Megee, who ran a hotel and store in Canton, was the source for a great number of supplies for the vessel at Whampoa such as paint brushes, tools, arrack, paint, oil, yellow paint, etc., all obviously necessary to keep up the *Governor Endicott.* However, interlaced among the ship's supplies are an interesting number of more personal orders: 34 gallons of rum (for the crew), one-half gallon of brandy, and two more bottles of brandy.

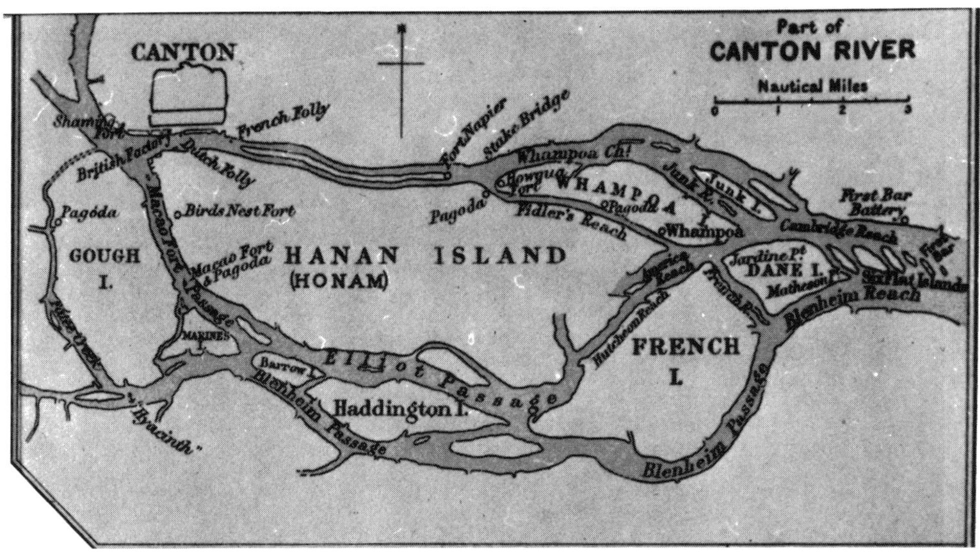

Shreve wrote a note to himself to see if there was any market at Canton for a crew member's ten boxes of American shaving soap. He needed several personal items throughout his stay in Canton: tooth powder, salt, "teeth" brushes, mustard and writing paper. For the medicine box at Whampoa he purchased mercurial pills, landanium (liquid opium), cream of Tartar, blistering salve, and sundry other medications and palliatives needed by the crew living on board.

On August 8, in between his errand-running, Shreve received an unusual letter from the crew at Whampoa, asking for the removal of James Richardson as "he is entoxicated [*sic*] and abuses all hands he himself wishing to leave the Ship it seems he does not care what he dose [*sic*] and we cannot get along with in pease [*sic*] yesterday in particular he told Mr. Carwick that the Ships crew were going to murder him . . . . we are all happy and comfortable except with the Mischiefmaking young man." The letter was signed by the entire crew, and on the following day Shreve wrote to Carwick to pay Richardson his wages and release him.

For his small orders from home Captain Shreve went to a number of different dealers, but tried to get as many of the things at one place as possible. He priced children's dinner sets at Old Synchong's for Pickman, and finally, by adding and subtracting various items, came within the limited price and managed to buy 20 pieces for $4. Yinqua supplied a lacquer tea caddy that Shreve wanted for his cousin Thomas Shreve, who lived in Alexandria, and Yinqua also was to make the lacquer waiters for Dudley Pickman. Pickman's waiters came to a total of $14.25 for twelve. They were "black ground with but little ornamented, strong and fit for use." William Proctor had six similar waiters, also from Yinqua, for $6.50, a lacquer cigar box and a tea caddy. Yinqua was given four weeks to complete the orders. Hupshong supplied boxes of china, probably those bought for Pickering Dodge. The tortoise-shell combs for Charles Thorndike were bought of Yushing. The total cost for them was $254.64, and Shreve seems to have done an excellent job of selecting the exact combs Thorndike wanted.

One of Shreve's most important purchases was the silver he bought from Synshing, possibly the maker who marked his pieces *SS*. He purchased six silver tumblers for his cousin in Alexandria, two dozen silver teaspoons, and one dozen each of table and dessert spoons. Under his memorandum of articles "taken into houses expenses" is listed a number of additional pieces of silver which he bought for himself at the same time: fish knife, soup ladle, cream pot, tongue scraper, and flatware, for a total cost of $175.38. For gifts, he purchased an ivory fan for a Mrs. Fowle of Alexandria ($5.00), a bolt of handsome silk for his wife, two pots of sweet meats, an ivory seal for a Mr. Tucker, and various and sundry small items which added up to $224.02.

His personal orders are among the most interesting since they are so diverse: a lady's parasol, $5.50; six mother-of-pearl spoons, $.50; ten tin saucers for Mandarin cups, $1.67; two "teeth" brush cases with covers; two "conscience" cups; two tubs of sugar candy; and several jars of dried candy and preserves, which his wife always asked him to bring home. In having his cargo loaded at Whampoa, he made a particular point of telling Carwick to place the sugar candy "where it can be got at." For his cabin, he had the cabinetmaker Angow of Carpenter Square make a rattan cot bottom 6 feet long and 26 inches wide for $2.50, the job to be completed in four days.

Shreve had a rather sizable dinner bill from William F. Megee for 78
meals from May 18 to November 1. The meals were 40 cents apiece and most
were billed in groups of four which would imply that the Captain and friends
often dined together. Henry Carwick must have come to Canton to visit a
number of times (on one such visit he had his portrait painted), since his bill 4
from Megee indicated that he ate eight meals including breakfast, dinner and
tiffin from May to November. Mr. Mansfield, the second officer, also ate at
Megee's and seems to have had a minor drinking problem: "May 25, Tiffin,
1 pint wine; Aug. 20, Breakfast, 1 bottle port, 2 gin and water; Sept. 22,
Tiffin, 3 glasses Brandy and water."

The bills of lading for the cargo were signed in late November, and the *Governor Endicott* left Whampoa shortly after for Boston. Duties for the cargo were paid in late April, and the silverware, silks, china, nankeens, canes and candy that Shreve had purchased for himself were charged the high sum of $3,945.28 on an estimated value of $20,000. On May 7, Benjamin Shreve paid the crew their final wages and in the next few weeks he settled his last financial business of the trip. The following year Shreve was again headed for Canton on the *Comet* to make another profitable voyage.

5. The silk merchant Eshing, painted by Spoilum, before 1809. Oil on canvas, 27″ × 21″. *Peabody Museum, Salem.*

1. Spoilum and His Followers

The China trade portraitists working for the Western market followed the trends of portraiture in the West. The early portraits (1785–1820) reflect the Neoclassical styles of portraiture so popular in England, France and America. The later portraits, from 1820 to mid-century, are more in the English Romantic style represented by George Chinnery, William Beechey and Sir Thomas Lawrence. Portraits executed after the mid-century depended heavily on photography, and were usually painted from daguerreotypes or in the style of photographs. This decline is also observable in the West to a great degree, except for the work of the major portraitists.

The earliest portraits of Western merchants executed by Chinese painters are the most interesting, and, in a way, surprising to those not familiar with Chinese export painting before the arrival of George Chinnery in China. One of the earliest known portraitists was the artist Spoilum, who was working in Canton from circa 1785 to 1810. His portraits are not only of Western merchants but of many of the Chinese Hong merchants with whom they did business. The earliest reference, 1789, to this artist is found in a description of the trip of a Hawaiian royal tourist, Tianna, who had sat for Spoilum and was very pleased with the results. "But of all the various articles which formed his present wealth, his fancy was most delighted with a portrait of himself, painted by Spoilum. . . . The painter had indeed most faithfully represented the lineaments of his countenance."[1]

One of the best known portraits attributed to Spoilum is that of the silk merchant Eshing. The portrait of Eshing is known to have been "painted before 1809" and was an early gift to the East India Marine Society, now the Peabody Museum.[2] The painting is distinctive in several respects and reflects the work of a Chinese artist moving into the Western style of painting from traditional flat Chinese portraiture.[3] The face is painted in flesh tones which have an overall light quality. Behind the shoulder is a lighter area, one of this

6. Member of the British East India Company, by Spoilum, circa 1800. Oil on canvas, 17″ × 13½″. *Collection of Graham Hood.*

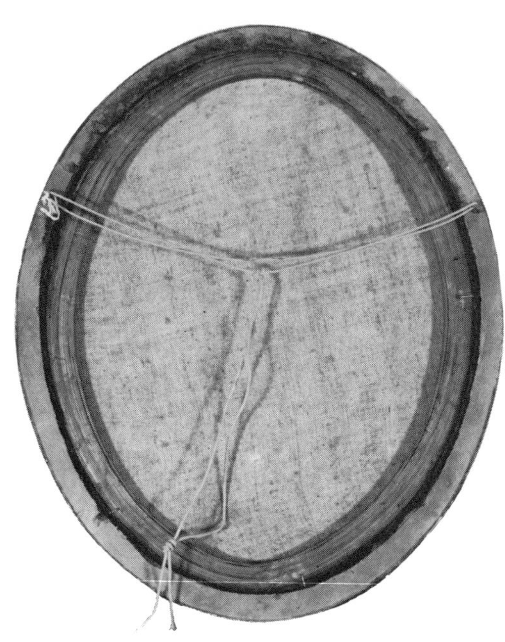

7. Stretchers and canvas and back of frame to portrait by Spoilum of member of the East India Company (*Illus. 6*).

8. Member of the British East India Company, by Spoilum, circa 1800. Oil on canvas, 17″ × 13½″. *Author's Collection.*

9. A man from Dorchester, Massachusetts, by Spoilum, circa 1805. Oil on canvas, 17″ × 13½″. *Author's Collection.*

painter's easily recognizable characteristics. The eyes are painted with a great deal of sensitivity and there is an excellent feeling for the personality of the sitter. The mouth has a slight smile and is upturned at the left side, another characteristic of Spoilum's style. The background of the portrait and the coat are relatively flat. This flatness is the element most reminiscent of his native Chinese style of portraiture.

Spoilum appears to be the first major Chinese artist to have executed a group of portraits in the Western style of painting for the export market, and he was considered "the celebrated artist of China, and perhaps the only one in his line, throughout that extensive empire."[4] ("The only one in his line" probably means the only one painting in the Western style.) Some other painters, working between 1810 and 1825, seem to have developed their styles of portraiture from Spoilum, since they have so many of his characteristics, the shadow behind the head and the delicate palette as well as a similar treatment of mouths and eyes. None of these followers seems to have possessed Spoilum's skill and attractive presentation of character. These later painters also undoubtedly worked in the Canton area close to the hongs.

Spoilum was in fairly frequent contact with the Western population from which he drew many of his sitters. Since it was nearly impossible for a Western merchant to venture into other parts of Canton, his studio must have been situated in the Western sector, perhaps on Old China Street. One of the key paintings in the identification of Spoilum's style is the oval portrait
of a member of the British East India Company, painted around 1800. The *6*
portrait was executed on hand-primed canvas and stretched on oval laminated
pieces of wood. The frame is an exact copy of an American or English frame, *7*
and was made in the same manner as those used on the China trade reverse paintings on glass. The portrait demonstrates that the artist worked in both rectangular ("Eshing") and oval formats. The sitter has the light flesh tones of the Eshing figure, a similar upturned smile on his mouth, and one eye placed slightly higher than the other. The coat is painted in the flat style of Eshing's robe, although the painter has used gold to pick out the braid of the coat and the gold buttons with their English lions rampant.

Of the same size as the portrait of the East India merchant are two other oval portraits, one of a man reputed to be from Dorchester, Massachusetts, the other of a young Englishman. In the second, the pale skin tones, *8, 9*
treatment of the eyes and the smile positively identify it as by Spoilum, the "Eshing" painter. The background is the same light blue-grey shade, with the shadow rising to the right of the head and neck, as seen in the East India merchant portrait. The gold braid of the coat is again applied in gold paint. The two English sitters also have their hair tied back with a black ribbon. The portrait of the younger merchant has been relined in England, and the original laminated stretchers have been lost. The portrait of the man from Dorchester, painted in the same manner as the other two ovals, with the same facial characteristics, is on laminated stretchers like the East India merchant portrait and has a similar gold frame, a copy of a Western moulding. The dates for all three of the oval portraits seem to be very close: somewhere between 1795 and 1810. A portrait of Samuel Blanchard of Boston by Spilum [*sic*] states it was painted in Canton, China in 1790—just one year after the first reference to Spoilum by Meares, which was crucial in identifying the painter.

An important pair of portraits by Spoilum gives us an exact working

10. William Story of Salem, Massachusetts, painted by Spoilum, during a trip to Canton in 1804. Oil on canvas, 27″ × 22$\frac{1}{4}$″. *Peabody Museum, Salem.*

date for the artist and suggests that he sometimes executed portraits as pairs. A portrait of James Cary (1777–1812), obviously stylistically related to the other paintings by Spoilum, complete with the shadows and light blue-grey background, still has its original label which reads: "James Cary portrait, taken in Canton, February 10, 1802. Aged 24 yrs. 11 months, 10 days." A companion to this portrait is one of the same size and palette, with a matching Western-style frame. The label reads, "I have this day given this picture of Chung Qua, a Chinese Mandarin, to James Hussey Cary [*signed*] Love, Brickman." Both portraits are on hand-primed canvas, identical in their weave and priming to that used for the portraits of the man from Dorchester and the East India merchant. Both Cary paintings retain their original stretchers, which, although of wood, are made in the Chinese manner for rectangular port paintings in that period. Thus, from this pair, it may be assumed that Spoilum did portraits in pairs of the Western merchant and his Chinese counterpart. Three other similar portraits of Chinese merchants are known, all stylistically close to the Chung Qua and Eshing, with the same placement of hands, treatment of face with the smile and slightly tilted eyes, and the light shadow behind the head.

Another portrait, very much like that of James Cary, is of William Story *10*
of Salem and Marblehead, Massachusetts. Captain Story was master of the *Friendship*, out of Salem on a voyage to Russia, the Mediterranean and Canton from 1801 to 1804.[5] The portrait of Story, in his 1804 dress, was unquestionably painted on this trip to Canton. The painting is very bold, with a good incisive grasp of the man's personality. The background light and other stylistic attributes of the hand of Spoilum are all readily identifiable.

A large number of other paintings by Spoilum has recently been discovered. Many of these had previously been attributed to American, French and Dutch portraitists, but all are clearly by Spoilum. One of the finest portraits to be reattributed is one of Captain Benjamin Smith, a recent gift to the Whitney Museum of American Art. This is the most ambitious of the paintings, with a handsome background of tree, sky, ocean and a finely painted ship. This background may be a clue to the discovery of paintings of other subjects, such as port scenes and ship portraits, which could well have been executed by Spoilum. It is possible that portraits by this highly competent painter will be found in every major Eastern seaport city; more than twenty-five are known to exist at present.

That Spoilum inspired or had an influence on other Chinese painters working for the Western market becomes evident with the study of several other Chinese portraits of early Western merchants trading in Canton.

One group of paintings can be put together to form the oeuvres of the "Carwick" painter, so called for the portrait of Henry Carwick, possibly
painted in Canton in 1819. Carwick was first mate on the *Governor Endicott* *11*
under Benjamin Shreve from 1819 to 1821.[6] Here the style is reminiscent of Spoilum, but the portrait lacks his crisp delineation and ability to capture character. Two or three similar portraits, with their less crisp backgrounds and darkening face tones, suggest the painter worked in the period from 1805 to 1825. A portrait of Cornelius Soule of Providence, Rhode Island, may have been painted by the Carwick painter, too; it has a similar palette and identical treatment of the eyes and face.

A portrait of William Townsend of Providence, Rhode Island, is by
another follower of Spoilum whose name is unknown. Townsend recorded in *12*

11. Portrait of Henry Carwick, by an unidentified artist, painted in 1820. Oil on canvas, $23\frac{3}{4}'' \times 18''$. *Peabody Museum, Salem.*

his journal for November, 1818, that he was very sick, and was concerned about being well enough to continue to sit for his portrait, which was being painted by one of the artists close by the hongs.[7]

13 A portrait of an unidentified young Salem man shows the work of yet another painter, who was very much influenced by Spoilum's style and was, possibly, a student of the master. The use of a blue-grey background with shadow, the flat blue coat with gold buttons and the well delineated features all point to the earlier painter, but the portrait is a much more primitive work than any of Spoilum's portraits.

Two or three other portraitists can be stylistically identified or grouped together from the large number of existing portraits of American merchants of this period. In all, judging from the number of portraits extant which were painted between 1800 and 1825, it would appear that Spoilum was followed by a half-dozen portraitists who had learned to paint in his style, but still had individual characteristics by which they might be distinguished.[8]

Spoilum was perhaps the most important early painter working in Canton, and he had great influence on the portrait painters who followed him in the next decade. In the middle of the 1820's, a large and significant change

12. William H. Townsend, painted in Canton in November, 1818. Artist unidentified. Oil on canvas, $23\frac{1}{2}'' \times 17\frac{3}{4}''$. *Rhode Island Historical Society.*

13. Young Man from Salem, Massachusetts, circa 1820. Follower of Spoilum. Oil on canvas, 23″ × 18″. *Private Collection.*

took place in the style of portraiture executed for the Western market. Changes in tastes in the West effected a momentous change in the style of painting by the Chinese portraitists. With the advent of George Chinnery and other painters in the English Grand Style, the Chinese artist adopted an English style of portraiture and abandoned the Neoclassical–Chinese style as represented by Spoilum.

14. Israel Porter Williams of Salem, Massachusetts, circa 1820. Artist unidentified. Oil on canvas, 24″ × 18″. *Peabody Museum, Salem.*

15. Stephen Dexter, by Spoilum, circa 1805. Oil on canvas, $23\frac{3}{8}$″ × $17\frac{1}{2}$″. *Rhode Island Historical Society.*

Notes

1. *Extracts from Voyages in the Years 1788 and 1789 from China . . . by John Meares.* 2 Vols., Legographic Press: London, 1791. Hawaiian Historical Society Reprint, 1787, '88, '89, p. 33.
2. The portrait of Eshing is listed in the catalogue of the East India Marine Society as having been given by a particular merchant; however, a check of earlier records before 1821 proves this erroneous. The painting was definitely given to the Society before 1809. This important painter has just recently been identified as Spoilum; he was known before only as the "Eshing painter." Hence, the importance of this painting.
3. An observation made by D. Roger Howlett, to whom I am indebted for much of this type of information.
4. *Extracts from Voyages . . . by John Meares,* p. 33.
5. Peabody Museum records.
6. Shreve Papers, ship *Governor Endicott,* 1819–1821, Peabody Museum. Although Carwick stayed with the vessel at anchor at Whampoa Reach, his hotel bills in Canton indicate he came up to Canton to visit at least eight times. The portrait was undoubtedly painted on one of these trips.
7. Journal of William H. Townsend, Rhode Island Historical Society.
8. A large number of portraits of this period exist, and an exhibition of them should be organized in an attempt to sort out the artists and their exact periods and styles. A number of institutions own portraits of this type: New Haven Colony Historical Society, Peabody Museum, Salem; Essex Institute; Whitney Museum; Rhode Island Historical Society; Historical Society of Pennsylvania; Girard College; Rhode Island School of Design; Henry Francis du Pont Winterthur Museum.

16. Anders Ljungstedt, Swedish Consul to China, by George Chinnery, circa 1835. Oil on canvas, $9\frac{1}{2}'' \times 7\frac{3}{4}''$. *Peabody Museum, Salem.*

2. George Chinnery and Lam Qua

Portrait of Lam Qua, wood cut from a French newspaper of 1848. Approximately, $2\frac{1}{2}'' \times 2\frac{1}{2}''$. *Collection of Francis B. Lothrop.*

The extent of George Chinnery's influence on the Chinese painters in Canton and Macao after 1825 has never been satisfactorily measured. It is clear from the styles of some artists working in oils then that their techniques had been derived in large part from that manner of English painting best represented by Chinnery. Many characteristics of his portraiture begin to appear in a number of Chinese portraits for the Western market, and it is doubtful if anyone else could have exerted much influence in this area.

George Chinnery was born in London in 1774 and showed an early
talent for painting; by the time he was twenty-four he had exhibited 21 paint- 18
ings at the Royal Academy. He had married at the age of twenty-one and gone to live in Ireland, his wife's home. He was back in London in 1802, and that same year he left for India without wife and children. His marriage had been an unfortunate one, and it was to plague him most of his life. Chinnery met with considerable success in India, both in Madras and Calcutta, and painted some magnificent portraits of the best known figures in both English and Indian society and politics. Chinnery brought his wife and family to India in 1818, but by 1823, bothered by debt and wife, he left for Serampore. In 1825 he went to Macao and Canton, where he was to stay until his death in 1852. In China he met with success, and he painted many of the prominent people of the Western colony. His superb portraits of Chinese merchants, American men and women and Englishmen and their wives gave him an unexcelled reputation on the China coast. That a man of his stature, in a colony the size of Macao and Canton, should have influenced some of the native Chinese export painters around him is only natural. With J. M. W. Turner and T. Girtin, Chinnery had studied under Sir Joshua Reynolds and developed swift and confident brushwork and a drawing technique which is only seen in a major academic artist. If he had remained in England or Ireland, he would undoubtedly have reached the same heights as his contemporaries Sir Thomas Lawrence, George Romney and Sir William Beechey.

Chinnery undoubtedly had Chinese students. Lam Qua is known to have studied and lived with him in the 1820's, and his Chinese student was to become the most prominent of the Chinese painters working in the English manner.[1] According to a Fearon family tradition, Lam Qua was a houseboy in their household in Macao at the time of Chinnery's arrival. When Chinnery arrived in China, Christopher Fearon set up a studio for him in the garden, and Lam Qua, who began by cleaning his brushes, became his first pupil. Lam Qua may have known how to paint before Chinnery arrived, but it is not likely. A highly informative and important portrait of Chinnery by Lam
22 Qua illustrates his work before he had fully learned to paint successfully in the English Grand Style.[2]

Pupils doubtlessly began their careers by copying their master's sketches to fill double orders, then graduated to their own studios and painted small portraits in the English manner for those who could not afford to sit for a Chinnery painting. Robert Bennet Forbes wrote of having sat for a portrait by Chinnery which was then sent to Lam Qua for copying.[3] Protin Qua is another Chinese student mentioned in the period, but no works by him are known to exist.

The prices for a Lam Qua copy can be gathered from a note in the Latimer Papers, although the size of the portrait is not given: "1832. paid Lamqua for Copy of portrait, $26.50."[4] Many of the portraits of prominent Westerners, which have been tentatively attributed to Chinnery, are most probably by Lam Qua (or a follower), since they lack some of the quality and dash so characteristic of the best Chinnery portraits as exemplified by those
16 of Harriet Low and Sir Anders Ljungstedt.

In a portrait like the small painting of S. Weir Lewis of Philadelphia,
23 all the elements of Chinnery's English style, as adapted by Lam Qua, can be found: the touches of red around the nose and mouth, the use of a freely painted drapery background and the compositional placement of the figure.

Lam Qua and Chinnery had a falling out, which led to considerable rivalry in Canton. A significant note by "Old Nick," a French traveler, on the Chinnery–Lam Qua relationship, and the reasons for its final dissolution, establishes quite conclusively the tension behind the later bitterness between them. After a description of Lam Qua's studio, "Old Nick" comments,

> Then there are a certain number of studies borrowed from Chinnery by his student though Chinnery maintains he neither loaned them nor gave them nor sold them. Between these two men exists a rivalry that is all the more lively due to the fact that they lived together. To hear Chinnery talk, Lam Qua is a subaltern, a wretchedly bad painter whose sole merit comes from having stolen from him some models and some methods. To hear Lam Qua talk, he was the favorite student, the assistant to the English painter. Chinnery whose talent is far superior to that of Lam Qua asks 50 to 100 piastres for the same portrait that the native artist makes for 15 to 20; and because his are cheaper, untutored people frequently prefer to give their business to Lam Qua, Whence the hatred.[5]

Far more than a copyist or a "wretchedly bad painter," Lam Qua was to become the most celebrated Chinese painter in the English style in Canton. Over his door was a sign which read: "Lam Qua, English and Chinese painter."[6] Another viewer records his sign as reading, "Lam Qua Handsome face-painter."[7] That Lam Qua was highly respected in Canton is obvious from a remark by Osmond Tiffany, Jr., who visited the portraitist's studio in 1844.

17. Houqua, attributed to Lam Qua, thought to have been given to Robert Bennet Forbes by Houqua, late 1830's. Oil on canvas, 30″ × 25″. *Museum of the American China Trade.*

> The prince of Canton limners is Lam Qua, who is celebrated throughout China, and is indeed an excellent painter. He takes portraits in the European style, and his coloring is admirable. His facility in catching a likeness is unrivalled, but wo [*sic*] betide if you are ugly, for Lam Qua is no flatterer. I might repeat a dozen stories of his bluntness, but they have probably found their way into print.[8]

Tiffany described the interior of the studio and those works and artists, other than Chinnery, that had influenced Lam Qua's painting style.

> His walls are decorated with his own copies of English paintings,[9] and he possesses the engraved works of several British artists.[10] His admiration of Sir Thomas Lawrence is profound. . . .[11] Lam Qua's portraits of Chinese mandarins or hong merchants are scarcely to be excelled. He not only gives the dress and face, but throws a perfectly characteristic expression into the countenance, and introduces as an accessory a Chinese landscape very successfully.[12]

Lam Qua exhibited at the Royal Academy in London "Head of an Old Man," in 1835 and, in 1845, "Captain Hall".[13] He was the first Chinese working in the Western manner to exhibit in America. In 1841, in the March exhibition of the Apollo Club in New York, Lam Qua was represented by a

18. Self-portrait of George Chinnery, circa 1840. Oil on canvas, 9½″ × 7¼″. *Peabody Museum, Salem.*

19. The Chinese merchant Samqua, by Lam Qua, before 1850. Oil on canvas, $25\frac{1}{4}'' \times 32\frac{3}{4}''$. One of the five merchant portraits painted for Augustine Heard and exhibited at the Boston Athenaeum in 1851. *Peabody Museum, Salem.*

"Portrait of Moushing, Tea Merchant, Canton, China," which was listed as owned by Talbot Olyphant and Co.[14] In 1851, under a misspelled version of his name, the catalogue for the Pennsylvania Academy of Fine Arts indicates he exhibited three paintings: "#187, Portrait of a gentleman," "#407½, Napoleon and his Son" and "#416, Sir Henry Pottinger."[15] All the paintings were owned by A. A. Ritchie, the Philadelphia engraver. In 1860, under his correct name, Lam Qua again exhibited at the Academy. Number 52 was "A portrait by a Chinese artist [*sic*]," owned by C. Gullager.[16]

In 1851, five Lam Qua portraits of Chinese merchants, including the Hong merchant Houqua, were exhibited at the Boston Athenaeum, according
to the exhibition list for that year.[17] The five portraits had been shipped to *19*
America for Augustine Heard of Ipswich, Massachusetts. Still in existence, study of them reveals what a superb portraitist Lam Qua could be. Freely and incisively painted in the best English style, they are personal and appealing, with no indications of copying. They are some of the finest portraits ever done of the Chinese merchants who dealt with the Westerners. The Houqua portrait is equal in quality to a portrait by the most academic American painter of the period.

A French traveler, M. La Vollée, who had visited Lam Qua's shop in Canton, saw the paintings in Boston and wrote an article for the *Revue de Paris,* which was later translated and published in the *Bulletin of the American Art Union.* "We saw at the Athenaeum exhibition in Boston, this summer, four or five portraits by this artist of Chinese dignitaries, which would not

20. Portrait of Doctor Peter Parker and his student Kwan Ato operating on a patient, by Lam Qua, circa 1845. Oil on canvas, size unknown. Kwan Ato was Lam Qua's nephew. *Privately owned.*

have disgraced a clever European painter. That of HouQua [*sic*], the celebrated Hong merchant who died a year or two since, was particularly meritorious. It was well modeled and full of character."[18]

Many of the portraits of the merchant Houqua, either three-quarter-length or seated full-length on a throne with a trellis upper left, were very possibly copied by Lam Qua (or his studio) after the original(s) by Chinnery.[19] The only Houqua portrait generally accepted as being a genuine Chinnery is the one from the Plowden family, owned by the Hong Kong Shanghai Banking Corporation, which is full length.[20] Many portraits of Houqua of a similar composition are obviously by the hand of Lam Qua or his studio. A study of many of the known waist-length portraits of Houqua reveals that they are also by Lam Qua (and his followers). The superb Houqua portrait exhibited at the Boston Athenaeum is, of course, a documented Lam Qua, and an equally fine portrait, owned by the Museum of the American China Trade, can also be readily accepted as by his hand, and not that of the Englishman. The portrait was given to Robert Bennet Forbes upon his departure
17 from Canton in 1840. These portraits, just short of the work of Chinnery himself, have the incisiveness so aptly described by Tiffany. The delicate handling around the eyes and the refined mouth are the work of a major painter who has learned to paint in the English Grand Style.[21] One of the finest small paintings by Lam Qua is of Ah You, the Tanka boat girl. The painting is very close to the work of Chinnery, with its bold brush stroking and

21. The Hongs at Canton, circa 1835, attributed to Lam Qua studio. Oil on canvas, 18″ × 23″. *Vose Galleries of Boston.*

brilliant palette. Painted in the 1850's, the portrait with landscape has a full Chinese inscription on the back stating it is the work of Lam Qua.

The most important single body of work by Lam Qua in existence is a complete surprise to most scholars of the China trade, because of its very unusual subject matter. Dr. Peter Parker, who took his medical degree at Yale in 1834, a missionary and surgeon in China, commissioned Lam Qua, circa 1850, to paint a large number of portraits of his patients in the Canton *27*
Hospital.[22] These somewhat gruesome paintings of subjects with noticeable pathological conditions provide a startling insight into the painter's ability and style. Some reach the heights of the finest English portraiture as represented by Sir Thomas Lawrence or Sir William Beechey. Those with landscape backgrounds are painted with the broad swift brush strokes of the English landscape school and provide an important comparison to the port scenes with landscapes which can be attributed to Lam Qua. Lam Qua painted a half-length portrait of Dr. Parker[23] as well as a small painting of Parker seated in his room overlooking the park at Canton.[24] In that room, Parker's eldest *20*
Chinese student is examining a patient's eye. The student is none other than Lam Qua's nephew, Kwan Ato.

Lam Qua obviously had a number of Chinese artists working in his studio. References by visitors to the studio, although conflicting as to what these painters were executing, state there were between ten and twenty assistants. A passage from "Old Nick" adds to the confusion as to exactly how

22. Portrait of George Chinnery by Lam Qua, late 1820's. Oil on canvas, measurements unknown. *Private Collection.*

23. S. Weir Lewis, of Philadelphia, by Lam Qua, circa 1845. Oil on canvas, $9\frac{1}{2}'' \times 8\frac{1}{8}''$. *Collection of Alford Rudnick.*

24. Boating on a river, circa 1845, attributed to Lam Qua studio. Oil on canvas, $10\frac{3}{4}'' \times 17''$. *Private Collection.*

and what the painters were painting. "Lam Qua is the first among the artists of the nation to have copied European methods, but far from founding a school, he has quite readily taken into his employ a number of Chinese workers whom he allows to work as they wish and whose work he sells."[25] It was inevitable, however, that these painters should pick up Lam Qua's style. From the great number of portraits extant in Lam Qua's style, but not up to his standards, it may be assumed that other painters in the studio were copying his work, as he had copied Chinnery's. Tiffany stated, "Seated in the large room are a number of his pupils and assistants, copying for foreigners, or painting on the bamboo [pith] paper."[26] Lam Qua probably executed paintings from life and important commissions, while the assistants copied and fulfilled standard orders.[27] La Vollée gives an excellent description of how Lam Qua worked. After seating the subject in a large bamboo chair,

> Lam-qua painted rapidly. His first sketch was already made. . . . It showed great certainty of hand, and was not without resemblance, although the artist had had but three sittings. . . . The best painters, especially portrait painters, buy other paints of the English. Lam-qua had near him a box divided into compartments in which were arranged in order about twenty different colors, prepared before hand in porcelain cups. A drawer contained as many small phials of the same colors in a powdered state. In the bottom of the box were placed brushes of every size and degree of fineness. . . . An apprentice stood behind Lam-qua to renew the water in the cup and wipe the brushes while

25. The Hongs at Canton, shortly after the fire of 1842, attributed to the Lam Qua studio. Note the removal of the British hong. Oil on canvas, 11½″ × 22″. *Museum of the American China Trade.*

> his illustrious master attacked the face of the Englishman. Lam-qua stopped at intervals—left pencils and palette and retired a distance in order to see the effect of his work, with which he appeared, according to custom, to be well satisfied.

"Old Nick's" descriptions provide the information that Lam Qua lived on China Street, and that the house had three floors; a shop occupied the bottom one where there were numerous watercolors arranged in cases and the stock of things one would find in a Western stationery store. Lam Qua's workshop was on the second floor. La Vollée wrote,

> Lam Qua then introduced us into the outer apartment, which was a sort of workshop. Here were twenty youths copying drawings upon great rolls of white or yellow paper, or upon that fine pith which we in Europe obstinately call rice-paper, although there is no rice in it. . . . It would take a day to pass in review the pictures, the rolls of drawings and albums heaped up in the shop of Lam Qua. This picture business in China is immense.[28]

A number of watercolor albums exist, and in one particularly important set of street trades each piece is signed lower right: "Lam qua Pinxit, China Street, Canton." The *pinxit* had been adopted from the English tradition of signing a painting. Another album of Chinese figures has a penciled inscription underneath the "Lam Qua" written inside the cover reading, "The Sir
Thomas Lawrence of China." A price for this type of watercolor can be ob- *88*
tained from the Latimer Papers: "1833. paid Lamqua 1 book 12 paintings 8, 1 picture 15—$23."[29]

The few Chinese painters working in the Chinnery (or English) manner, whether connected directly with Lam Qua or not, did not execute

26. View of the Joss House, Macao, circa 1843, attributed to the Lam Qua studio. Oil on canvas, $11\frac{1}{2}'' \times 19\frac{3}{4}''$. *Museum of the American China Trade.*

only portraits, which are the most readily identifiable stylistically, but also landscapes and port scenes. Most of the port scenes, however, are not in the standard formats. They are often more personal statements, painted from angles and in locations not often seen. To tag the large, sweeping harbor views of the 1840's to the 1860's as "Chinnery's" or "School of Chinnery" is erroneous. Few of these standardized views were done in the English style of painting, as represented by Chinnery or Lam Qua, but rather they were executed in the Italian, French or Dutch port tradition.

The port views by the followers of Chinnery or Lam Qua tend to depict the buildings as low and stumpy (as they actually appeared) rather than in the long attenuated style of the port painters working in the tradi-
21 tional manner. A pair of views of Canton, circa 1835, depicts the hongs and the park from an unusual vantage point, and reveals the fresh, fluid brushwork and use of light so characteristic of Chinnery's painting. The paintings are not by the Englishman, but they are most certainly by the hand of Lam Qua. The palette is bright and fresh and employs the colors seen in the medical paintings. This particular pair shows Lam Qua at his best in landscape
24 painting. Another painting of a number of Chinese persons in a boat on the river near Canton is executed in the broad painterly style of the two views above, and it can be attributed to the Lam Qua studio.

A set of four port and river scenes in the Museum of the American China Trade is thought to be from the Lam Qua studio, if not by his own
25 hand. The painting of Canton is extremely important, since it shows the port

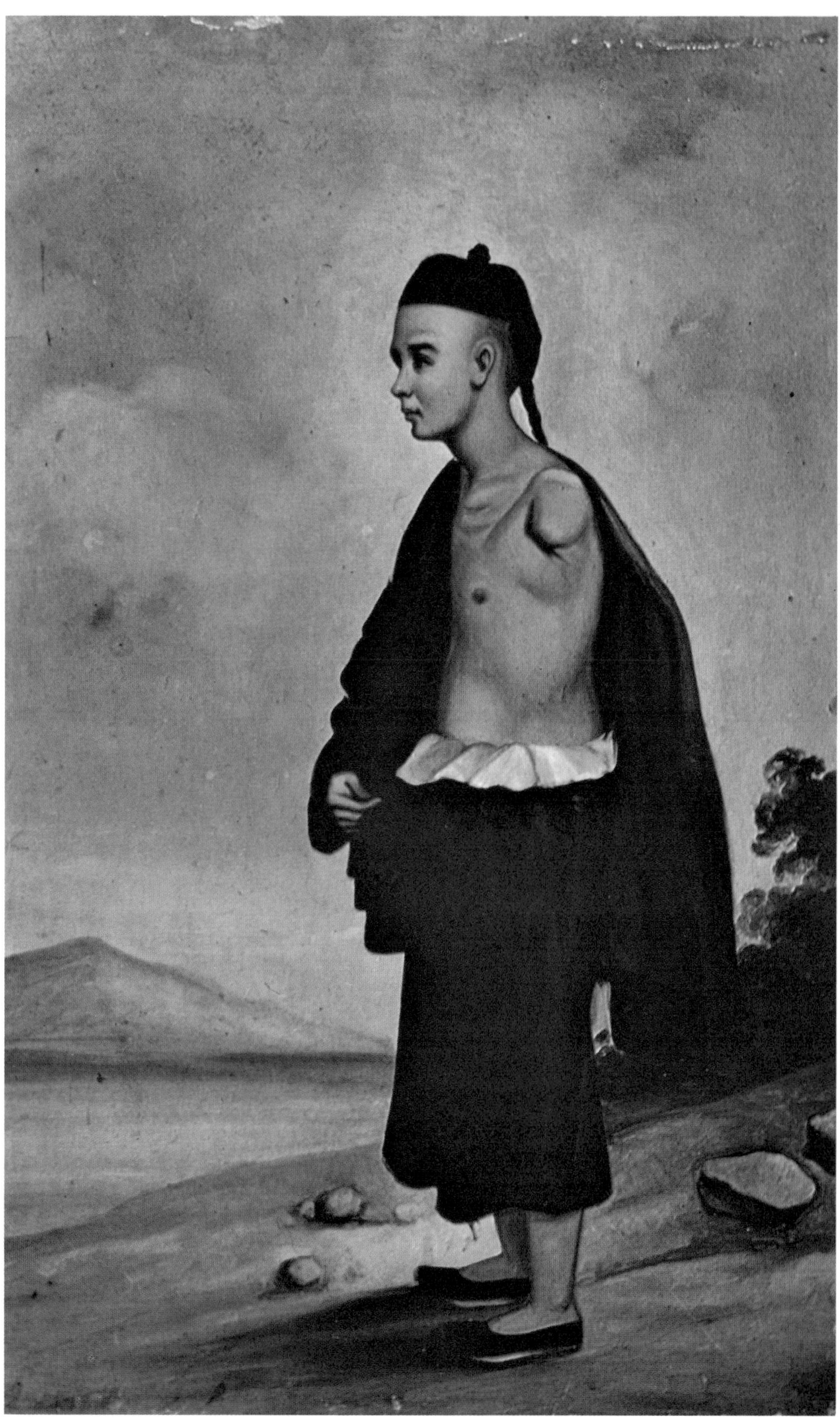

27. Patient from the Canton Hospital, 1840's, by Lam Qua. Oil on canvas, 26″ × 18″. *Yale University Medical Library.*

28. The Chinese merchant Houqua, by Tingqua (inscribed on back), circa 1840. Watercolor on ivory, $6\frac{3}{4}'' \times 4\frac{1}{2}''$. *The Metropolitan Museum of Art, Gift of Mrs. John de Peyster, 1966.*

shortly after the fire of 1842, when the English hong had not yet been rebuilt.[30] The gardens and park are placed in front of the American buildings, and it may be assumed that the painting was executed around 1845. The style of the four paintings is very broad and English in concept, and all are of excellent quality. The painting of the Joss House, Macao, Inner Harbor, in
26 the same set, is compositionally very close to a painting of the same view by George Chinnery which is in the Peabody Museum. The angle is slightly different, but the "Lam Qua" painting could possibly have been based on a watercolor or drawing by Chinnery, which might have been one of those mentioned by Tiffany as being in the Lam Qua studio.

Lam Qua had a younger brother, Tingqua, who was to become one of the most important Chinese watercolorists executing works in the Western style. "Tingqua is a younger brother of Lam Qua and was instructed by him in the use of the pencil. Lam Qua is chiefly employed on portraits, while Tingqua confines himself to miniatures and sketches."[31] Tingqua's studio was at 16 New China Street, Canton. A miniature of Houqua, watercolor on
28 ivory, is signed by Tingqua, and it may well have been based on a Lam Qua portrait, which was in turn based on a Chinnery. Copying of one another's works and compositions seems to have been common among the Chinese painters working for the export market.

It will take a tremendous amount of additional research to determine just how many of the Chinese painters were working in the style of Chinnery. Their names are barely known today. Lam Qua will unquestionably remain the most important painter in this group, and his studio will remain the source of a great quantity of the paintings produced from the 1830's through the 1850's. The paintings by Lam Qua and those which are believed to have come from his studio are generally of high quality; very much in the English portraiture style, they are some of the most impressive paintings executed for the Western market.

Notes

1. Information with the portrait.
2. Privately owned. Given away by Chinnery in 1837 or 1838.
3. Forbes Correspondence, Massachusetts Historical Society.
4. John R. Latimer Papers, Library of Congress. Another price source is William Fane de Salis, *Reminiscences of Travel in China and India in 1848*. London: Waterlow and Sons, 1892, p. 12. The traveler describes his negotiations with Lam Qua in the studio: "Thence my friend took me to Lamqua's studio—Lamqua, the great painter, the Millais or Ouless of South China. He had a keen eye to business, and was most anxious to get a commission to paint. He offered to paint me English fashion (that is in good drawing and perspective); or China fashion, (out of all drawing proportion and perspective)—China fashion to be £8, English fashion £10. He could paint in both styles, and it was indifferent to him which. He was, I understood, considered a very fair artist, and had a considerable *clientèle* both among the Portuguese and the natives, as well as the Europeans at Canton and Hong Kong. After thanking him for his courteous reception, but declining his professional offers of service. . . . "
5. *La Chine Ouverte* par "Old Nick" [Paul Émile Daurand Forgues]. Paris: H. Fournier, 1845, p. 56. I am indebted to David Brubaker of Boston for translations from the French.
6. From an article in *L'Artiste: Revue de Paris,* 1849, by M. La Vollée, which appeared in translation in *The Bulletin of the American Art Union,* 1850.
7. "Old Nick," *La Chine Ouverte,* p. 56.
8. Osmond Tiffany, Jr., *The Canton Chinese, or the American Sojourn in the Celestial Empire.* Boston and Cambridge: James Monroe and Co., 1849, p. 85.
9. A copy of a print or painting of Napoleon was exhibited at the Pennsylvania Academy of Fine Arts in 1851.
10. Vast numbers of English engravings and mezzotints found their way to China. Several were used as the source of inspiration for the decoration of export porcelain and the reverse paintings on glass. Merchants such as Houqua valued them very highly, and Bryant Tilden, in 1816, mentions the engravings hanging on the walls of Houqua's house in Honam.
11. On the binder of a set of watercolors is written, under Lam Qua's name, "The Sir Thomas Lawrence of China."
12. Tiffany, *The Canton Chinese,* p. 85.
13. "Cantonese Chinnerys: Portraits of How-Qua and other China Trade Paintings," Albert Ten Eyck Gardiner, *The Art Quarterly,* Winter, 1953, p. 316.
14. Exhibition records for the Apollo Association, New York, and the American Art Union, New York.
15. Exhibition records of the Pennsylvania Academy of Fine Arts, Philadelphia.
16. *Ibid.*
17. Exhibition records of the Boston Athenaeum.
18. Gardiner, quoting La Vollée, *The Art Quarterly,* p. 316.
19. The concept of "studio" will be explained below, but it is here used to describe paintings that might have been done by Chinese artists who had learned to paint in Lam Qua's style and might have worked for him.
20. The painting of this subject at the Metropolitan Museum of Art, New York, is unquestionably a Lam Qua, and not a Chinnery. A portrait owned by the descendants of Benjamin Chew Wilcocks, of similar composition, is also not a Chinnery, but a Lam Qua. Two other similar portraits are at India House, New York, and the National Gallery, Dublin, Ireland.
21. Several fine portraits of merchants, fitting Tiffany's description are in Brighton Pavilion, Brighton, England, and a group is in the small China Trade Museum in Macao, China, as well as in City Hall, Hong Kong. Of the number of handsome portraits of Chinese merchants which exist in America today, a good portion can be considered to be by Lam Qua or his workers.
22. *User's Guide to the Yale Medical Library, Historical Collections,* New Haven, Connecticut, Jan., 1970, p. 17. Eighty-six of the paintings are at Yale; another 23 are at Gordon Museum, Guy's Hospital, London.
23. Collection of the Yale University Medical Library and on exhibition there.
24. Only a photograph has been seen by the author; the painting was, many years ago, in the possession of Dr. Peter Parker's grandson.
25. "Old Nick," *La Chine Ouverte,* p. 57.
26. Tiffany, *The Canton Chinese,* p. 85.
27. Gardiner, quoting La Vollée, *The Art Quarterly,* p. 317.
28. *Ibid.*
29. Latimer Papers, Library of Congress.
30. La Vollée wrote: "'Look at this' said Mr. B. showing to me a copy they were making, 'more than ten times I have pointed out to Lam-qua the incorrectness of this picture. He will obstinately persist in leaving here the English factory which was burnt during the war, and there an open space which is now covered with houses.'"
31. *Chinese Repository,* Vol. XVI, No. 5 (May, 1847). Tingqua was thirty-eight at this time.

29. Mother and child by Yeuqua, circa 1875. Original label on back of stretchers. Oil on canvas, $23\frac{1}{2}'' \times 17\frac{3}{4}''$. *Childs Gallery.*

3. Later Portrait Painters and Photographers

Portraits of the 1820's and 1830's, when done by a competent artist from an actual sitting, take on the appearance of a Western portrait such as those of Thomas Sully or Sir Thomas Lawrence. Portraits of Americans from the second quarter of the nineteenth century, executed in the Chinnery–Lam Qua style, are generally competent and American in feeling, but evince a rather stilted quality and lack the full modeling and brilliant brushwork of Chinnery and Lam Qua themselves. Nor do they have the handsome flat decorative quality or charm of the Spoilum portraits.

With the introduction of photography in China in the 1840's, the concept of portraiture changed considerably, as it was handled by ordinary port painters.[1] Increasingly, portraits were based on daguerreotypes or photographs rather than sittings. Westerners who brought photographs from home
could have them copied skillfully by a number of painters in either watercolor *30*
on ivory, or, enlarged, in oils on canvas. Mention has been made of the workers in the Lam Qua studio who painted on ivory. A portrait miniature of
a member of the Heard family, painted around 1850, has Sunqua's name on *31*
the back panel. A group of three portraits of the Captain Oliver Lane family has Chow Kwa's label on the backing of the frames. The three, painted circa 1850, are of extraordinary quality and must have been done with fine brushes and painstaking care. Several English and American accounts relate with amazement the Chinese ability to copy on ivory in the miniature technique. Rear Admiral George H. Preble commented in his diary, September 24, 1854, "The daguerreotypes of the family which you sent me I am having copied on ivory by old Loequa. I called on the painter today. He has the dresses painted but the faces of all but Fannie and Lizzie are yet blank. . . . I hope the painter will be able to secure a good likeness of all, as he says he can."[2]

Many portraits of ship captains and traders in the 1850's and 1860's

NOTICE.

SHOULD THE PICTURE SPOT OR MILDEW WHILST ON BOARD, THROUGH ANY VAPOUR CONSEQUENT ON BOARD STEAMER, THE PICTURE CAN BE WASHED IN COLD WATER WITH A LITTLE SOAP AND AFTR-WARDS POLISHED (VARNISH.)

YEU-QUA, No.-93, Queen's Road.

were done from sittings, and two portraits in the Peabody Museum, of a Captain Fuller and Captain Francis Babbidge, are good examples of standard Chinese portraiture for the export market at mid-century. They look somewhat Chinese in treatment, but exhibit a very definite Western approach to painting. Despite this, however, they are a far cry from the Chinnery–Lam Qua portraits of the 1820's through 1850's. Aside from those portraits which are done from life, there were a number of full-size portraits, in oils on canvas, which were based as early as the mid-century on daguerreotypes. These are, for the most part, little more than slavish copies of photographs.

As the century progressed, most of the portraits were executed in Hong Kong and Shanghai, and they displayed less and less quality and painting technique. Depending increasingly on photography, the painters finally turned to enlarging photographs and painting over them. A number of studios arose on Queens Road in Hong Kong which could render these services.[3] The ship painters of the third quarter of the nineteenth century turned to photography also, not so much for their ship paintings but for the other pictures they executed, and a number of labels state that they would do enlargements of all types. On the reverse of a photograph of 1868, Lai Sung declared that he was a photographic artist at No. 419 Queens Road. Wing Chong, who executed a ship portrait now in the Peabody Museum, is listed on the back of an 1870's photograph: "Cheong Heng and Wing Chong, Photographers and Portrait Painters, No. 66 Queens Road. . . ." A torn label on the back of the painting of the ship *Houqua,* circa 1860, reveals the end of the artist's name "—ua" and the following, "Marine Ship Portrait and Chart Painter, also Daguerrotype Copier, Hong Kong." The ship painters, therefore, were doing portraits and photography as well. Hing Qua, who painted a number of large and rather mediocre ship portraits, announced on one of his labels, "Hingqua Portrait and Chart Painter, Hong Kong," with no mention whatsoever of his ship painting. A large double portrait of man and wife, circa 1870, which bears this label, was done in a palette similar to that of the ship paintings. It is difficult to judge whether the portrait was done from sittings or from a photograph, but it would seem to be from the latter because of its stilted flat quality.

30. Portrait of a young woman, by Yeuqua, circa 1880. Original label on inside of silk covered base. Watercolor on ivory, $3\frac{1}{2}'' \times 2\frac{1}{2}''$. *Ronald Bourgeault.*

Many portraits painted between 1860 and the 1880's bear Yeuqua's
label and depend heavily on photography and the use of a strong blue color.
His portraits are rather overbearing and Victorian in coloring and mediocre
in quality. A portrait of a mother and child, with his label, circa 1875, was 29
based on a photograph, although that artist had done more creative work
in port scenes and junks at sea. Yeuqua's labels are most informative, since
they give instructions on the care of the paintings. A label on the stretchers
of an oil portrait reads, "should the picture spot or mildew whilst on board,
through any vapour consequent on board steamer, the picture can be washed
in cold water with a little soap and afterwards polished." The instructions for
one of his miniatures on ivory read, "NOTICE If this Ivory Miniature gets
damp or spotted, take out the glass and place the picture in the Sun for 10

31. John Heard of Ipswich, Massachusetts. Inscribed "SUNQUA" on back panel, circa 1850. Watercolor on ivory, $4\frac{5}{8}'' \times 3\frac{3}{8}''$. *Privately owned.*

32. A woman and two children, attributed to Youqua, circa 1845. Oil on canvas, $12\frac{3}{4}'' \times 11''$.
Childs Gallery.

minutes, and afterwards clean it with a feather or dry handkerchief." Most of Yeuqua's portraits, both in oil on canvas or watercolor on ivory, appear to be based on daguerreotypes and photographs rather than sittings.

A number of existing photographs of Western merchants and their families were taken by Chinese photographers. Many of them are of the same quality as pictures taken in this country during the same period. Several are posed and amusing, although others are quite professional. The photographers also took pictures of areas around Canton, Hong Kong and Shanghai, views which provide great insight into Chinese coastal life in the second half of the nineteenth century. A particularly entertaining advertising card is that of Ying Cheong of Shanghai, which carries a photograph of two little Chinese boys—one with a gun—in Western dress coats and top hats. The back of the card announced that Ying Cheong was a "Portrait Group and Architectural Photographer" on Canton Road, Shanghai, and that he had "Views for Sale." These painters-turned-photographers and the photographers played an invaluable part in preserving for the twentieth century a view of Western life in China in the nineteenth century.

With the advent of photography in the West and China, there was far less demand for oil portraiture. The portraits done in the West toward the end of the nineteenth century were executed for social, political and professional reasons, and were no longer the mere limning of friend, relative or loved one. Renderings in the English Grand Style, as executed by the Chinese artists, were inexpensive, and paintings of considerable style were available to those Westerners in China who could not or would not have sat for a native artist of comparable quality at home. Later Chinese painters adapted to the times by producing photographs, miniatures from photographs and full-size portraits which filled the demand for representations but were not comparable as works of art to some of the portraits done before 1850.

Notes

1. Photography may have been introduced to China by William W. Wood of Philadelphia, who was editor and compositor for the *Canton Register,* the first foreign newspaper in China, in 1831. W. C. Hunter states he introduced photography to Manila. (W. C. Hunter, *The Fan Kwae in Canton before the Treaty Days.* London: Kegan Paul, Trench & Co., 1882, p. 113.)
2. Rear Admiral George Henry Preble, USN, *The Opening of Japan; a Diary of Discovery in the Far East, 1853–1856.* Norman, Okla.: University of Oklahoma, p. 254.
3. An 1880's photograph of the 60's block of Queens Road shows almost a half-dozen photographers in this area alone. From the number of photographers' advertising cards which have survived, it is obvious the number engaged in this profession must have been great.

33. Chinese artist painting a landscape, artist unidentified, circa 1840. *The British Museum.*

4. Painters of Port Views and Ships

The identity of the Chinese painters and their paintings is entangled in a mass of labels, misfact, attributed paintings and hundreds of undocumented works of considerable quality. The painters all undoubtedly executed port scenes, landscapes, portraits, and works based on English prints. Tremendous quantities of paintings exist, but few are documented or give any clue as to who the painter might have been or by whom he was influenced to paint in the Western style. The earliest paintings of Canton, which are some of the best port paintings ever executed, usually have no labels and give no indication of date or artist. The bills of lading and historical references to the exportation of paintings give no definite names or studio addresses. Only five or six artists' names of the period from 1795 to 1825 are known, and these can be associated with only a few paintings. A set of English aquatints of the street trades of Canton, published in 1797, carries the legend that the prints are from the originals by Pu Qua.[1] Whether or not this artist was also a painter of port scenes is not known. A painting of the Macao Customs House, inscribed 1814, is by the painter Mayhing, but it is difficult to associate the style with any other paintings of this approximate period.[2]

That a tremendous quantity of paintings came out of China at the end of the eighteenth and the beginning of the nineteenth century is proven by the number of paintings still in existence and the lists of pictures in ships' bills of lading. A bill of lading from the *Minerva* of Salem, which returned from Canton in 1801, lists 21 pictures, 13 of which were packed in one box.[3] It is impossible from this brief reference to know if the pictures were port scenes, portraits or watercolors. Sullivan Dorr of Providence, Rhode Island, sent four port scenes of Bogert [*sic*], Whampoa, Canton and Macao, to his brother in 1800.[4] Around 1800, a number of portraits of Salem merchants, by Spoilum, were brought back and are still in existence. The Peabody Museum in Salem owns a collection of views of Canton, 1790 to 1820, which

34. The Fire at Canton, 1822, by the Master of the Fire of 1822. Oil on canvas, $7\frac{1}{4}'' \times 11''$. In set of three. *Private Collection.*

are of superb quality and detail, and could well have been painted by someone as competent as Spoilum, since he undoubtedly painted port scenes as well as portraits. A large painting of Canton, painted about 1785, uses much the
C. 3 same palette as Spoilum's portraits, but it is difficult to judge how the painter's style might have been applied in a port scene. The canvas of a number of the early views is quite similar to that of the portraits, and the stretchers are also of like construction. No actual painters' names however, come to light as possible delineators of these views. The famous pair of paintings of a Chinese
36 Court of Inquiry concerning British sailors and the front of the hongs at Canton (the former in the possession of the Peabody Museum, the later at Winterthur) are by an artist of tremendous skill, and could well have been done by one of the early portraitists, because of the number of miniature faces which are seen throughout the paintings.

The relationship between the Chinese student and the Western painter who could have taught him how to develop a Western style is undetermined before the Chinnery period. It is known that several of the mid-eighteenth century Chinese port painters learned to paint from Castiligione and other Jesuit missionaries. A great number of European artists were in Canton and Macao before the period of 1815: Thomas Hickey, J. Webber, William Alexander, the Daniells, and others who were either full-fledged artists on

35. Jamestown, St. Helena, by the Master of the Fire of 1822, circa 1815. Oil on brass, $4\frac{1}{4}'' \times 5\frac{1}{2}''$. *Childs Gallery.*

official voyages or simply amateur painters. Any one of these men could have had a tremendous influence on port painting and portraiture. It is quite obvious that someone like Spoilum must have known how to paint in the native Chinese style of portraiture, since his Western portraits maintain the flat nonperspective qualities of the native school; however, the use of shadow and slight modeling clearly comes from a Western concept. The presence of the Dutch and Portuguese in China for such a long period of time must have been felt by the artists who wished to fill foreign commissions. In style, many of the smaller port scenes are very close to the Dutch school of painting of the late seventeenth century with their little buildings and figures and exacting attention to details, and these scenes reflect the Lowlands artists' viewpoint on the part of the Chinese painters.

The "Master of the Fire of 1822," so called for painting a set of three
small oils depicting the burning of Canton in 1822, with his attention to the *34*
most minute details and his ability to include so much in such a small area, is a member of this school. Another two paintings, views of Canton and Whampoa, are certainly by his hand, with their finely painted buildings and beautiful, sweeping panoramic landscapes and skies. This painter could

36. The Court of Inquiry, possibly by Spoilum, circa 1807. Companion painting to a view of the front of the hongs at Winterthur Museum. Oil on canvas, $28\frac{3}{8}'' \times 40\frac{1}{4}''$. *Peabody Museum, Salem.*

well have executed a number of the early large views of the ports, such as
the superb set at Winterthur, circa 1815. It is difficult to judge exactly what
his style would have been in working on a larger scale. The composition for
these larger paintings is identical, however, to those of his smaller paintings
on canvas or brass. That he is as competent as many European painters of
the period is clear through a close examination of his work. A set of four
35 superb miniature paintings on brass of Canton, Whampoa, Jamestown (St.
Helena) and Capetown, South Africa, is also unquestionably by the "Master
of 1822." A matching view of Capetown, another view of Jamestown and a
view of Macao, all the same size as the above set and also painted on brass,
are in the Peabody Museum. A painting of the fire of 1822 on brass, matching one of the views in the set of three paintings on canvas of the fire, uses
the same technique and is the same size as the two sets of views on brass
discussed. A copy in oil on canvas of the Providence Marine certificate could
37 well be by the "Master of 1822," with its careful delineation and copying of
the vignette views of Providence and vessels at sea.

37. Providence Marine Society certificate, circa 1805. Made out for John Updike. Artist unidentified, possibly the Master of 1822. This is an exact copy of the engraved Providence Marine Society certificate. Oil on canvas, 13½″ × 18¾″. *Rhode Island Historical Society.*

Although a painter like the "Master of 1822" could work in a highly personalized manner with a great feeling for light and atmosphere, he was bound by a certain convention in composition seen throughout innumerable port views. The artists were willing to record every change which took place in the arrangement of the fences, buildings, and flags at the Canton waterfront, but they remained within a tight compositional vocabulary that was repeated over and over again. Each of the views of Canton (*see Appendix C illustrations*) has recorded the changes which have taken place over a span of twenty years, 1800 to 1820, but each uses the same compositional treatment of junks and other vessels at anchor in the foreground. This placement of the vessels was to be used continuously, by countless artists, throughout the late eighteenth and the first half of the nineteenth century. Whether the compositional arrangement was introduced by a Western painter and repeated by the Chinese artists is not known; however, it is obvious that there was a strong prototype for all the paintings.

There are few ship portraits in existence which were painted in the first period of the American contact with China, from 1785 to 1815. Although the painters filled commissions for portraits of officers, evidently few painted ship portraits. A decent number, however, must have been executed because of the Western demand for such paintings. A painting of the ship *President Adams* for the American market, dated 1812, would seem to be one of the
earliest recorded ship portraits.[5] The handling of the water and the tight *38*
drafting style of the ship are very reminiscent of several of the views of Canton of the period, and the painting may well have been executed by one of the port painters. There is little question that a Chinese painter could

38. Wreck of the ship *President Adams,* Sept. 9, 1812. Artist unidentified. Oil on canvas, 18″ × 23¾″. *Museum of the American China Trade.*

and would fill any commission for a Westerner. A goodly number of portrait painters are very possibly the painters of ports and ships, and vice versa.

A problem has arisen at this particular point in the study of port painters which has done a great deal to hinder present-day understanding of the subject. In the past few years there have been several publications and art market references attributing paintings by Chinese artists to the "School of George Chinnery." In most cases, this attribution is an impossibility, since many of the port scenes, so called, were painted well before 1825, the date of Chinnery's arrival at Canton. To label a painting of 1800 as "School of Chinnery" is an anachronism. The painters of the early views obviously learned to paint in the Western manner from other visiting artists working on the China coast. Many of the Chinese painters worked in the Italian or Dutch vein, rather than the English, too. Scenes of strongly colored skies and bright blue waters with streaking of white are much more reminiscent of the works of Italian port painters than of the English style as represented by someone like Chinnery.

The names of the artists working for the export market after 1830 are better known. One of the first to actually sign his own work on the front of the canvas was Sunqua (1830–1870), a painter working at Canton and Macao. The signature is usually in small block letters in the lower righthand corner of the painting, like a Western artist's signature. Sunqua's earliest works are easily identifiable by their distinctive compositions and palette
40 tonalities. A typical ship painting has the ship neatly placed in the water with a view of the island of Lin Tin behind.[6] The water is painted in a rather free

39. Cemetery at Whampoa Reach, by Sunqua (original label on back), circa 1850. Oil on canvas, 17″ × 30″. *Peabody Museum, Salem.*

manner with white highlights on the waves and a streak of light running across it in the foreground. The hills beyond and the sky have a warm color in them, and the overall palette is delicate and light. The ships are often a bit small for the canvas size, especially when compared with the placement of the vessels by the Hong Kong painters in the later period of 1850 to 1880.

A large number of Sunqua's ship portraits, most of them signed, is housed at the Peabody Museum, and the group forms an important study collection for his early style. Most have either Lin Tin or Whampoa Reach as a background, and those focused on the anchorage often include small boats or junks. Sunqua's other early works are port scenes and unusual subjects such as a view of the cemetery at Whampoa Reach (two versions are
known). In a work such as the cemetery, one finds the keys to Sunqua's *39*
early painting: the attenuated figures heightened with white, the meticulous technique of drawing trees and a penetrating use of light in the water and foliage. There is a crispness to the early paintings which is missing from the paintings to come later. A view of Dutch Folly Fort shows him at his best,
with his carefully controlled composition, a fine delicate palette and the *B. 12*
swift, sure rendering of boats and figures.

A body of work, of the period 1825 to 1840, exists which has been tentatively attributed to Sunqua, but which seems on closer examination to be by another hand. One of the painters of this group can be called the "Master of the *Greyhound*" after a painting in the Peabody Museum. A
superb painting, using many of Sunqua's technical devices (including the *43*
writing of the ship's name on the front of the canvas) and approximately

40. Bark *Cynthia* off Lin Tin, signed "Sunqua" lower right, circa 1840. Oil on canvas, 17½″ × 23″. *Peabody Museum, Salem.*

the same palette, the "*Greyhound*" still differs in so many ways that it cannot be considered to be Sunqua's. Dated 1827, the painting has strong drafting techniques and rigging details that set it apart from the paintings by or attributed to Sunqua. (There is always the slight possibility that this picture represents Sunqua's very earliest painting style.)[7] The water has a crisper handling, with strong accents on the crests of the waves. The ship is extremely well drawn, with fine attention to detail, and the treatment of the figures is realistic and convincing. A painting of a Russell and Company vessel anchored somewhere on the Pearl River is by the same hand as the
41 "*Greyhound*" and displays competent draftsmanship and finely painted water. Closely allied to these two paintings and undoubtedly by the same artist is a painting of the *Levant* and *Milo* again of similar palette and technique to the other two paintings. The ships are executed with a tight draftsmanship

and have a certain amount of flatness and distortion about the bow and stern; a characteristic which is not evident in the broadside views of the *Greyhound* and the Russell ship.

Another painter in this early period of ship portraiture is the painter of the "*Henry Tuke*" and the "*Beaver*" (the former in the Peabody Museum, the latter at Mystic Seaport), both painted around 1825. The *Tuke* painter has a drafting manner like that of the *Greyhound* painter and a related palette, but his treatment of water and trees is very different. Sunqua, the "Master of the *Greyhound*" and the painter of the "*Henry Tuke*" seem to make up 42
the three major artists working in Canton, Lin Tin and the Whampoa area, painting ship portraits in the period before 1840. As the port paintings seem to reflect a certain formula of painting in the Western style, so do the ship paintings have their formulas for placement and execution.

There are a number of very fine paintings of the ports before 1840 which are not attributable to any of the artists or groups previously mentioned, but do deserve note for their outstanding quality and interesting compositions. A set of six paintings (of Boca Tigris, Canton, Dutch Folly Fort, Whampoa and two of Macao) is most distinctive in treatment and at first observation seems not unlike the work of the painter of the *Henry Tuke*. They lack, however, his landscape technique and must be by another, 44
as yet unidentified painter. The water in the paintings is conceived as long streaks of green-blue and brown, and is unlike water depicted in any other port scenes. The Peabody Museum also owns a highly individual and attractive pair of views of Macao, both from unusual angles, which, because of the buildings visible, must have been painted in the period of 1830 to 1840. These are ambitious compositions with a bright palette of blues and purples.

After the painters of the 1830's and earlier, there arose another group of painters for the Western market who had learned to paint in a much freer and looser style, possibly through the influence of Western painters, such as George Chinnery, who were residing in Canton and Macao. Undoubtedly, as taste changed in the West, styles of paintings purchased by the foreigners in China changed as well. The earlier port scenes and portraits reflect the European and American taste for the Neoclassical, whereas the views after the 1840's reflect the Romantic trends in England, the Continent and America. The tightly structured drawing (and the Dutch landscape feeling) of the earlier paintings disappears, and looser, more Western approaches to painting, similar to those of the European port artists, develop among the Chinese painters. With the opening of Hong Kong, many of the artists moved their studios there or maintained one in Hong Kong as well as one in Canton. A great deal of confusion arises in this period because of the changes in technique, and it is difficult to determine if a painter is adapting to the stylistic trends or if another man has assumed his name, a not uncommon occurrence.

The grouping of Canton, Macao, Whampoa and Boca Tigris in a set for the export market is a typical arrangement of four views before the opening of the treaty ports in the 1840's; after that date, the sets more often included Hong Kong rather than Boca Tigris, or were expanded to six paintings with the addition of Hong Kong and Shanghai. Sullivan Dorr of Providence bought one of the typical early sets of four in 1800.[8]

A set of four paintings of Macao, Boca Tigris, Whampoa and Canton, signed in block letters SUNQUA, is important for illustrating the changes

41. Russell and Company ship at anchor, by the "Greyhound" painter (possibly Sunqua?), circa 1835. Oil on canvas, $21\frac{3}{4}'' \times 29\frac{1}{4}''$. *Museum of the American China Trade.*

that took place in that painter's style. Painted around 1840, they are on nearly-square canvases, and the views of Whampoa and Canton reveal what was to be his style through the 1850's, while the other two reflect his style of the 1830's. There was a very definite stylistic change; so much so that there has been some question as to whether there were two painters who signed their works "Sunqua."[9] Sunqua's later paintings are not generally signed, but have small oval labels with the name SUNQUA in block red letters pasted on the backs of the stretchers or frames. These labels are of several types, and one includes the word "Macao" which would suggest that he had moved his studio from China Street, Canton, where he was recorded as being in the mid-1830's.

A view of Hong Kong in the 1850's bears a Sunqua label, and is a clue to the identity of a set of four paintings of Macao, Canton, Whampoa and Hong Kong that can thereby definitely be attributed to Sunqua. The paintings are extremely important for clarifying the changes that Sunqua had made by the 1850's, and they are done on the rectangular canvases of that period rather than the nearly-square canvas of the earlier paintings. His later style is more attuned to the works of the other port painters of the mid-century, but his technique has developed out of his previous work. The brushwork is more fluid, the compositions better arranged and the palette stronger. The new technique lacks the tight precision of the earlier style, and the delicate treatment seen in a painting such as that of Dutch Folly Fort is missing. The view of Hong Kong bearing his label exactly

42. Ship *Henry Tuke* at Whampoa Anchorage, by the "Henry Tuke" painter, circa 1835. Oil on canvas, $17\frac{1}{4}'' \times 23''$. *Peabody Museum, Salem.*

matches, in every detail, composition and palette, the view of Hong Kong in the set of four attributed to Sunqua. The Canton is very similar to that view in the early set (on the nearly-square canvases) and gives a clear idea of Sunqua's compositional arrangement when painting that port. The Macao is painted from a rather unusual angle—from out in the harbor looking straight at the Praya Grande and front row of buildings. This particular compositional arrangement is significant, since other paintings, on a larger scale, done in this manner can be attributed to him. A pair of long, large paintings of Macao from the open water exist which have all the elements of Sunqua's painting, including the treatment of figures, water and buildings. One is framed in a wide lacquered Bolection moulding which gives it the look of an overmantel panel. The two are identical and would seem to have been painted by Sunqua. With the view in the Bolection frame is a large view of Canton, which had been brought back by the same trader. The view of Canton is very close in composition and execution to the Canton view of the 1850's set by Sunqua mentioned above. These later paintings have one common characteristic: the faces of the figures have no features. This characteristic, however, is not peculiar to Sunqua only at this time.

Two paintings of ships by Sunqua, both painted in the 1860's, are signed in the lower right with the identical signature seen on his early paintings inscribed on the front of the canvas. Both are nearly square in composition and are the same size as those ship paintings of the 1830's. Here is an obvious regression to his earlier style. The paintings, however,

43. *Greyhound* to Canton, China, 1827, by the "Greyhound" painter. Oil on canvas, $17\frac{1}{2}'' \times 23\frac{1}{4}''$. *Peabody Museum, Salem.*

44. The hongs at Canton, artist unidentified, circa 1841. Oil on canvas, $17\frac{1}{2}'' \times 23''$. *Peabody Museum, Salem.*

45. The Burning of the Hongs at Canton, by Sunqua, 1856. Original label on stretchers. Oil on canvas, 17″ × 29½″. *Peabody Museum, Salem.*

have little similarity in execution to the early ship portraits. The handling of the water, the compositional placement of the vessel and the handling of the rigging and ship are all quite different. Some traces of his former technique can be seen in the use of light and the highlighting of the water.

Sunqua or his studio also worked in watercolor on either pith paper or English paper, and did superb miniatures on ivory, either from life or based on daguerreotypes. These are all discussed in subsequent chapters.

A second painter of great prominence in the mid-nineteenth century is Youqua. There is a minor problem of identity with Youqua, since there is also a Yeuqua in Hong Kong. However, the painting techniques, which at first glance would seem somewhat similar because of like palettes, upon close examination, are very different. In an early view of Macao (bearing his early label), Youqua uses the almost-square canvases popular with Sunqua. The later paintings described below are on long rectangular canvases. His earlier paintings show elements of his more developed style, but are somewhat less ambitious in composition and technique.

Youqua is an extremely competent painter, as proven by a very im-
46 pressive large view of Whampoa Anchorage (the companion paintings of this set of four exist, and the view of Canton would suggest that the set was painted around 1850).[10] Handsomely executed, the painting has a very distinctive palette with a heavy use of purple-blues in the sky and water. The boats and buildings are well delineated with very fluid brushwork, and the

figures and water are highlighted with white. The composition is very ambitious, but the whole works well for a painting of its size. The handling of the paint is extraordinarily pleasing, and the painting style and technique would stand up well in the West when compared with European or American painting of landscape and shore.

Bearing in mind the competence and ability shown in the Whampoa painting (and the remaining three in the set), it is possible to attribute a group of four highly important port paintings to Youqua with a great deal of surety.[11] The four, some of the largest views of the Chinese ports known
to exist, are of monumental quality and composition. Depicting Hong Kong, *49*
Canton, Whampoa Reach and Macao, the paintings must have been painted by the most significant Chinese artist working for the Western market in the mid-nineteenth century. In color, style, composition and handling of the skies, and the overall execution, the large set of four is very close to the Youqua of Whampoa Anchorage.

Through comparisons of these paintings with other labeled and documented Youqua port scenes, the attribution becomes more positive. The most conclusive evidence is a Chinese inscription on the sail of a junk in the view of Canton, which when translated freely states the set was painted in Honam by Youk Lin, which, when transliterated into a Western form of Chinese names, would be *Mr. You (k)* or "Youqua." The differences in the treatment of water in the four paintings can be explained by one characteristic of Chinese export artists. The port painters were meticulous in defining water and were careful to differentiate between river and sea water, and the water of the inner and outer harbors of Macao. When this is taken into consideration, one realizes that what may at first appear to be a stylistic difference in the handling of water, which would imply a different artist, is in actuality a distinctive treatment for each type of water represented.

In the oeuvres of Youqua are also found portraits of young ladies
which were undoubtedly based on European prints, landscapes and water- *32*
colors on both English paper and pith paper. Highly competent and attractive in color, the portraits are convincingly rendered and should have been popular decorative pieces in the mid-nineteenth century. There are examples of Chinese garden scenes and landscapes of considerable skill which bear the Youqua labels, but they lack the fine use of paint and the great attention to detail that one finds in his best port scenes. Youqua's earliest label lists 34 Old Street (Canton) as his address, while his later label carries the additional address of 107 Queensroad (Hong Kong), which confirms the fact that he worked in both ports. Perhaps the lesser garden scenes were
painted by assistants working under his tutelage in the studios (*see Chap. 5*). *69*
Youqua may well have executed portraits from life or miniatures from daguerreotypes, but no example has come to light up to the present time. A most amusing and innovative still life painting of fruits and vegetables (formerly misattributed and published as Lam Qua and Yamqua)[12] has
Youqua's label and clearly shows he is an unusual artist who could paint *47*
highly original paintings in the Western genre for a foreign market.

The painter Yeuqua is similar to Youqua in many ways, but he lacks the competence and the compositional strengths so obvious in the latter. A view of Shanghai, with a Yeuqua label, sharply points out the differences in the two painters. Here the composition is strung out, with the boats randomly placed and a certain disinterest in overall composition. The palette is

46. The Whampoa Anchorage, by Youqua, circa 1850. Oil on canvas, 27″ × 44″. *Peabody Museum, Salem.* (Overleaf)

47. Still life of fruit, by Youqua, circa 1850. Original label on stretchers with both Canton Hong Kong addresses. Oil on canvas, 23″ × 28¾″. *Peabody Museum, Salem.*

48 similar to that of Youqua, but it lacks his refinement of coloration. Several
paintings of the 1860's through the 1880's bear Yeuqua's label, complete with instructions as to how to care for the paintings.[13] A good many of these later paintings are portraits of girls and children and the wives of sea captains, either based on photographs or executed from life. The paintings are done in a rather heavy-handed manner and depend a great deal on the use of blue paints, a characteristic of all types of painting for the export market in the third quarter of the nineteenth century.

B.15 Yeuqua painted a large number of ship portraits, many of them of
the later steam and sail vessels. The two most interesting paintings by him
50 to date are copies in oil of paintings or watercolors of two Lynn, Massachu-
setts, vessels which were painted off Elsinore Castle in Denmark by either C. Clausen or Jacob Peterson. Yeuqua has copied the original paintings exactly, and has even included the famed castle. The paintings undoubtedly hung in a ship's cabin, and the owner must have wanted them duplicated for a friend by a Chinese artist.

A photograph taken by a Chinese artist of Queens Road in Hong Kong in the early 1880's shows a sign for Yeuqua's studio at the far left, and judging from the numbers of the adjoining buildings, his address would seem to have been 64. This is a different address from the one on his previous labels of 107 Queens Road.

One problem in attributing Chinese port and ship paintings to particular painters is that so many of the artists worked with lesser painters to

48. View of the Bund at Shanghai, by Yeuqua, circa 1860. Original label with 93 Queensroad, Hong Kong, address on stretchers. Oil on canvas, 16¾" × 29". *Peabody Museum, Salem.*

execute the innumerable works demanded for export. In much the same manner as Sir Joshua Reynolds and other great Western painters, the Chinese maintained studios to work on their paintings, and the master's style comes through even though an assistant has worked on a painting. Many of the assistants were to do the watercolors and pith paper albums, with the major paintings left to the "Master" himself. It is possible to distinguish the individual styles of the port painters and their studios and to group them accordingly. In the same way, the works of Reynolds, Gainsborough and Constable can be distinguished and placed together, although it is known that each had several followers or students who painted in the master's individual style.

Although Youqua is unquestionably the finest painter of this period on a large scale, there are numerous other painters of the third quarter of the nineteenth century who could execute an extraordinarily competent commission for a Western client. Namcheong is a painter of both ships and port scenes whose compositional devices and use of light make him readily identifiable. His most common paintings are vertical ovals of the small vessels and landscape around the Whampoa Anchorage pagoda and the French and Dutch Folly forts. Several of these still exist, and all have the *51*
same palette and play of light on the foreground water.[14] Many of the paintings bear the small red stamp NAMCHEONG PAINTER on one or more places on the back of the canvas or stretchers. There are enough ovals

49. View of Canton, by Youqua, circa 1855. Signed in Chinese in sail of junk to far left. Oil on canvas, $31\frac{1}{4}'' \times 57\frac{3}{4}''$.
Peabody Museum, Salem.

of identical composition to suggest that he or his studio used the format repeatedly.

Namcheong's large ship portraits, usually painted at the Whampoa Anchorage (it is suggested that his studio was at Whampoa, since so many of his paintings use the Whampoa area as a background or for subject matter), are handsome in composition and palette and very well executed. A
52 large painting of the *Victory,* owned by Captain Oliver Lane of Annisquam, Massachusetts, who sailed to China around 1860, shows a broadside view of the vessel with a Chinese junk and other small shipping and Whampoa in the background.[15] Namcheong's handling of the junk to the right is free and painterly, and the junk is a compositional addition seen in most of his other ship portraits. The painting is stamped twice on the reverse of the canvas NAMCHEONG PAINTER. A number of paintings commissioned by Thomas Hunt of Salem seem to have been executed by Namcheong in the 1850's. Hunt ran a ships' chandlery at Whampoa with James Cook and James Endicott. He and his family lived aboard a houseboat at Whampoa which was anchored with the numerous other Hunt vessels used for storage, freight transportation from Whampoa to Canton, ocean travel and the chandlery. The bulk of the group of paintings is now in the Peabody Museum, complete with diagrams of the vessels and their functions which were drawn and annotated by Hunt himself. A view of the Hunt boatyard and dry dock at Whampoa, with the schooners *Brenda* and *Minna,* is signed by Namcheong

50. Ship *Rasselas* of Lynn off Elsinore Castle, Denmark, by Yeuqua, circa 1850. Name originally on reverse of canvas. Copied from a European watercolor. Oil on canvas, $17\frac{1}{2}'' \times 23''$. *Lynn Historical Society.*

and was part of the Hunt bequest. 53

Several other paintings of the large Hunt fleet at anchor at Whampoa would also seem to be by Namcheong, as they are easily associated with the signed painting and have stylistic similarities to his other signed works. Three large views of Whampoa, each with innumerable vessels of many
sizes and purposes (including the Hunt houseboat, the floating *Bethel* and 54
the small river schooners), all flying the red, blue and white Hunt house flag, are similar to the signed Namcheongs in their palette, treatment of sky and use of light and detail. The attribution becomes even more positive when a comparison is made with a broadside view of the ship *Lantao,* owned by Hunt, which is almost identical to the signed Namcheong "*Victory.*" Alike in size, compositional arrangement and treatment of light, the two paintings evidence the style developed by Namcheong for his broadside ship portraits. Since the *Lantao* was also in the Hunt group, it would seem that Hunt had commissioned the entire group from Namcheong. It would appear, therefore, that it was not unusual for a Westerner to use the same painter repeatedly for portraying his vessels and for recording the ports he visited, much in the same way that John Singleton Copley might have been commissioned to paint an entire family. Another ship painting attributable to Namcheong is of the *Wild Pigeon,*[16] built by George Raynes of Newburyport, which is the same size as the "*Victory*" and "*Lantao*" and uses the same compositional devices and colors for the water and sky.

Namcheong was a good, competent painter who was able to work on a large scale; he lacked, however, the refinement of touch and the ability to render figures and smaller vessels convincingly, skills that were to set Youqua so far apart from the other port painters. The heavy figures, the rather clumsy treatment of buildings and the awkwardness with which the vessels sit in the water show Namcheong not to be a highly academic painter. The broadside ship portraits employ similar enough technique and composition to make other attributions to Namcheong viable.

In the mid-1850's and '60's several other artists' names constantly appear, but few of these artists possessed great skill or worked above the level of the average competent painter for the export market. Further research will be necessary to establish more information about the painters and what they were selling. In many instances, the painters of port scenes were painters of ships and portraits, and vice versa, but it is difficult to know how many were so versatile without definite signed examples.

The *Typhoon* painter (circa 1850), called after the ship he painted, is
55 one artist recognizable by his style, but his name still eludes research. His light grey-blue palettes and delicate handling of the ships and rigging are unlike the works of any other painter of the period. Two other ship paintings possibly by him, of the *Gamecock* and the *Hollander,* are of similar size and show a similar light palette and compositional treatment. All three paintings have one characteristic in common which helps to define this painter: the names of the ships on the pennants are in each case reversed.

The quality of the painting of most of the artists in the third quarter of the nineteenth century is inconsistent and is not nearly so high as that of
56 the *Typhoon* painter or Namcheong. Lai Sung, a painter of large and small paintings in the 1860's through the '80's (mostly broadside views of ships), is competent, but his paintings are repetitive and his brushwork careless. Predominantly painted in hard blues, the paintings invariably have a view of Hong Kong in the background. The stencil, which Lai Sung used on the back of his canvases, in heavy black letters gave his location as Hong Kong. The paintings have a certain dash and are very dramatic on first appearance, but the quality is certainly not that of the port painters of the earlier period or of a Youqua.

Hing Qua is another painter of the third quarter of the nineteenth century who was prolific and able, but his paintings fall within a set formula, and, hence, become repetitious and dull when seen in quantity. Several paintings by him in the Peabody Museum provide a study collection of his work which is helpful in establishing in what ways his work varied from the other painters. Hing Qua did a number of different types of paintings, such as portraits, charts, etc., and this fact is set forth on his label.[17] His existing portraits are rather heavy and Victorian in color and composition, and are often based on early photographs of the sitters rather than done from life. Hing Qua's most common label was a small oval with a red line around the edge with his name and his specialties in the center. (Many of the best labeled Chinese paintings have been lost to researches through relinings of original canvases and the removal and disposal of the original stretchers and frames.) The influences on the painting styles of these later artists may have come more from the Mediterranean school of marine painters than from the earlier English or Dutch schools. The painters of the late-nineteenth century were competent and could execute a very presentable painting, but the care-

51. Nine-stage pagoda at Whampoa Reach, by Namcheong, circa 1850. Original stamp on back of canvas. Oil on canvas, 20″ × 15″. *Childs Gallery.*

52. Ship *Victory* at Whampoa, circa 1850, by Namcheong. Oil on canvas, 27″ × 36″. *Collection of Nina Fletcher Little.*

53. Whampoa shipyard with vessels *Brenda* and *Minna,* by Namcheong, circa 1850. Original stamp on back of canvas. Oil on canvas, 17¼″ × 33″. Painting originally owned by Thomas Hunt. *Peabody Museum, Salem.*

54. The Hunt fleet at Whampoa, circa 1850, attributed to Namcheong. Oil on canvas, $33\frac{3}{4}'' \times 57\frac{1}{2}''$. *Peabody Museum, Salem.*

ful renditions and delicate palettes of the previous seventy-five years had given way to a more highly commercial and garishly decorative quality. It might be said the paintings became attractive to a "tourist" market, where concern for size and color was greater than for subtlety and quality of execution.

Other painters whose names are known in the 1860's through the '80's and who, for the most part, executed ship portraits are Hung Qua, Wing Chong, Woo Cheong, Taicheong, Qua Sees, Lai Fong, W. E. Chung, Lee Heng, Pun Woo and Yat On. Unfortunately, only isolated examples of these painters' works exist, and it is difficult at the present time to establish a particular style or format for each. The examples that exist for Lee Heng, Taicheong and Lai Fong (who worked in Calcutta) show them to be capable artists working much in the manner of Lai Sung and Hing Qua. The most important and interesting painting to date by a member of this group is of the bark *Dirigo;* it is a copy by Taicheong of a C. Clausen or Jacob Peterson watercolor or oil.[18] Very similar to the two copies by Yeuqua discussed previously, Taicheong has included Elsinore Castle in the background. The painting is handled in much the same way a member of this European port school would handle it. The practice of copying a Western ship painting does not seem uncommon, since a picture of the *Aurora* in the Peabody Museum appears to have been based on a Samuel Walters or David McFarlane, complete to the white cliffs of Dover in the background.

Painters such as Namcheong, Lai Sung and Hing Qua mainly concentrated on delineations of ships and port scenes, although they would often fill portrait and other commissions. Occasionally, in the study of port painters, a man comes to light who painted all types of work for export, and a large enough body of his work exists to be able to examine all the various services he advertised. Such a painter was Chow Kwa, who, from the limited information available, must have had his studio in Shanghai from approximately 1855 to 1880. His label is a small one printed with his name only in black ink.[19] In one rare instance he signed a view of Shanghai on the front of the canvas in block letters in the manner of Sunqua. One painting of the
58 Shanghai house of Augustine Heard of Ipswich, Massachusetts, owner of
Heard and Company, bears a typical Chow Kwa label on the back of the stretcher.[20] The painting is pleasing and shows the artist to be an excellent limner. It is interesting to note there is another view of this house from the same vantage point which may also be by Chow Kwa or a member of his studio. An actual photograph of the Heard House, taken in the 1870's, clearly
59 shows that both paintings depict the house very accurately, with attention
to details such as the open and closed exterior shutters. Another painting of two unidentified houses at Shanghai, also bearing the Chow Kwa label, reveals the same skill in drafting and a palette similar to the painting of the Heard House. The foreground treatment and the figures are alike in both paintings, and the paintings establish a technique for Chow Kwa which is readily identifiable. That Chow Kwa was a diverse and highly skillful painter is illustrated through a set of three extraordinary miniatures of members of the Captain Oliver Lane family of Massachusetts. The superb miniatures were undoubtedly copied from daguerreotypes of the subjects, which were taken to China by Lane.[21] One or two other known paintings by Chow Kwa are also of Shanghai or Shanghai houses, and this would tend to confirm the fact that this was the location of his studio.

55. Ship *Typhoon* at Whampoa, by "Typhoon" painter, circa 1860. Oil on canvas, 17″ × 21¼″. *Peabody Museum, Salem.*

There was an incredible number of port scenes and ship portraits painted in the nineteenth century that we cannot attribute to a particular artist. A great deal of research will be necessary to determine who some of the other painters may have been and how many studios there actually were. Bryant Tilden mentions, in 1816, some thirty places in the vicinity of the Canton hongs where he could buy pith paper watercolors, but since several dealers in general merchandise handled these, the number of artists' studios at that time may be fewer. The painters of the eighteenth century are a perplexing problem, since so few names or labels have emerged from that period. There were many paintings of Chinese gardens and views, based on Western prints and of great competence, done at the end of the eighteenth century. All similar in style and technique, there are few clues to the painters' names. The quality of the port paintings and ship portraits of the nineteenth century varies markedly, and it is possible that those of lesser quality were executed in the studios of the "masters" by assistants. Just like the painters of the Mediterranean ports, the style of each painter and his studio is identifiable, and the paintings can be grouped according to style; in the years to come it is hoped that more of these artists and their studios will be identified and individuated.

56. Ship *Shirley* off Hong Kong, by Lai Sung, circa 1860. Original stencil, "Lai Sung," on reverse of canvas. Oil on canvas, $27\frac{3}{4}'' \times 38\frac{1}{2}''$. *Peabody Museum, Salem.*

57. Ship *Surprise* at Whampoa, artist unidentified, circa 1855. Oil on canvas, $26\frac{1}{2}'' \times 35''$. *Peabody Museum, Salem.*

58. House of Augustine Heard and Co., Shanghai, by Chow Kwa, circa 1865. Original Chow Kwa label on back of stretcher. Oil on canvas, $16\frac{1}{4}'' \times 21\frac{3}{4}''$. *Peabody Museum, Salem.*

59. Photograph of the house of Augustine Heard and Co., Shanghai, circa 1870. 8″ × 10″. *Peabody Museum, Salem.*

The frames and stretchers (or strainers) on the China export paintings are important guides for general dating. Below are illustrated and described the more typical frames for each major stylistic period from 1790 to 1870. Although these frames were in vogue for particular time-spans, many continued to be used after their initial popularity had waned.

60. Detail of a frame to a reverse painting on glass, circa 1810. This design is typical of the frame mouldings used by the Chinese artists on the early paintings and the reverse paintings on glass. These period gold leaf frames were in direct copy of English frames.

61. Detail of a mirror frame, circa 1820. The frame is carved and gilded exactly like an American or English frame of the period. Note the addition of the gold balls.

62. Detail of the back of a frame with its original fitted back panel. These panels were used for reverse paintings on glass and mirror backs. Note the small wooden "tabs" that fit into slots to hold the panel in place.

63. Detail of a carved and gilded frame of the period 1825–1860. These frames, magnificently carved and very Western in feeling, were often used on portraits by Chinnery and Lam Qua; they also appear on port scenes and other paintings of the period.

64. Detail of a bevelled frame on a port scene of circa 1840. This smooth bevelled moulding, often painted, gilded or left natural, was often used on Sunqua's ship paintings and other port and ship portraits of the period from 1825 to 1860. Port scenes and some portraits of 1790–1825 were often framed in flat mouldings, sometimes with an inner gilded edge, which were painted black. In rare instances, carved rosettes or decorations were applied to the corners.

65. Detail of a typical China trade strainer (stretcher) showing its construction. This type of strainer was used throughout the nineteenth century. The pieces are cut and the corners are placed at a right angle so they overlap, and then are held together by four small wooden pegs driven down through the two pieces of wood. The underside facing the painting is often bevelled to prevent abrasion of the canvas from behind.

66. Detail of the popular "Chinese Chippendale" frame found on the majority of port scenes painted from 1830–1880. The frames were usually painted a deep brown-black lacquer, and had an inner edge, either plain or carved, of gold leaf. The frame was also extremely popular for portraits and other paintings.

67. Detail of an ornate, overly decorated, carved and pierced frame, circa 1870. This style of frame was popular throughout the nineteenth century and was often used for framing waterors and pith papers as well as port scenes, ship portraits and portraits. The design is of complex landscapes, and Chinese figures with pavilion and gardens.

Notes

1. Hand-colored stipple engravings: "Pu-Qua Delin. Dadley London, Sculpt., Published May 4, 1799, by W. Miller, Old Bond Street, London."
2. "Custon House on the River between Canton and Whampoa Painted by Mayhing, China Street Canton. Purchased by Charles Copeland Midshipman, Hon[ble] Com[py] Ship 'Surat Castle' from the Artist. 8th January 1813."
3. Customs House Records, for 1799–1800, Salem, Massachusetts.
4. "Letters of Sullivan Dorr," ed. by Howard Corning, *Proceedings of the Massachusetts Historical Society,* Vol. LXVII, 1945. Letter to Ebenezer Dorr, Jr., Jan. 14, 1800.
5. Two other ship portraits are known which are undoubtedly by the same hand: one privately owned; the other exhibited at the Loan Exhibition at the University Hospital Antiques Show, 1972. The latter ship is the *Montesquieu.*
6. Lin Tin was the island in the mouth of the Pearl River where most of the opium hulks were at anchor and where the "troublesome article" was traded.
7. This question, and the question of whether or not Sunqua did the Russell & Co. vessel and the *Levant* and *Milo,* has been discussed extensively. He is known to have signed a watercolor or pith of the *Levant* and *Milo* of approximately the same composition.
8. Set purchased for his brother in Providence; see *Proceedings of the Massachusetts Historical Society,* Vol. LXVII.
9. Sunqua is the most perplexing of the artists; his career is long and his style changes. The author believes he is one artist only, and the two later paintings signed *Sunqua* seem to confirm it.
10. The Canton view has the church built circa 1848.
11. The set, now in the Peabody Museum, was given by Beverley Robinson of New York, and it is probably the most important large set of port scenes of this period now known, for quality, condition and detail.
12. The label was misread as *Yamqua* and the painting listed as such in the catalogue of the "Marine Paintings and Drawings in the Peabody Museum," by M. V. and Dorothy Brewington. Salem, Mass., 1968. The label was again misread as *Lamqua,* and the painting exhibited and published in "Chinnery (1774–1852) & other Artists of the Chinese Scene." Peabody Museum: Salem, Mass., 1967.
13. See Chapter 3 for direct citation of these informative and unusual labels.
14. A particularly good and typical pair may be seen at the Fogg Museum, Harvard University, Cambridge, Mass. Approximately four sets have been identified.
15. Lane brought back a great number of China trade artifacts and paintings, and the contents of the Lane House, dispersed in the late 1950's, were an excellent record of the types of paintings, etc., which were purchased by a mid-nineteenth century trader.
16. The painting was exhibited at the 1941 Metropolitan Museum of Art show, "The China Trade and its Influences," and was recently sold at auction.
17. A label by an unidentified painter named Hung Qua, is one of the most informative to date: "Marine, ship and portrait painter, photos copied on ivory, photographs enlarged & coloured in oil, all kinds of pictures framed, plain music copying with neatness, landscape pictures and photographic materials always for sale, terms moderate, No. 58 Wellington St. Hong Kong."
18. C. Clausen (worked second quarter of the nineteenth century) and Jacob Petersen (1774–1854) were both Danish artists working near Elsinore Castle, executing fine watercolors of ships. The Peabody Museum has several examples of the works of both.
19. This seems to be the only label he used. A view of Shanghai, privately owned, is signed "Chow Kwa" on the front.
20. Heard and Company's houses in Shanghai, Hong Kong and Macao were frequently painted, and many copies exist of these handsome residences.
21. The miniature portrait of Mrs. Oliver Lane, although based on a daguerreotype, is of the same composition as a life-size three-quarter-length American oil portrait of her.

68. Chinese garden scene, one of a set of four of the seasons, artist unidentified, circle of Spoilum, circa 1800. Oil on canvas, 25″ × 37″. *Privately owned.*

5. Genre Painting and Copies of Western Art

The Chinese painters working for the export market executed a large body of work that does not fit within the categories of port scenes, ship paintings, or portraits. These other paintings were unquestionably done by many of the same artists executing the more standard orders, since several of them show identical stylistic handling. Few of the more unusual paintings are signed, and it is difficult to establish who the painters might have been.

Chinese landscape and garden scenes, painted in oil, were very popular from the end of the eighteenth century through the nineteenth. Those painted in the 1790's and slightly later are often large ($3\frac{1}{2}$ or 4 feet in some instances) and of superb quality. One set of four defines the seasons in an allegorical manner. The large Chinese figures in the foreground on the garden terraces must have been painted by an extremely competent artist: *68*
possibly one of the men who did the large port views of Canton in this period or a painter like the one who executed the Court of Inquiry (*see Illus. 36*). The palettes are magnificent, with a strong use of bright colors and electric blues. In many ways this impressive set is reminiscent of the paintings on glass and the gouaches of Fatqua.[1]

The garden scenes of the nineteenth century are usually less ambitious and not so well conceived. Some fine ones do exist, however, such as a labeled pair by Youqua (or his studio) now at Mystic Seaport. These show *69*
Youqua to be as competent in landscape as he was in the large port scenes and copies of portraits of European ladies.

A large, important set of four oils on canvas from the first quarter of the nineteenth century depicts an archery contest, boating on the river and other phases of Chinese life. One is an unusual night scene of a pleasure *70*
boat lighted with lanterns. Each painting is very large by export standards, 32 by 50 inches, and is of stunning quality. Again, these are reminiscent of a set of gouaches by Fatqua (*see Chap. 6*). The fact that paintings of this size

69. Chinese garden scene by Youqua, circa 1845. Oil on canvas, $17\frac{1}{2}'' \times 23''$. *Mystic Seaport, Mystic, Connecticut.*

and subject were done for the trade indicates the extraordinary degree of Western interest in various facets of Chinese life. Having little opportunity to observe Chinese life other than on visits to the estates of some of the wealthy Hong merchants, Western traders obviously enjoyed having a part of this way of life permanently recorded in the paintings they purchased to take home with them. The Westerners looked forward with great anticipation to visiting Houqua's fabulous gardens at his estate in Honam.[2] Two watercolors by Tingqua are labeled "Houqua's Gardens," and depict views of the lush plantings, gazebos and pavilions, all connected by bridges and pools.[3]

Sets of paintings showing the Chinese in various phases of domestic
71 and social life were also painted for export, and often followed the same subject matter as the watercolors and gouaches on pith paper. Popular themes were tea-drinking, ladies being attended and dressed by servants, card-playing and other games, and garden parties. Many are of extremely fine quality and very well painted. Those executed towards the middle of the nineteenth century, except canvases by Youqua and other painters of comparable skill, tend to be somewhat sloppy in painting and drafting. The interiors are excellent, however, as studies of Chinese-style household furniture, and accessories, often including bamboo seats and stools, and wood and brass dressing mirrors similar to those exported to the West. The gardens and terraces are particularly interesting as illustrations of the custom of planting flowers and small trees in pots and urns rather than directly in

70. Boating in the evening, artist unidentified, circa 1840. One of a set of four large paintings depicting Chinese life. Oil on canvas, 32¾″ × 49½″. *Photograph courtesy Childs Gallery.*

the ground. Bonsai trees and indigenous Chinese flowering plants can be readily identified.

Certainly one of the most charming of all the garden scenes is one
with a Western (possibly American) woman and her baby sitting in a bam- 72
boo extension chair.[4] The garden is ornate and quite beautiful: a small gazebo in the middle of a pond, several garden structures, and a moon gate in the wall beyond. Possibly the garden belonged to a wealthy Chinese Hong merchant of the mid-century. The painting is a portrait of a particular woman whose child was born in the Orient, and, from the mother's hair style and dress, the painting was probably done around 1850. An interesting note is the series of Western-style lighting fixtures which hangs in the garden house to the right. Those on the ground floor have globes with prisms; the one on the second level is a familiar late Empire oil lamp, which hangs from three brass chains and supports a glass globe.

Oil paintings on canvas based on Western prints were exported as well. The best of them are extremely faithful to the originals and, hence, are often difficult to distinguish from English or American paintings. The subjects were very diverse, like those of the paintings on glass, and run the gamut of nineteenth-century tastes and interests. English satirical subjects and prints after Gainsborough and Reynolds portraits of ladies were copied. A particularly amusing satirical one, after an unknown print, depicts a dance
or reception. The lady to the left in this scene has just fainted after realizing 73
her friend's retainer is wearing the same ball gown. The painting is obviously

71. Chinese domestic scene, artist unidentified, circa 1835. Oil on canvas, 19″ × 25″. *Photograph courtesy Childs Gallery.*

72. Garden scene with an American woman, artist unidentified, circa 1850. Oil on canvas, 15″ × 24″. *Private Collection.*

73. An evening gathering, artist unidentified, circa 1840. Based on an unidentified European print. Oil on canvas, 12″ × 15″. *Peabody Museum, Salem.*

74. Brocket Hall, England, artist unidentified, circa 1810. Based on an English print. Oil on canvas, 21″ × 27″. *Author's Collection.*

75. Chinese landscape in the European manner, circle of Spoilum, circa 1810. Oil on canvas, 25″ × $36\frac{5}{8}$″. *Metropolitan Museum of Art, Gift of the Members of the Committee of the Bertha King Bankard Memorial Fund,* 1946.

Chinese in execution and certain details, such as the dropped glove, are poorly drawn. The picture was executed around 1840 and is on its original Chinese stretchers; it is framed in the period black "Chinese Chippendale" frame found on ship paintings and port scenes of the period.

A magnificent view of an English country estate, painted circa 1800,
74 is copied from an English print of Brocket Hall. It is of such superb quality
that it could easily be taken for a Western painting. The canvas, however,
is Chinese, and the large concave gold Regency frame is joined and gilded
in the Chinese manner. Several other Chinese paintings of English estates
do exist, and they were probably copied from the same prints that were
brought to China for the porcelain decorators to copy onto dinner and
tea services. The Metropolitan Museum owns a handsome nineteenth-
75 century painting of a Chinese landscape handled very much in the style of
an Anglo-Dutch landscape of the early eighteenth century. The composition and treatment reflect the influence of Hobbema or Ruysdael. An influence of this type is likely, since so many of the port paintings of the same
period reflect Dutch and English painting traditions. A second, and larger,
version of this painting is also known to exist.[5]

Many of the watercolors on pith paper used European prints and
drawings as sources of inspiration. Still lifes of fruits and flowers, caricatures, and satirical prints were all copied. Tingqua's gouache and watercolor
91, 95 still lifes and figures were based on prints or watercolors of Western derivation.[6] Again, the prints were readily available in China, having been sent out
for copying by porcelain decorators. The watercolors, on fans, of French
court scenes and mythological and allegorical designs were also copied from
prints which had been used for porcelain designs.[7]

Notes

1. See Chapters 6 and 7 for a full description of his work.
2. Extensive descriptions of visits to the gardens of various Chinese merchants can be found in the papers of Bryant Tilden in the Peabody Museum, Salem.
3. Heard Collection, Peabody Museum, Salem.
4. The painting has an American provenance, and it is thought to represent an American woman.
5. Privately owned, Philadelphia. This painting also reflects a heavy Dutch treatment, and for years it was thought to have been the work of a Western painter.
6. See Chapter 6 for illustrations.
7. See Chapter 11 for illustrations.

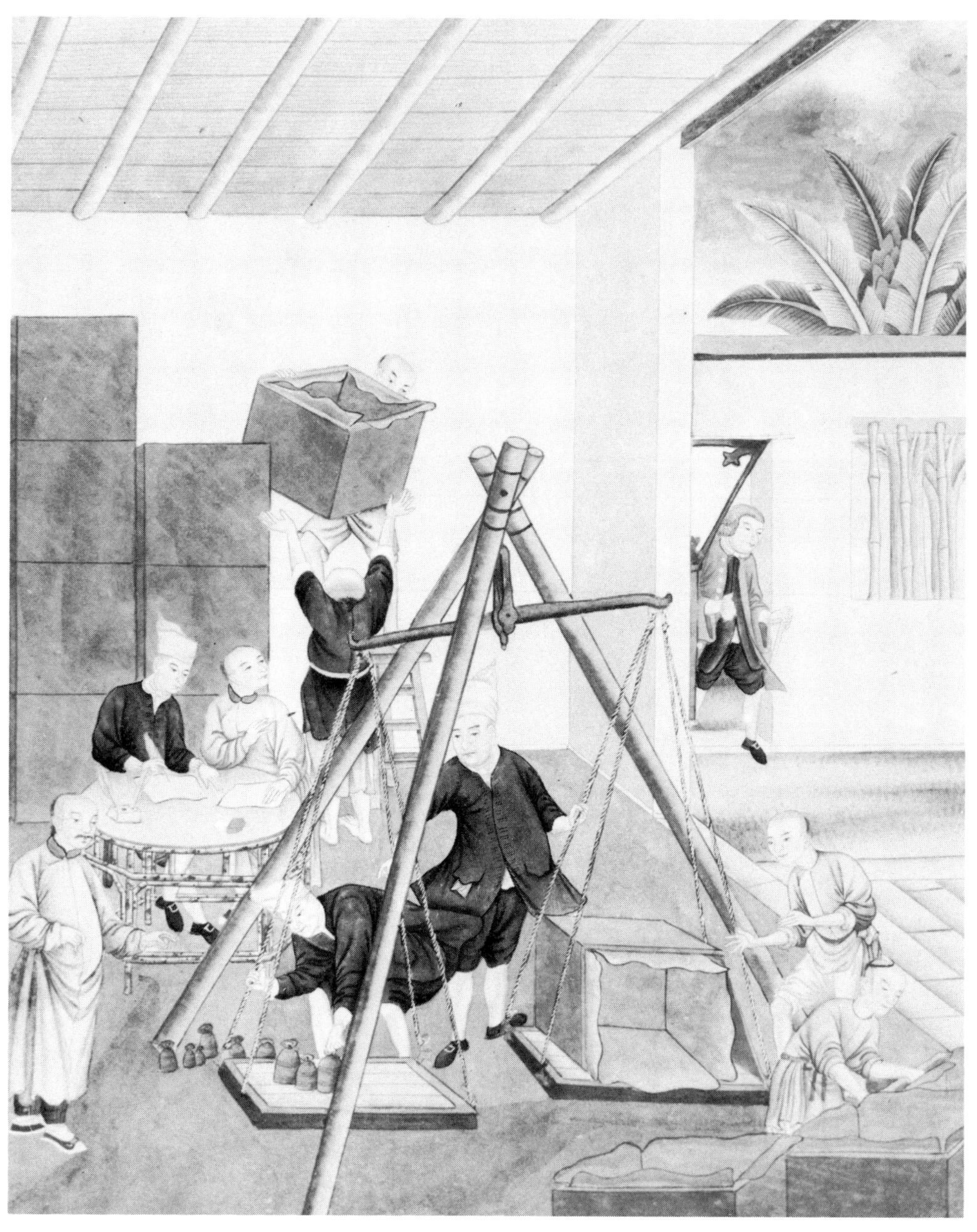

76. Merchants buying tea, artist unidentified, circa 1780. Watercolor on paper, 13″ × 9″. *Collection of Endowment Management, Boston.*

77. Canton, circa 1760, artist unidentified. One of a set of four forming a panorama of the entire Canton waterfront. Gouache on silk, $18\frac{3}{4}$″ × 29″. *Peabody Museum, Salem.* (*Opposite*)

6. Watercolors and Gouaches

The watercolors and gouaches for the export market were even more avidly purchased by American merchants than the oil paintings because of their convenient size and relatively low price. The watercolorists were in many instances the same painters who worked in oil on canvas, although there were those who worked only in watercolor or gouache. Little is known of the earliest watercolorists working for the export market; like the oil painters of the period, they remain quite anonymous unless a reference was found in a shipping document or book, or an English printer gave the Chinese painter credit for his original drawing.

The eighteenth-century watercolors showing Westerners in the Orient were often done in a more Chinese style than those seen after 1800. Figures were drawn with a certain amount of modeling, and perspective was employed in painting the buildings and landscapes, but the overall appearance was definitely Chinese. A set of four watercolors of Dutch merchants super-

78. The *Canton* East Indiaman, artist unidentified, circa 1797. Watercolor on paper, 17″ × 20¼″. *Photograph courtesy Childs Gallery.*

vising the purchasing and packing of tea, circa 1780, clearly illustrates the eighteenth-century export style. Bright and colorful, the set is on English 76 rather than Chinese paper. This type of vertical composition and Chinese style was to be used for the many series of watercolors, such as the porcelain-making set, that were painted before 1790. A magnificent album of grisaille watercolors of numerous Chinese ports and cities is painted very much in the manner of native Chinese scroll painting with sweeping panoramas and delicate brushwork. A set such as this must have been executed by a painter fully familiar with traditional Chinese painting who was just beginning to paint in a Western style. A similar set in light watercolor now in the British Museum employs the same techniques and brushwork and confirms the development of this type of painting for the export market before 1800.[1]

The few existing large eighteenth-century watercolors or gouaches of the ports are impressive in size, extremely accurate in detail, and delicate in palette. Four paintings in a set, gouache on silk, join together to make a 77 panorama of the Canton waterfront about 1760. The horizon line is very low in the composition with a large smooth sky area above. The paintings are very Chinese in feeling and seem to come out of the Chinese landscape school of painting despite their Western perspective and treatment of details. In the mid-eighteenth century, the export market painting in watercolor or gouache on silk still remains very much in the indigenous Chinese tradition. This set has serenity and simplicity that are not found in the port scenes after 1800. Another pair of gouaches, of similar style and technique, shows Whampoa Reach and Dutch Folly Fort as they were about 1760. Also of large size and on silk, they have the same low horizon and sweeping skies.

The composition of the section of the panorama which shows the Canton hongs is similar to a view of the city in oil painted around 1785.[2] Both C 3 the gouache and the oil have the same low horizon, simple sky and a generally uncluttered aspect to the composition. Although undoubtedly painted by different artists, the paintings reveal a particular style developed for the export market in painting. The delicate colors, the clear blues and the greys of the painting and the gouache reveal the use of the same palette, regardless of the medium. A Chinese watercolor of an English vessel, the "Canton East 78 Indiaman," painted in 1797, illustrates the fine Chinese drafting techniques used in ship watercolors around 1800. Somewhat flat and decorative, it is reminiscent of the early port scenes on silk. The simplicity and coolness of this export technique are no longer seen after the introduction of the more Western style of painting to the Chinese artists.

These early watercolor views on silk did not find their way to America. By the time the Americans had entered the China trade, the demand was for port scenes in oil; or later, on Western paper or pith paper. After 1790, then, the Chinese artists executed most of their watercolors for the trade on Western paper. The watermarks on these British and American papers have proved very useful in helping to establish dates for the watercolors laid upon them. The watermarks of J. Whatman of London and A. Cowan and Son, also of London, are common. Benjamin Shreve of Salem mentions taking 90 reams of paper to Canton for sale in 1816.[3] Supplying the Chinese with the raw materials for a product which was to be sold to the West was not unusual, since it happened in many fields of manufacture. The other paper commonly used for watercolors and gouaches, after 1800, was pith, which has been mistakenly called "rice" paper. A description of pith paper and its man-

79. An Emperor's audience, artist unidentified, circa 1810. Gouache on silk, 30″ × 37½″. *Private Collection.*

80. Western merchant negotiating for the purchase of tea, artist unidentified, circa 1790. Watercolor on paper, $14\frac{3}{8}'' \times 18\frac{3}{8}''$. *Private Collection.*

81. Glazing porcelain, artist unknown, circa 1790. Watercolor on paper, 14″ × 18″. *Peabody Museum, Salem.*

ufacture appears in the catalogue of the Chinese section of the Philadelphia Centennial International Exhibition of 1876: "The so called rice paper is made of pith of the Aralia papyrifera. The pith is soaked before cutting; the workman then applies the blade to the cylinders of pith, and, turning them round dexterously, pares them from the circumference to the center, making a rolled layer of equal thickness throughout."[4] The pith paper was a very fragile medium to work on, and many of those watercolors which have survived are cracked and broken. The standard technique for mounting was to place the pith on another type of paper, bind the pith edges with Chinese silk ribbon and bind the pages, usually in groups of twelve according to subject matter, between album covers of woven geometric fabrics.

Many of the watercolors were done in sets, such as groups of port scenes, the trades, shop interiors, and Chinese scenes and landscapes. Single large subjects were executed as well. The folio size, and larger, watercolors of the period 1790 to 1820 which are still extant display superb quality and
79 show great attention to coloring and detail. A watercolor of an Imperial audience given by the Emperor Chia Ching (1791–1820) is complex in com-

82. Chinese room interior, artist unidentified, circa 1830. Watercolor on paper, 15″ × 17″. *Childs Gallery.*

position and magnificent in handling of colors and paint. Each face and figure is carefully planned and the whole is unified and pleasing. Another version, identical except for size and the change of one figure, now at Brighton Pavilion, was brought back to England about 1800 by Richard Hill, a supercargo of the East India Company.[5]

Watercolors in sets of between 12 and 36 pictures, showing the growing, processing and shipping of tea, the making of porcelain, the silk industry and tea culture, were popular from the middle of the eighteenth century through the nineteenth, since they explained the products that were being sent to the West. The most desired of all the watercolors in the series were the ones that actually showed the Western merchants or supercargos negotiating with the Chinese merchants. A superb example, with a European *80*
figure in late-eighteenth century dress, exemplifies the quality of painting the artists could attain. The watercolors depicting craft and manufacturing processes vary in complexity of composition and detail, but the finest became some of the most desirable export watercolors painted. The tea-culture series represented all the processes from the growing of the tea to its final shipment and sale. Since tea was a major commodity in the trade, the water-

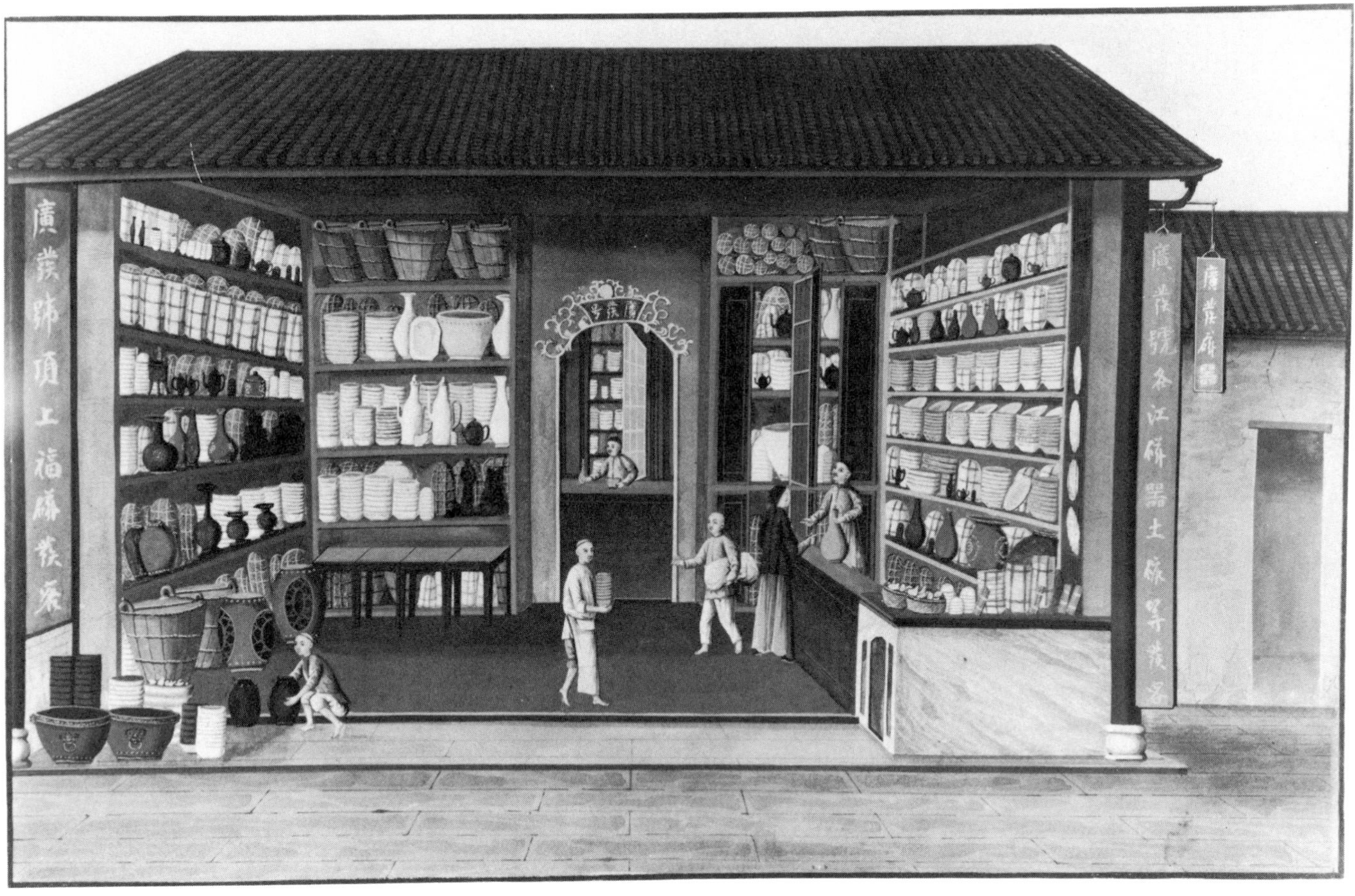

83. Interior of a porcelain shop, artist unidentified, circa 1835. Gouache on paper, 9″ × 14″. One of a set of 13 steps in the making of porcelain. *Peabody Museum, Salem.*

colors found a ready market. The series depicting the making of porcelain
81 is considered the most important, since every step of the process from the digging of the clay to the glazing and final shop sale was recorded. The eighteenth-century watercolors of porcelain manufacture were in the style of the four watercolors of the Dutch merchants buying tea (*see Illus. 76*); the perspective was more Chinese than Western, and the figures maintained a flat Chinese look much like those in the early wallpapers.

After 1800, watercolors depicting the porcelain industry were often done in full rich colors and show more than one step of manufacture on each sheet. The large silk-industry depictions have handsome landscape backgrounds and show great detail, and, like the other sets, were often done on English paper. Smaller sets of the industries were executed after the 1820's and were bound together either as separate trades or as compilations of several different ones. In this period the trades were also painted in small size on pith paper and bound in albums. It is not uncommon to find some parts to each trade series, but not complete series, bound with subjects from the other trades or completely different subjects. The selection of subject matter may well have been left to the individual purchaser.

Occasional sets of botanical watercolors of indigenous Chinese flowers were executed, but they are rare. Usually of staggering quality, the watercolors are extremely precise and accurate. The flowers are in rich delicate

84. Chinese winter scene, by Fatqua, stamped on reverse, paper dated 1824. Gouache on paper, 18″ × 24″. *Photograph courtesy Childs Gallery.*

colors that are far from the palettes used by the later port artists in the middle of the nineteenth century.

A set of watercolors, circa 1830, showed room settings of native furni- 82
ture. Accurate in detail and subtle in color, the set would have given a Westerner of the period an excellent idea of a Chinese household, complete with its scrolls and decorative accessories. A set of watercolors of lanterns, close in period, illustrates the profuse variety of lighting fixtures the Chinese house might have. These two sets indicate an interest on the part of the Westerner in native Chinese furnishings as well as in those objects made solely to appeal to a foreign market.

Series of watercolors of the interiors of the various shops making products for the export trade gave the Westerner a rare glimpse of the articles available for purchase. These views provide the best documentary evidence possible in that regard. The interiors of lacquerware shops are filled with tables, boxes, screens and oddities of all shapes and sizes. The pewter and fan shops display items often or seldom seen. The bamboo furniture shops have the familiar rattan and bamboo chairs and settees of the "Brighton Pavilion"
style. In the porcelain shops are arrayed hundreds of pieces of porcelain 83
readily identifiable by the collector of China trade porcelains. Perhaps the shop which gives the greatest surprise is one where furniture in the Western style is being made. Here are Empire scroll-arm chairs, gate-leg tables, chests,

85. Boy selling birds, artist unidentified, circa 1840. Watercolor on paper, 9″ × 12″. From a series of 99 Street Trades of China. *Private Collection.*

tip-top tables, settees, couches and chests of drawers, most of which do not appear to be Chinese at all.

One of the few watercolorists known by name in the first part of the nineteenth century is Fatqua, particularly noted for his superb paintings on glass after Western prints.[6] A series of three very handsome, large gouache Chinese landscapes on watermarked J. Whatman paper of 1824 bears his
84 name. A winter scene with figures has the red stamp "Fatqua" on the back of the paper, a highly unusual mark to find on a watercolor. The gouaches make extensive use of the technique applied to a reverse painting on glass, and have highlights of white on the trees and figures which endow them with a great deal of style.

Some of the most common albums for the Western market were those
85 consisting of from one to four hundred watercolors of the various street trades of Canton. Popular from the late-eighteenth century, one early set was copied in 1799 by a London publisher, who printed in the lower corner of the stipple engravings "Pu Qua Canton, Delin." Although this is an important early note of an artist's name, no actual work by Pu Qua has come to light. The subjects of the street trades were to be copied again and again, and even by the mid-nineteenth century, the artists were still using the same compositions and formats established in the late-eighteenth century. The quality tends to vary considerably, but even in 1860 some of the watercolors were

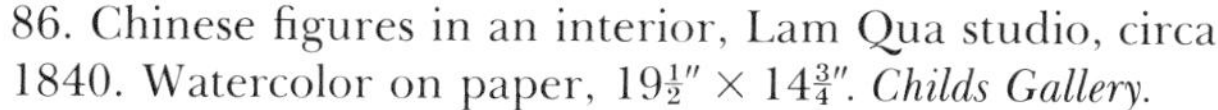

86. Chinese figures in an interior, Lam Qua studio, circa 1840. Watercolor on paper, $19\frac{1}{2}'' \times 14\frac{3}{4}''$. *Childs Gallery.*

87. Woodblock stamp on the reverse of Illus. 86, Lam Qua studio, circa 1845. *Childs Gallery.*

comparable to those that had been done seventy years before.

It is in the period from 1815 to 1870 that one sees the greatest export of Chinese watercolors for the foreign trade. In effect the picture postcards of the day, they were readily available on any subject, and for a reasonable enough price to make purchases of entire sets or mixed groups possible. (As with the oil paintings, the names of the artists or the studios become known only through labels and signatures.) The scenes of Chinese manufactories, discussed above, remained in vogue, as did garden scenes or scenes of every-day life. Many were executed on a large scale, on English paper, and they represent some of the finest watercolors done for export.

A large watercolor of a Mandarin and his wife sipping tea in a Chinese
interior gives an important clue as to how these sets might have been painted. *86*
In this set showing different facets of Chinese life, the watercolors are all executed on English paper of around 1840. On the back of the watercolor mentioned is an outline for a completely different subject: a court parade. On
close examination, this outline proves not to be drawn in pen and ink or *87*
pencil; it is, rather, a light woodblock print. The use of a woodblock printing process for the initial step of a watercolor or gouache would explain how the subject could be repeated so often by the Chinese artist or his studio, with so

88. Chinese figure in a Western chair, by Lam Qua (studio), circa 1845. Watercolor on paper, 13″ × 9″. *Peabody Museum, Salem.*

little variation among sets. If this process is valid for much of the painting of the export watercolors, one can more easily understand why certain views and scenes, figures and landscapes, are seen repeatedly in China trade albums. A description of Lam Qua's studio provides another observation on the watercolorists and their methods: "The design is usually limited to a mechanical tracing made very easy by the extreme transparency of the paper. Each artist has a collection of printed outlines and from them he chooses at will the elements of each composition; a boat, a mandarin, a bird, anything that pleases him."[7] After the outline was traced, the colors were filled in. The technique was undoubtedly used for the street scenes which were on very thin paper and bound in albums.

The views of the ports were always in heavy demand, since, before the introduction of the photograph, Western merchants had only this means of showing their families at home exactly where they had been. Like the paintings, the most typical sets found bound together, before the opening of Hong

89. Interior of the studio of Tingqua, by Tingqua, circa 1855. Gouache on paper, $6\frac{3}{4}'' \times 10''$. *Author's Collection.*

Kong and Shanghai in the early 1840's, were Boca Tigris, Macao, Whampoa and Canton. River scenes and Chinese landscapes were sometimes included to make a larger and more impressive album. Occasionally, an entire panorama of the Pearl River from Whampoa to Canton was painted. Although pieces of such panoramas exist, complete ones are extremely rare. One complete set consists of ten sections, and two additional views of Macao and Boca Tigris. The watercolors are of the highest quality, and were painted around 1830. The individual scenes have borders with margins beyond, but the landscape and river continue from one to another; if the margins were trimmed, the panorama would be uninterrupted.

As in all fields, the most interesting and the most important items are the most unusual and unexpected ones. The Chinese could and would copy anything available to them, as proven by the designs on export porcelain. Several watercolors by Chinese painters exist which are copied from European prints or books. Albums illustrating the costumes and appearances of people throughout the world were copied from Western books of a similar nature. The albums are so well done and so expertly copied that it is difficult to accept them as being by an Oriental hand.

Pith paper samples.

Caricatures of Westerners were done from humorous prints, and floral still lifes were made from foreign floral engravings and color prints.[8] A rare pair of watercolors of a Mandarin and his wife by the Lam Qua studio, circa 1845, depicts them sitting in a pair of Regency armchairs. The inclusion 88
of Western furniture forms, lighting devices, watches, and clocks in watercolors of native subjects illustrates the Chinese fascination with foreign objects.

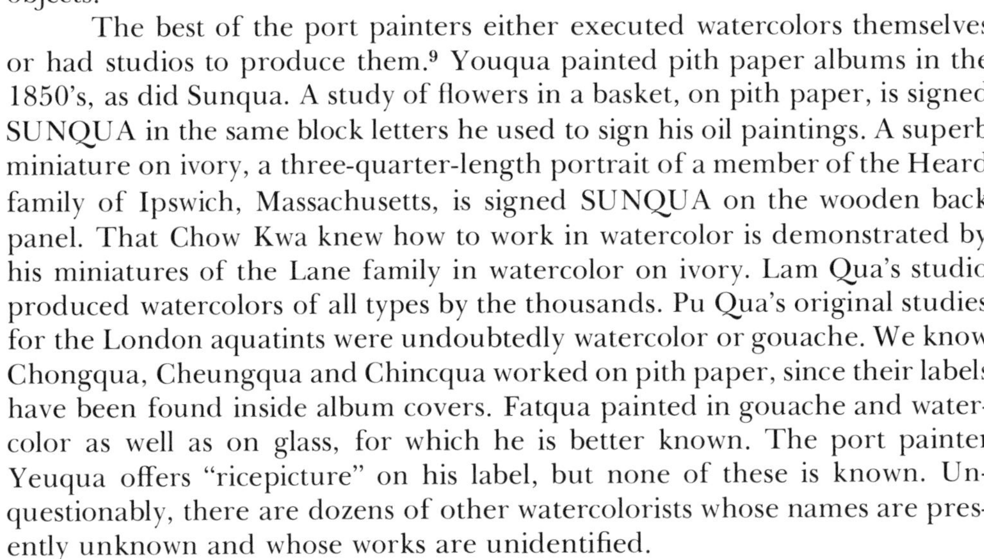

The best of the port painters either executed watercolors themselves or had studios to produce them.[9] Youqua painted pith paper albums in the 1850's, as did Sunqua. A study of flowers in a basket, on pith paper, is signed SUNQUA in the same block letters he used to sign his oil paintings. A superb miniature on ivory, a three-quarter-length portrait of a member of the Heard family of Ipswich, Massachusetts, is signed SUNQUA on the wooden back 31
panel. That Chow Kwa knew how to work in watercolor is demonstrated by his miniatures of the Lane family in watercolor on ivory. Lam Qua's studio produced watercolors of all types by the thousands. Pu Qua's original studies for the London aquatints were undoubtedly watercolor or gouache. We know Chongqua, Cheungqua and Chincqua worked on pith paper, since their labels have been found inside album covers. Fatqua painted in gouache and watercolor as well as on glass, for which he is better known. The port painter Yeuqua offers "ricepicture" on his label, but none of these is known. Unquestionably, there are dozens of other watercolorists whose names are presently unknown and whose works are unidentified.

Of all the watercolorists, the best known, and possibly the most proficient in Canton during the mid-nineteenth century, was Tingqua. The younger brother of Lam Qua, from whom he learned to draw, Tingqua seems to have worked only in watercolor and gouache in either miniature or standard formats.[10] Possibly the single most important scene he painted was a watercolor of his own studio, an invaluable document in the study of Chinese painters working for the Western market. Two versions of the subject exist, but the important one for identification has the name "Tingqua" written
89 across the top. The scene shows a studio, some two or three stories above

90. "An American Scene from a Sketch by an Amateur," by Tingqua, circa 1855. Gouache on paper, 5″ × 7″. *Peabody Museum, Salem.*

ground, at his address of 16 New China Street, Canton, with three artists painting at their own work tables.[11] In the center of the room in front of the studio hangs a Western oil lamp fixture; in the studio hang two Chinese lanterns outfitted with tassels. The studio and the anteroom are both furnished in the Chinese style, and the wood tables have marble inset tops. Along the walls are tiers of paintings, many of which are readily identifiable. On the left are Chinese landscapes and a row of portraits which could well be examples of the artist's Western style portraiture. On the right, the top row is of Chinese ladies, while the row below contains port views.[12] The only two ports which can be discerned are views of the Praya Grande at Macao from the north and south. These views are probably large watercolors, since no signed or labeled Tingqua oils are known, and contemporary references state he worked in watercolor rather than oil, leaving the latter art to his brother. The unsigned watercolor of Tingqua's studio comes from the collection of Augustine Heard, and with it are two sets of 56 and 34 watercolors, all of equal quality and interest. Among the subjects are views of Hong Kong and Canton, the forts along the river, storage warehouses, flowers, birds, different types of Chinese river craft, landscapes, and an unusual side view of the Western church at Canton with the park and hongs to the left. The most unusual watercolors in the group are a series of men and women of the

91. Floral still life, by Tingqua, circa 1855. Gouache on paper, $9\frac{1}{8}'' \times 12\frac{3}{4}''$. *Peabody Museum, Salem.*

92. Heard and Co. House, Canton, circa 1855, by Tingqua. Gouache on paper, $9\frac{1}{4}'' \times 12\frac{3}{4}''$. *Peabody Museum, Salem.*

93. Canton waterfront with steamer *Spark,* by Tingqua, circa 1855. Gouache on paper, $8\frac{1}{2}'' \times 10\frac{1}{2}''$. *Peabody Museum, Salem.*

Philippines, two extraordinary still lifes of flowers and fruit and an unusual 91
watercolor identified in a Western hand as "An American Scene from a Sketch
by an Amateur." The watercolors of the Filipinos were copied by Tingqua 90
from a series of watercolors done by an export artist from the Philippines, 94
Tristiniano Asumpción.[13] Tingqua was probably given the set to copy by a
merchant who had purchased them in the Philippine Islands.

Two particularly important views are of Heard's own company build- 92
ing at Canton, which is the last large building to the right in the row of hongs
as seen after the fire of 1842.[14] There are several watercolors from the tea,
silk and rice-culture series, but the sets are not complete. In all, the 90 Heard
watercolors give an incisive look at the production of an artist working for the
export market in the mid-nineteenth century.

With the watercolor albums by Tingqua from the Heard Collection are four bound albums of tradesmen and other subjects, done in pen and ink. The drawings show Tingqua (or his studio) to be an excellent draftsman, and the representations of 360 tradesmen of Canton are all creative and attractive in composition and design. The fourth album of the group has 10 sets of 12 drawings each. Depicted are gambling, boats, ladies, idols, tumbling, rice-culture, etc. The drawings so closely approximate in composition other watercolors of the trades and street scenes from the Tingqua studio, that it would seem they may be the prototypes, or possibly the outlines from which the artisans in the studio worked. The albums have TINGQUA stamped on each cover in large block letters, and this spelling settles the scholarly discussion as to whether his name was spelled "Tinqua" or "Tingqua."[15]

There is considerable variation in the quality of the Heard Tingqua watercolors, and one may assume that several of them, as with other watercolors, were worked on by the assistants in the studio and not by the master himself. The best are of superb quality, the lesser have weaknesses in drawing and delineation. All, however, reflect the palette and style of Tingqua, and are readily identifiable as having come from his studio.

Through these important albums of watercolors and drawings in the
Heard collection, numerous other watercolors of a very similar nature can
be identified and tentatively attributed to Tingqua. An historically important
watercolor of the Canton waterfront, painted in 1855, shows men loading tea 93
in the foreground and the entire hong area at Canton, with river traffic, in
the background.[16] Down the side of the view is a description of the occupants
of each of the buildings.[17] An inscription on the back, in English, reads: "A
Chinese painting of the Foreign Factories at Canton by Tinqua [*sic*] of 16
New China Street, Canton, January 1855." Four or five other versions of this
view exist, each approximately the same size and in the same style and handling.[18] There is little doubt that they were all from the Tingqua studio.[19]

The Tingqua view of Macao in the Heard Collection shows a woman
with a baby on her back walking along the Praya Grande. Another set of five B 2
watercolors at the Peabody Museum and one set on pith paper in private
hands, both similar in size to the Heard views, present views of Macao of
identical format and with the same woman and child. The view of Canton in
the first set is identical to that described above, but lacks the key to the buildings on the side of the paper. The views which complete this set are of
Whampoa Reach, Hong Kong and a very unusual view of Angier Point, Java.
This last view includes a group of Westerners in red uniforms and white
outfits rowing ashore. Doubtless Tingqua copied the subject from a foreign

94. Mestigo, by Tristiniano Asumpción, Manila, circa 1845. Watercolor on paper, $10\frac{1}{2}'' \times 7\frac{1}{4}''$. *Author's Collection.*

95. Mestigo, by Tingqua, circa 1855, copied from a watercolor by Asumpción. Gouache on paper, 13″ × 10″. *Peabody Museum, Salem.*

sketch or print. The entire set is unquestionably by Tingqua or his studio, since the views so closely relate to the Heard set.

Tingqua was very diverse in his choice of subject matter and he was one of the most innovative of the port painters working in watercolor. Two unique views of Macao, circa 1850, here attributed through association and stylistic relationship to Tingqua, are drawn from vantage points never used by other port artists.[20] Of approximately the same size as the other documented Tingqua watercolors, they are of fine quality and carry his delicate brush technique and purply blue skies. The leaves of the trees are highlighted with white and executed in very precise strokes, a characteristic of all his work whether done by him or his assistants. With these two views is a third; another version of the Praya Grande at Macao with mother and child, exactly like those discussed above.

Little is known of Tingqua's larger work but a view of Macao from the ocean, painted circa 1855, may provide a clue.[21] If the individual elements of the water, buildings, vessels, mountains, figures and trees are compared in detail with the smaller known Tingqua watercolors, striking similarities may be found. The palette is very much that of Tingqua with its heavy use of blues and purples and the sweeping white clouds. The water has the same white crests and sweeps as the Heard views of the ports and river. The trees and mountains are treated in a similar manner, and the overall composition marks the work of a major watercolorist such as Tingqua. Since there are so many elements of his style present, the large watercolor must be judged to be his work.

Tingqua's brother Lam Qua was known to have painted many portraits of Houqua in the Chinnery style, so it would seem plausible to assume
28 that Tingqua had also painted him. A superb miniature on ivory of Houqua signed by him exists, and another portrait of the famous merchant, in watercolor on paper, has been attributed to him.[22]

A group of three watercolors of Shanghai houses of the 1860's and 1870's is attributed to the same unknown painter. The first of the three is
96 of the Low House at Shanghai.[23] The view is executed in opaque watercolor and is very well drawn. The figures and trees are painted darkly and are in heavy contrast to the stark white outlines of the house. The second water-
97 color depicts the buildings of Russell and Company in Shanghai, and is painted in a similar technique, with identical handling of the figures and trees. There is a dark quality to this watercolor also. The third view is of a house in the "stick" style, which would appear to have been built in the third quarter of the nineteenth century. Under the house is the caption, "A House in the American Legation, Shanghai," and the watercolor is dated 1862. Again, the same heavy opaque quality of the others and the same small distortions in the perspective may be noted. The group is obviously by the same painter or studio, but, at present, painter or studio remains anonymous.[24]

There are few watercolors after 1880 that carry on the tradition of Chinese watercolors for the export market. The demand for such paintings had seriously diminished with the introduction of the camera, and several of the port painters became photographers. The only watercolor lines that remained popular as tourist items were the decorative pith paper albums, and the tiny drawings on pith of a single figure, fish, or shell, which were sold in little fabric-covered boxes with glass lids.

96. Low House, Shanghai, artist unidentified, circa 1865. Watercolor on paper, 10″ × 14″. *Photograph courtesy Childs Gallery.*

97. Buildings of Russell and Co., Shanghai, artist unidentified, circa 1875. Watercolor on paper, approximately 18″ × 28″. *Peabody Museum, Salem.*

The dating of the watercolors on pith paper has been the subject of considerable controversy, but it is doubtful if this medium was used before 1800. An anonymous set of pith paper watercolors of diverse Chinese subjects was mounted on English paper watermarked "A. Cowan and Son, 1828." The quality of the watercolors is good, and there is more attention to color and detail than in the later albums. A set of port scenes consisting of Macao, Canton, Boca Tigris and Whampoa is extant along with a letter of presentation from the donor watermarked 1821; the view of Canton, however, shows that port as it appeared around 1835. The subjects for the pith papers, as for the watercolors on other papers, were endless: mandarins, theater scenes, birds, flowers, the ever-popular tortures, ports, landscapes, ladies, tea culture, etc. The best quality port scenes, boats, flowers and birds are the most desirable of all subjects.

A description of Lam Qua's studio in the 1840's gives a note on the albums:

> Here it is that are painted those little silk covered albums which are sent to England and the United States and even to France and contain representations of animals, flowers, landscapes, the different manufacturing processes, the costumes of mandarins, the various kinds of punishments, etc. There is no art in this. It is purely a mechanical operation, in which the system of division of labor is faithfully practised. One painter makes trees all his life, another figures; this one draws feet and hands, that one houses. Thus each acquires in his line a certain perfection, particularly in the finish of details, but none of them is capable of undertaking an entire painting.[25]

A description of the trade in pith paper watercolors comes from another visitor's account of 1844.

> In every artist's studio are to be found the paintings on what is called rice paper. This is very delicate and brittle, and nothing can exceed the splendor of the colors employed in representing the trades, occupations, life ceremonies, religions, etc. of the Chinese, which all appear in perfect truth in these productions. Everything enacted in life, from the highest pageants of religious ceremonial down to the lowest scenes of shameless debauchery, are given in the paintings. Not only the proper colors, but the exact attitudes of the figures are worthy of admiration. Then there are landscapes, boats, birds, animals, fruit, flowers, fish and vegetables, and all may be obtained for a very reasonable sum, in boxes, or bound up in books. They cost, for the usual class of excellence, from one to two dollars a dozen. . . . Or you may order a set comprising the emperor and empress, and the chief mandarins, and court ladies, in the most magnificent attire, and finished like miniatures, for eight dollars.[26]

A reference was made in 1835 to there being some thirty shops in the vicinity of the hongs where the watercolors on pith paper could be purchased.[27]

The colors used at the beginning of the nineteenth century tended to be rather delicate, while those used after the mid-century became increasingly hard, with a very heavy use of garish blues, greens and reds. The watercolors on pith paper were rarely signed, but in this later period labels, which were pasted inside the front covers, were used to identify the painter or studio. The more traditional label is an octagonal piece of white paper with a red outer border and the artist's name in red letters. The port and ship painter Sunqua used these labels, as did a number of other painters such as Lam Qua and Youqua.[28]

Although the works of the later painters may have been crude and gaudy, several superb watercolors on pith were executed in the middle years of the nineteenth century. A floral watercolor in this medium, brought to *98*
Salem in 1830 by Mrs. Thomas Hunt who had lived at Whampoa, shows the great competence of the best studio at the time.[29] With the watercolor is Youqua's label, which is identical to that used on his port scenes and other paintings. Also with the watercolor is a note that it was done by the "celebrated" Chinese painter, Youqua.

The watercolors on pith, of all possible subjects, either mounted in albums or placed in small fabric-covered boxes were great tourist attractions at the time of the Centennial International Exhibition of 1876 in Philadelphia.[30] At the exhibition, the catalogue to the Chinese booth listed dozens of albums of pith watercolors on all possible subjects. Regrettably, no artists' names were mentioned. In the last years of the nineteenth century, several boxes of minute watercolors, completely labeled with the painters' names, were readily available tourist items.

Judging from the tremendous quantities of watercolors on pith and Western paper that are extant today, there must have been a tremendous demand in the nineteenth century for those which so aptly and skillfully described a foreign existence to the Westerner. The watercolors were some of the most exciting and topical items made for export, and they are important today as an accurate reflection of Western life in China in the nineteenth century. The watercolors also depicted those phases of Chinese life which fascinated the Westerner but defied description to friends and family at home. Before the advent of the camera, this medium played an extremely vital role in revealing Oriental culture to the West.

98. Floral still life, by Youqua, circa 1855. Gouache on pith paper, $6\frac{1}{2}'' \times 9\frac{1}{2}''$. *Peabody Museum, Salem.*

Notes

1. Illustrated in Soame Jenyns and Margaret Jourdain, *Chinese Export Art of the 18th Century*. Middlesex: Spring Books, 1967, #49, p. 98.
2. In the Peabody Museum, Salem. See Appendix C, Illus. C-3.
3. Shreve papers for the voyage of the brig *Canton,* Peabody Museum, Salem.
4. "A Catalogue of the Imperial Maritime Customs Collection," United States International Exhibition, Philadelphia, 1876. Published in Shanghai, 1876. Dept. II, Manutures, Class 259. Peabody Museum, Salem.
5. Illustrated in Jenyns and Jourdain, *Chinese Export Art,* #50, p. 99.
6. Illustrated and described in Jenyns and Jourdain, *Chinese Export Art,* #67, p. 108. Label here misread as *Falqua.*
7. "Old Nick" (Forgues), *La Chîne Ouverte,* p. 58.
8. Often the same prints were used for the reverse paintings on glass and the decorations on export porcelain.
9. The word "watercolor" is used throughout this chapter for convenience's sake, although many of the watercolors are actually of a medium closer to gouache and its opacity.
10. *The Chinese Repository,* Vol. XVI, May, 1847, #5, p. 27, states, "Tingqua confines himself to miniatures and sketches."
11. The address comes from the back of the watercolor of the Canton waterfront in the collection of the Museum of the American China Trade, Milton, Massachusetts.
12. It is difficult to distinguish the individual views in the version illustrated; they are clearly shown on the version owned by the Peabody Museum.
13. Little is known about this artist from Manila; his working dates are probably the second quarter of the nineteenth century.
14. This building was also shared by Jardine Matheson.
15. "Tinqua" was the spelling in Western handwriting on the back of the watercolor in the collection of the Museum of the American China Trade. All the period references and the albums in the Peabody Museum are marked "Tingqua." I mistakenly spelled his name "Tinqua" throughout the catalogue, "China Trade Paintings and Other Objects," Peabody Museum, 1970.
16. The watercolor with the name "Tinqua" and the address on the back.
17. The key is: #1, King & Co.; #2, Lindsay & Co.; #3, Wetmore & Co.; #4, Russell & Co.; #5, Nye & Co.; #6, Church; #7, Cassumbhon Nathabhog & Co.; #8, Gibb Livingstone; #9, Holliday Wise & Co.; #10, Consul; #11, Vice-consul; #12, Augustine Heard & Co.; #13, Jardine Matheson & Co.; #14, The Club.
18. An interesting wood engraving was done from one of these versions for a Boston newspaper in the mid-1850's, marked as after an original watercolor by a Chinese artist.
19. All the versions are documented as being from Tingqua's studio or are with other watercolors which exhibit Tingqua's composition and technique.
20. Owned privately in England. Photographs available in the files of the Peabody Museum.
21. Owned by the Museum of Fine Arts, Boston; on loan to the Peabody Museum, Salem.
22. The watercolor on ivory, in the Metropolitan Museum, was given to Mr. David Washington Olyphant of Olyphant & Co., by Houqua. The second watercolor is in the Peabody Museum, Salem.
23. The watercolor of this house came from the Blydenburgh family, who did not own a house in Shanghai; however, family tradition has it that they stayed with the Lows. Photographs in the Peabody Museum, given by a member of the Low family, are of the interior and exterior of this same house.
24. If Chow Kwa worked in watercolor in this format, the paintings could be by him.
25. Gardiner, quoting La Vollée, in *The Art Quarterly,* 1953, p. 317.
26. Tiffany, *The Canton Chinese,* p. 84.
27. *Chinese Repository,* Vol. IV, Oct., 1835, #6.
28. Sunqua seems to be the only Chinese painter on pith paper who signed with block letters like his signature on his paintings. He also used a small red label in the albums in the period 1845 to 1860.
29. John Robinson scrapbook, Peabody Museum, Salem.
30. "A Catalogue of the Imperial Maritime Customs . . .," United States International Exhibition, Philadelphia, 1876.

99. Chinese landscape scene, reverse painting on glass, circa 1810, $21\frac{1}{4}'' \times 29''$. *Carrington Collection, Rhode Island Historical Society.*

7. Paintings on Glass

In England, in the mid-eighteenth century, there arose a tremendous demand for Chinese reverse paintings on glass of native figures or landscape scenes. Many of these had mirrored backgrounds or were the lower part of mirrored panels which would serve as pier or mantel glass,[1] either framed in English Chinoiserie or Chinese frames. From the end of the eighteenth and through the nineteenth century, because of the interest in things Neoclassical or exotic, this demand continued, and the most popular subjects for the American market were Chinese landscapes and garden scenes which gave a close look at native life. The early glass paintings, like the paintings in oil and watercolor, used delicate palettes and were of fine quality. As the nineteenth century progressed, however, the subjects became simpler and the artists began to concentrate on a single figure, usually that of a young lady. Many of these paintings also had mirrored or silvered backs, and were in fitted natural wood Chinese style frames (*see Chap. 4*).

A particularly fine example of a Chinese landscape with figures on glass was brought to this country by Edward Carrington of Providence, Rhode Island, in the first quarter of the nineteenth century. In this painting are found the soft colors and complex compositions that were seen in the eighteenth-century paintings on glass of Chinese subjects made for the English market. Later paintings lack the delicacy and refinement of this one and, like so many of the objects for export, reflect the more general "tourist" appeal of the manufactures of the mid- to late-nineteenth century.

By the end of the eighteenth century, another trend had developed: the exact copying by the Chinese of European and American prints onto sheets of glass, which were then framed in the Western style. This interest in reverse paintings on glass by the Chinese probably arose out of the popularity in England and on the Continent (as well as in America) of the transfer-prints on the back of glass sold by the print-hawkers of Europe. Rather than

100. The Annunciation, colored English mezzotint by Valentine Green after the painting by Maria Cosway, 1800. In original blue glass mat and frame. This type of framed print was the prototype for the Chinese glass paintings. $33\frac{1}{2}'' \times 27\frac{1}{4}''$. *Photograph courtesy Childs Gallery.*

having only a transferred print, the Western purchaser was able to obtain, through the skill of the Chinese artisan, an exact, colorful and handsome painting directly on glass. The date of the earliest importation of this type of painting is uncertain; however, since most of the prints from which they were copied were published after the 1780's, it is doubtful if this vogue hit the Western hemisphere before the 1790's.

Reverse paintings on glass, as they are discovered today, are invariably in their original frames, which are exact copies of English or American

101. Shakespeare, *Merry Wives of Windsor,* Act III, Scene III, reverse painting on glass, circa 1810, $28\frac{1}{4}'' \times 22''$. From the engraving published by John and Josiah Boydell, 1803. *Arthur S. Vernay, New York.*

frames of the late eighteenth and early nineteenth century. Most have a dark blue-black border painted around the subject, on the same sheet of glass as the painting, obviously an imitation of the painted mats used in framing English and American engravings of the period. Notches in the back of the frames indicate that all originally had fitted back panels of wood to protect them. The panels were held in place by flat wood pins, a distinctly Chinese feature of frame construction. The frames are gold leafed and are made to look, both with carving and decoration, exactly like their Western prototypes.

102. The Lady in Milton's *Comus,* circa 1820, reverse painting on glass, 19¼″ × 24″. Based on the mezzotint by John Raphael Smith after the painting by Joseph Wright. *Author's Collection.*

Other than the Chinese use of pins and grooves, the most revealing indication of Chinese manufacture is their joinery.

Some of the paintings have Chinese characters on the lower part of the panel and the same characters repeated on the back of the frame. This was done so that the Chinese workmen would be able to put the right frame with the right panel. It is evident from a comparison of the Chinese glass paint-
100 ings with matted and framed Western prints of the period that some prints must have been taken to China in their mats and gold frames, and copied in toto by the Chinese artists; otherwise, there is no explanation for the simulated mat or for the design of the frames, which vary but are all in the Western mode. There are several references[2] to Western prints being taken to China for copying. The great quantities of export porcelain with Western print designs attest further to this importation.

An indication of the cost of these subjects can be obtained from a note by Sullivan Dorr of Providence, Rhode Island, in 1800. In a letter to Ebenezer Dorr he wrote of one painting, "Temple Fame on glass Box. 2," with a price of $16. This was a typical Neoclassical subject, which would have been appealing to American aesthetic tastes during the Federal period.

The prints copied by the Chinese range from mythological to political subjects, and include many religious, literary and historical depictions. Among the literary scenes are selections from Shakespeare, such as one
101 from the *Merry Wives of Windsor.* The prototypes for the Shakespeare subjects are found in the very popular engravings by celebrated English artists published in London by John and Josiah Boydell in 1803. The Chinese paint-

103. The Triumph of Virtue, circa 1810, reverse painting on glass. After an unknown English print. $26\frac{1}{2}'' \times 19\frac{1}{4}''$. *Author's Collection.*

104. The Widow of an Indian Chief watching the Arm [sic] of her decased [sic] Husband, reverse painting on glass, circa 1820, 17½″ × 23½″. Based on the mezzotint by John Raphael Smith after the painting by Joseph Wright. *New Haven Colony Historical Society.*

ing in this instance matches within a half-inch the size of the Boydell print of
the subject and is extremely faithful to it. It is important to note that the
Chinese were so exact in their copying that they inevitably made the copy on
glass the precise size of the print from which they were working. It is only in
109 rare instances, such as the paintings on glass of the "Landing of the Fathers,"
that they varied from the size because of a print too small to be effective as
a painting.

For beauty of execution and sheer quality, another literary subject,
102 "The Lady In Milton's Comus," is unexcelled. Close in technique to the original
painting upon which the print is based, it is far more than a slavish copy
of a print, which cannot be said of many of the China trade porcelains. The
scene is derived directly from the mezzotint engraved by John Raphael Smith
after the painting by Joseph Wright, and published by Thomas Palser in 1812.
The surface area of the painting is exactly the same size as that of the print,
and the gold script by a Chinese hand on the blue glass mat is a precise copy
of the engraved title of the print. "The Lady in Milton's Comus" is the only
one of the Chinese paintings examined which still retains its original cotton
padding between the glass and the joined wooden back panel to prevent
breakage.

A religious subject which reflects the great complexity of composition
103 which the Chinese were willing to undertake is "The Triumph of Virtue."
Another version of the subject has an entire poem of six lines written in gold
in the dark mat below. It is interesting to suggest here, after studying many

105. The loss of the *Halsewell* East Indiaman, reverse painting on glass, circa 1810, 18″ × 23″. After a print published in London in 1787. *Collection of J. A. Lloyd Hyde.*

of these more complex paintings and their prototype prints, that the prints were held to the surface of the glass, put to a strong light, while the outlines of the Western print were carefully copied to give exact size and representation. However, this fact does not in any way detract from the great skill that was needed to copy one of these prints so as to capture the tonal qualities and skin textures needed, which because of the medium, had to be applied well before the body painting of the subject began.

An unusual subject is "The Widow of an Indian Chief Watching the *104*
Arm [Arms] of her decased [deceased] Husband." The title illustrates the difficulty the Chinese artists had in copying in reverse a language that was totally alien to them. The print on which this was based is after a painting by Joseph Wright originally executed as a partner to the "Lady in Milton's Comus." The paintings were engraved and published as a pair and must have been sent as such to China, where they were copied and returned to the West. The painting is approximately the same size (18 by 24 inches) as most of the reverse paintings on glass executed in China, dimensions based on large-folio European or American mezzotints which, in turn, had been dictated in size by that of the prototype engravings.

Historical incidents and battles were as popular in paintings on glass
as they were in the engravings that inspired them. The "Loss of the Halsewell *105*
East Indiaman" is a most appropriate subject, since the ship represented was involved in the Oriental trade. A striking pair of glass paintings depicts two
incidents in General Cornwallis' battles at Mysore. The event illustrated in- *106*

106. To the Honourable the East India Company, Definitive Treaty by the Hostage Princes, one of a pair of reverse paintings on glass showing Cornwallis at Mysore, circa 1815, 18″ × 23″. After prints from the paintings by Mather Brown. *Privately owned.*

volves the surrender of Tippoo, the Sultan of Mysore and presentation of
two of the young princes, his sons, as captives. A painting on glass of the
"Battle of Lexington" is not only important historically as a subject painted in 107
China but also because the American print from which it was copied is known.
The painting is slightly larger than the print which was engraved by Cor- 108
nelius Tiebout, after the drawing by Elkanah Tisdale, and published by Tisdale in New York in 1798.

Another American historical subject of particular significance is the
"Landing of the Fathers at Plymouth,"[3] one of three known Chinese paint- 109
ings on glass of that event, each with some title variations and size differences. The problem of the prototype here is an extremely unusual one, since the Chinese almost always copied prints which were close to the size of the intended reverse painting, and the only possible known print for the painting to have been copied from measures $2\frac{3}{4}$ by 5 inches. The source for the paintings seems to be a small engraving by Samuel Hill, a Boston engraver who did views for the *Massachusetts Magazine* and other publications in the last quarter of the eighteenth century. A group of gentlemen in Boston who called themselves the "Sons of the Pilgrims" sent out an invitation to their first dinner on December 22, 1800, and Hill engraved the invitation with a view of the "Landing" in the top half and an inscription in the bottom half, with a rock in the lower corner inscribed with the Pilgrims' names. Since the three paintings on glass are all of different sizes, it would seem the Chinese were not working from one large mezzotint, but rather from the small Hill engraving, developing the design to whatever size the purchaser desired. There is, however, the possibility that an unrecorded larger print after the small engraving does exist. The title of one painting on glass is an exact copy of the line of engraving of the print, while that of another has a decided variation in the title with "The Landing of Our Forefathers." This painting, the largest of the three known versions, was brought from China to Boston about 1810 by Benjamin Wheeler, an American active in the China trade. The Chinese glass paintings of the "Landing" seem in turn to have been prototypes for other paintings of the early nineteenth century, since several watercolors and paintings exist which would appear to have been based on them, complete to the blue-black mat with inscription on the bottom.[4]

Only two paintings on glass currently known bear the label of the artist who painted them. On one, of Reynolds' "Snake Lady," the label reads, "Fatqua, painter in oils and watercolors and on glass, China Street, Canton." A Fatqua trade card, with identical wording, depicts a ship painting on an easel, a palette, paint pots, and brushes surrounding the lettering. The red stamp "Fatqua" also appears on a set of three large folio watercolors of Chinese views.[5] The second labeled painting on glass, of a female figure in an Empire gown, has a Fatqua label with similar wording on the back panel. An interesting note on glass paintings is provided by one twentieth-century writer on Chinese export art, and acknowledged by another: "Writing of paintings of this period, Sir George Staunton speaks of the closeness of the copies of European prints, which attracted the notice of a 'gentleman eminent for his taste in London' who had in his possession a coloured copy made in China of a print from a study of Sir Joshua Reynolds, which he deems not unworthy of being added to his collection of valuable paintings."[6] The dates of Staunton's writings, 1798, and of the glass painting of Reynolds' "Snake Lady" are so

107. Battle of Lexington, reverse painting on glass, circa 1810, $17\frac{1}{2}'' \times 23\frac{7}{8}''$. After the engraving by Tiebout after Tisdale. *The Henry Francis du Pont Winterthur Museum.*

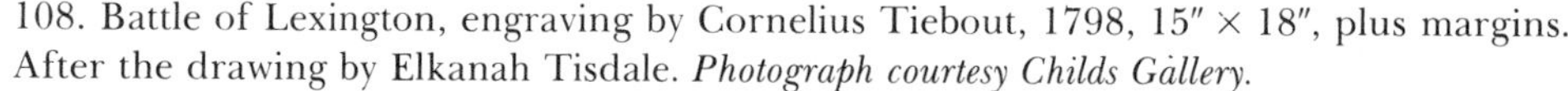

108. Battle of Lexington, engraving by Cornelius Tiebout, 1798, 15″ × 18″, plus margins. After the drawing by Elkanah Tisdale. *Photograph courtesy Childs Gallery.*

109. The landing of the Fathers at Plymouth, reverse painting on glass, circa 1815, 12″ × 19″. After the print by Samuel Hill. *Collection of Joseph T. Butler.*

close that the "Snake Lady" might indeed be the one referred to.

Some prints taken to China for copying inspired the decoration of both
export porcelain and the reverse paintings on glass. A painting on glass titled
"Fidelity" is based on the same print prototype as the decoration of a porce- *111*
lain saucer, made before 1808.[7] The painting is smaller than the others dis- *112*
cussed, and, therefore, must have been based on a print whose size was more
readily adaptable to the decoration of porcelain. There are large numbers of
the smaller paintings on glass, of single figures, genre scenes, the Seasons,
the Months and others which seem to have been as popular as the larger
paintings on glass based on the large-folio mezzotints or engravings.

The large portraits of George Washington on glass that were executed
by the Chinese are particularly important, and for many persons hard to
identify. The subject of George Washington (and his Apotheosis) was extremely popular with glass painters in America and Europe as well as with
the Chinese, and there has been a great deal of confusion as to which are by
whom.[8] At the beginning of the nineteenth century there was a mania for
Washingtoniana. The Washingtons that were copied by the Chinese were
undoubtedly copied from one of two portraits by Gilbert Stuart which were
known to have been taken to China.[9] All the known Chinese reverse paintings of Washington are of superb quality, of the same size as the Stuart panels *113*
or canvases from which they were copied, and are in the Washington "Athenaeum" portrait style.[10] That the Chinese were extremely adept in their
copying is evidenced by Stuart's action to secure an injunction against the
importation of these copies of his paintings from China.[11] Thus the Chinese
were in this instance working directly from a painting rather than a print.

There was also a considerable demand for the Chinese Washington portraits in oil on canvas. Edward Carrington was billed in 1805 for six paintings of the
114 Apotheosis of George Washington and for ten portraits of Washington.

The Washington portraits on glass are in wide gold frames typical of the type of moulding used on the Stuart originals, and they were very skillfully copied by the Chinese. Several versions of the "Apotheosis of Washington" exist in paintings on glass, and are undoubtedly like those mentioned in the Carrington bill.

The portraits of Washington appearing on the export porcelain jugs were probably copied from an American mezzotint or stipple engraving, which was, in turn, based on an American version of the Stuart Athenaeum portrait. Several of these prints, by engravers such as Edwin and Tiebout, are known in American print checklists.[12] The jugs at Winterthur and the Metropolitan Museum of Art show the meticulous care taken by the Chinese decorators to copy exactly in paint the effects of a mezzotint or engraving.

Another popular theme for both paintings on glass and export porce-
115 lain was the "Sailor's Farewell," a recurrent subject in late-eighteenth and early-nineteenth century decoration, especially popular with the wives and families of those who went to sea.

The China trade paintings on glass based on American prints are naturally of greater interest to American collectors than those based on English or Continental sources. One of the most popular of the American subjects was "Liberty," based on the Edward Savage engraving published in Philadelphia in 1798.[13] Paintings of "John Paul Jones," "America," "Battle of Lexington," "The Apotheosis of George Washington," allegorical Washington memorials, "The Landing of the Pilgrims," "George Washington," and similar historic and symbolic American subjects make up the list of the most desired paintings on glass brought back to this market. Various supposed captains' portraits are probably based on prints and are not actual portraits.

The painting on glass "America" is based on a large English print of the same subject, which is an allegory engraved by Joseph Strutt from the painting by Robert Edge Pine.[14] Although an extremely rare American version of this print,[15] a mixed media engraving by Amos Doolittle of New Haven, Connecticut, exists, it is doubtful if the painting on glass was copied from the American version.

The American traders at Canton did not limit themselves to purchasing only American subjects. Those of English derivation brought to this country are interesting for their variety and subject matter, which cover an extraordinary range. The pair of paintings of Cornwallis at Mysore was brought back from China in the first quarter of the nineteenth century by Captain Andrew Blanchard of Medford, Massachusetts. The large painting of the "Triumph of Virtue" descended in the famed Crowninshield shipping family of Salem. A painting "Cornelia, Mother of the Gracchi" carries a label stating that it was brought from China by William Sturgis of Boston in 1803. The "Fidelity" painting, mentioned previously, was owned by Paul Forbes, a member of the prominent Boston China trade family. Sets of paintings of the Months and Seasons, beautifully copied from known English prints, were brought to America by several merchants.[16]

110 Subjects such as "Sappho," "The Widow of an Indian Chief with Arms of her Deceased Husband," "Hebe," "The Lady in Milton's Comus," and "The Spirit of a Child in the Presence of the Almighty" are known to have

110. Sappho, reverse painting on glass, circa 1810, $19\frac{1}{2}'' \times 14\frac{1}{2}''$. Based on an unidentified print. *Author's Collection.*

111. Fidelity, reverse painting on glass, circa 1800, $9\frac{1}{4}'' \times 14\frac{3}{4}''$. Based on an unknown print. *Author's Collection.*

been brought from China by American captains or supercargos in the early nineteenth century. One large painting on glass appears to have been based either on a rare American print or an unknown English print of "The Resurrection of a Pious Mother and her Two Children." The American print, unusual for its large size in that period, is a stipple engraving by Thomas Clarke of New York, published by David Longworth, circa 1805.[17] Some variations between the painting on glass and the known American print would seem to indicate there may indeed have been an English version from which both the glass painting and the American print were copied, as in the case of "America."

Most of the large paintings on glass with their fine Neoclassical frames seem to have been executed early in the nineteenth century, judging from the character of the work and partly from the publication date of the prints which served as prototypes (from 1790 to 1815). These paintings seem to have enjoyed a relatively short vogue in comparison with most China trade objects,

112. China trade porcelain saucer, from a service made for Mary Hemphill of Wilmington, Delaware, circa 1808, diameter 5⅜″. Based on the same print of Fidelity as the painting on glass. *Historical Society of Delaware.*

since the majority are of consistently high quality, similar in execution, and apparently limited in quantity. Their popularity in the period was undoubtedly related to the strong Neoclassicism of the time, and the paintings were perfect complements to the other decorative arts. Few China trade objects maintained a high quality of execution and design over a long period of time, and so it was with the paintings on glass, too.

There are in existence several small paintings on glass, based on Reynolds or Gainsborough portraits of women and other smaller English prints of men and women, all executed between 1820 and the mid-nineteenth century. The quality of these is vastly inferior to the paintings discussed above, and seems to indicate a decline in interest on the part of both the artist and the purchaser. The brushwork is very loose with little or no attention to detail and no ambitious undertaking of a complex composition such as in the "Triumph of Virtue." The frames are less expertly copied, and so it seems

113. George Washington, reverse painting on glass, circa 1805, 29″ × 22″. After an original portrait by Gilbert Stuart. *Author's Collection.*

likely these productions were done in the second quarter of the century.

A small group of paintings on glass, not often seen because of their very nature, are those of pornographic subjects. The Chinese were great creators of erotica, both for themselves and for the trade, and in these paintings they displayed imagination and skill. Both Chinese and Western figures were depicted, and the small panels of glass were often inserted in the back panels of captains' shaving mirrors.

Because of their period and rarity, the fine China trade paintings on

114. George Washington, oil on canvas, by an unidentified Chinese artist, circa 1805, $28\frac{1}{2}'' \times 21\frac{3}{4}''$. Known to have been owned by Edward Carrington. After the original by Gilbert Stuart. *Rhode Island Historical Society.*

glass, both those of Chinese subjects and those based on Western prints, deserve more recognition. Some of the subjects may seem a bit saccharine today, but they are as representative of the taste of their own time as were the European religious and mythological subjects copied by the Chinese on porcelain. The skill required to execute a large painting on glass in reverse is even greater than that needed to decorate porcelain, and these paintings, with their historical and artistic interest, should finally receive at least as much appreciation.

115. The Sailor's Farewell, reverse painting on glass, circa 1810, 10″ × 8″. Based on an unknown print. This subject was extremely popular in the late eighteenth, early nineteenth centuries. *Childs Gallery.*

Notes

1. Jenyns and Jourdain, *Chinese Export Art,* p. 35.
2. *Proceedings of the Massachusetts Historical Society,* Vol. LXVII, Letter to Ebenezer Dorr, Jr., January 14, 1800, p. 204.
3. Title variations exist for the paintings on glass: "The Landing of Our Forefathers," "The Landing of the Fathers at Plymouth" and "The Landing of the Pilgrims."
4. For a complete discussion of this subject and the prototype prints, see *Antiques,* "Early Depictions of the Landing of Pilgrims," by Carl L. Crossman and Charles R. Strickland, November, 1970, p. 777.
5. Privately owned. This is the only instance known by the author of this small stamp being used by Fatqua.
6. Jenyns and Jourdain, *Chinese Export Art,* #67, p. 99.
7. The cup and saucer, in the Collection of the Historical Society of Delaware, Wilmington, bear the initials *MH* for "Mary Hemphill," who married Morgan Jones in 1808; this probably was part of her wedding china. Both her father and Jones were prominent merchants in Wilmington, trading with the West Indies and China. Information through courtesy of Dale Fields, Executive Director, Historical Society of Delaware.
8. The many smaller and less well executed reverse paintings on glass of Washington, done in America, were probably executed by minor painters of the 1840's through 1860's. William Matthew Prior is known to have done several of both Martha and George Washington.
9. In February, 1928, *Antiques* Magazine did an editorial page discussion of a reverse painting on glass of Washington, believed to have been done by a follower of Stuart because of its quality. In February, 1929, *Antiques* ran a correction on its editorial page in which the painting was attributed to a Chinese artist. Photographs of two other paintings, sent in by readers, that either had Chinese characters or were known to have been brought from China accompanied the article.
10. *Gilbert Stuart,* compiled by Lawrence Park, New York, 1926, Vol. II. One is listed as #111 under the portraits of Washington, oil on canvas 30″ × $25\frac{1}{4}$″. "This portrait was for many years in China, it was brought to England about 1850 and taken to America by a Boston trader." Fielding's listing is #68, reproduced, facing page 230. The second, #51, stated, "James Blight, an Indian trader, who according to Mason, 'took his portrait of Washington with him on a voyage to China. About 1800 or a little later, a number of portraits of Washington, on glass, were brought out of China and were offered for sale in Philadelphia till Stuart through the aid of Horace Binney, then a young lawyer, put an injunction on the sale.'" In Fielding, it is #50.

    The original portraits, owned by the Athenaeum, were the bases for a format of Stuart portraits of Washington, which was used repeatedly; i.e., head to shoulders.
11. *Ibid.*
12. David McNeely Stauffer, *American Engravers upon Copper and Steel,* Part II. Burt Franklin: New York, 1907; Tiebout, #3195; Edwin, #892–901; Hart, #369; Tiebout, #455.
13. Stauffer, *American Engravers,* Part II, #2761.
14. An impression of this print is owned by the Bostonian Society, Boston, which also owns the reverse painting on glass.
15. Stauffer, *American Engravers,* Part II, #522. An impression of this rare print is in the Museum of Fine Arts, Boston.
16. One set of "The Months" was brought to Salem by a merchant, circa 1810. Privately owned.
17. Stauffer, *American Engravers,* Part II, #417.

116. Interior of a shop making furniture in the Western style, circa 1830. Artist unknown. Gouache on paper, 11″ × 14″. *Ginsberg and Levy, New York.*

8. Furniture

Several very divergent types of furniture were manufactured by the Chinese cabinetmakers for the Western market from 1740 to 1870. The basic styles were furniture in the Western manner; bamboo furniture; campaign chests, desks and lap desks, trunks and sea chests; and furniture in the Chinese style. Chinese export watercolors of the interiors of the various furniture shops provide the finest visual and documentary record of the kinds of furniture being made.

Furniture in the Western style is the most difficult to identify, and there is in existence today a great quantity of American and English style furniture which has not been recognized as being of Chinese manufacture. Study through wood analysis and of construction and design is necessary to identify positively this important trade product. Since Americans were known to have taken American woods to China, it is possible that some pieces of furniture could have been made of American mahogany. The Chinese made chairs, settees and tables in the Queen Anne style with ball-and-claw or pad feet which are virtually indistinguishable from their Western prototypes except for their woods and construction. Because the Americans entered the trade late in the eighteenth century, few pieces of this earlier furniture found their way to the United States. The basic woods used for this type of furniture were Oriental rosewood and wood referred to as teak.[1]

The most typical furniture in the Western style made for the American market is in the Sheraton, Hepplewhite or early Empire taste.[2] Innumerable side and armchairs with reeded legs, turned-back rails and voluted arms exist and have been accepted as of American or European manufacture, when in reality they were made in China. Sullivan Dorr of Providence, Rhode Island, bought at Canton 12 chairs, 2 bedsteads and many other pieces of furniture in 1801.[3] What the style of the furniture might have been is unknown, but it was undoubtedly to the Federal taste. An 1820's watercolor of

117. Arm chair, circa 1825, in the Regency style. Oriental rosewood, 33½″ high. *Author's Collection.*

116 the interior of a cabinetmaker's shop illustrates the numerous forms and the diverse designs of furniture which could have been purchased by American merchants for use in the hongs or for export home to America. The style of the furniture comes as a complete surprise to those not familiar with the Western-type furniture made in China. The gateleg tables illustrated in the shop watercolor are not known in an actual example today.

Several chairs which match the scroll-arm chair exist; they are known to have been brought back by merchants in the China trade. Several documented chairs are excellent examples of those in the late Federal, early Empire style which found their way to New York, Boston and Philadelphia in considerable quantity. A handsome pair of chairs in the Sheraton style was made for Andreas Everardus Van Braam Houckgeest with his monogram carved in a shield below a carved ribbon in the center of the back splat. The chairs were undoubtedly for his house, "China Retreat," built in Philadelphia in 1795, and they are the finest examples of this type of late-eighteenth century furniture in the Western mode known to have been made for an American.[4] Houckgeest had spent the early 1790's in China as commercial director of the Dutch Company, and was one of the two ambassadors dispatched by the Dutch to congratulate the Emperor Ch'ien Lung on the sixtieth anniversary of his accession in 1794.[5]

A particularly important set of 16 chairs in the early Empire style,
120 with turned-back rail and saber legs, was brought back by a Captain Wills of
Newburyport, Massachusetts; he was engaged in the trade in the second quarter of the nineteenth century. The chairs are extraordinarily close to

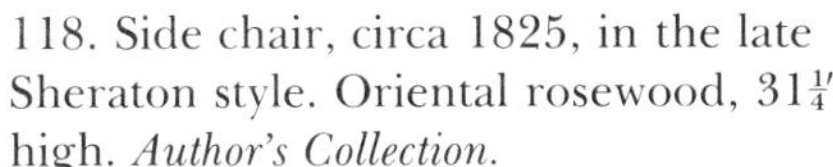

118. Side chair, circa 1825, in the late Sheraton style. Oriental rosewood, 31$\frac{1}{4}$″ high. *Author's Collection.*

119. Arm chair, circa 1825, in the late Sheraton style. Oriental rosewood, 31″ high. Possibly made for a member of the Lowell family, Boston. *Collection of Mr. E. J. L. Ropes.*

their American or English prototype, and are of especially fine design and
execution. The seats are cane, a characteristic of the majority of the Chinese
furniture to the Western taste. A set of Sheraton-style armchairs, with
reeded legs and rolled back rails was brought to Boston at approximately the *119*
same period. The design seems to have been popular in New England, since
several side and armchairs to other sets are in existence. *118*

Three récamiers which are identical in form to the one on which the
craftsman is working in the watercolor have been located. Very similar
in form to their Western prototypes, the details and proportions and the *121*
wood reveal their Chinese manufacture. The legs are too delicate and the carving of the taloned foot is weak, however. The rosette at the end of the arm roll on one of the récamiers, is, on close examination, not a rosette at all, but a Chinese dragon's head. The récamiers are extremely handsome and successful furniture forms with their caned seats and removable back panels. Many more must exist, unidentified as Chinese, in houses and historical collections along the Eastern seaboard.

There are in existence five Chippendale style camel-back sofas, which were undoubtedly all made in China, although there has been controversy over their place of manufacture because of the woods involved. All were probably made in Canton, and those of American woods were, possibly, made from woods brought to China by traders. A pair at Williamsburg is definitely of Chinese woods and manufacture. Very handsomely designed, with

120. Side chair, circa 1820, in the early Empire style. Oriental rosewood, 34½″ high. Known to have been brought back by Captain Wills of Newburyport, Mass. *Privately owned.*

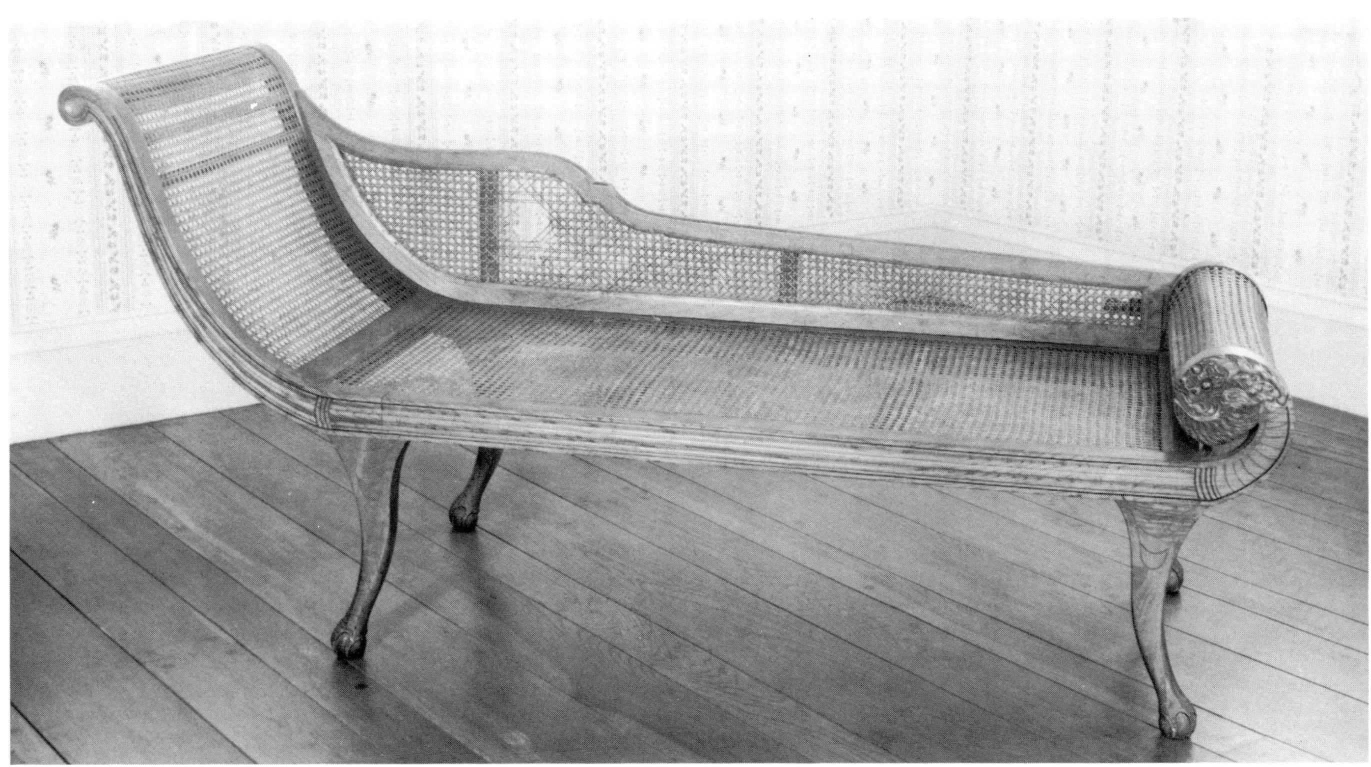

121. Récamier, circa 1815, in the Sheraton style, Cane and oriental woods, 31½″ high, 64″ long. Note dragon head on foot roll. *Photograph by permission of the Manchester Historical Society, Manchester, Mass.*

spade feet and rolled arms that end in carved rosettes, the sofas are caned on the backs, seats and arms. Two similar sofas, one at Winterthur and one at the 122
headquarters of the Society for the Preservation of New England Antiquities, are practically identical in construction and design, but they have been decorated with black paint and applied gold grape leaves to resemble lacquered furniture. The Winterthur sofa has a number of American woods in its construction, but it was known to have been used on a ship engaged in the China trade. Undoubtedly these sofas were all made in China, because of their similarity of construction and design, and many more must exist. The form is all but unknown in American furniture of the period (1800–1815).

Several tables in the Federal or Sheraton style were made and covered with lacquer; these are discussed in the chapter on lacquerware. None of the tripod base tip-top tables shown in the watercolor has been identified. Future wood analysis on doubtful tables will be necessary to establish their country of origin.

Many of the objects in the watercolor of the shop are familiar to those interested in China trade objects: the chest with the brass-bound mounts and corners, the tall chests with myriad drawers and the cane and wood settees.
The floor trunks were usually made of camphorwood and had brass tabs and 124
corners for decoration and protection. The locks and handles were made in China also, but were copies of English examples. The chests were made in all

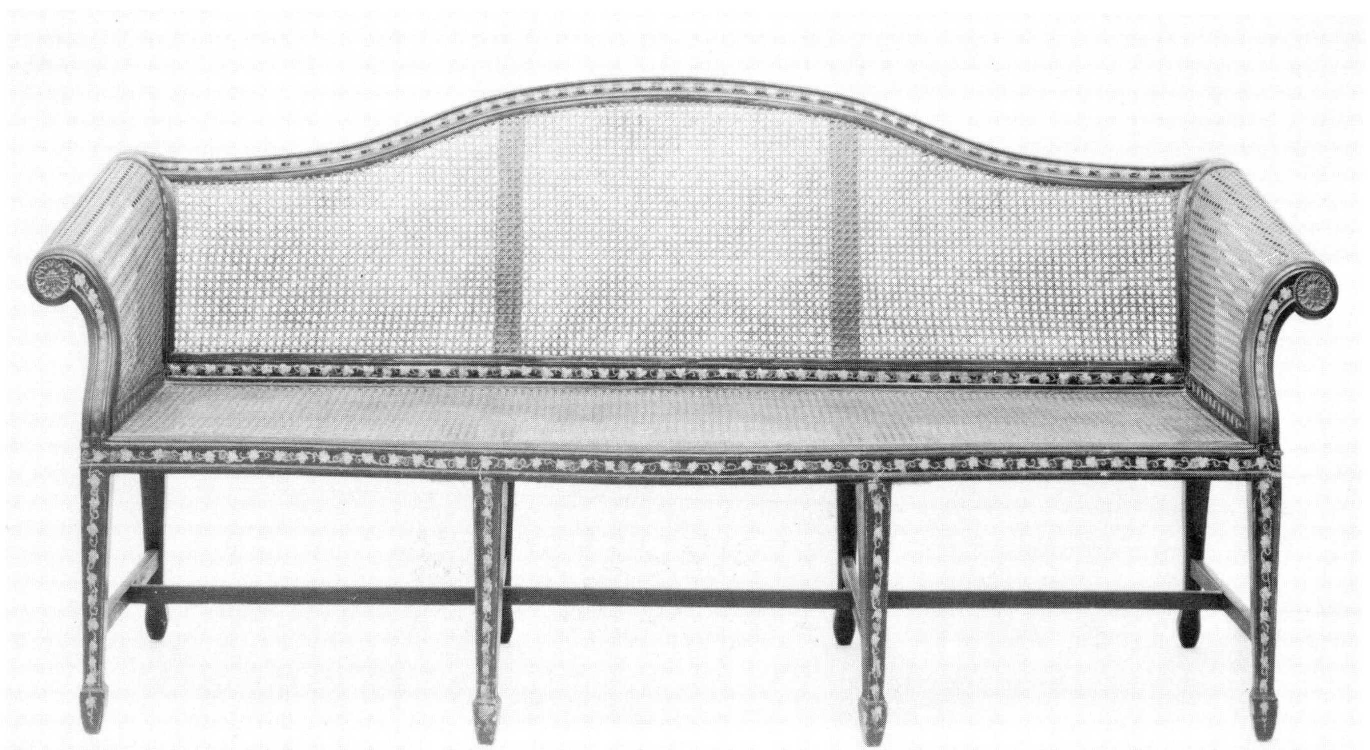

122. Settee, circa 1810, in the Hepplewhite style. Cane and painted and decorated wood. Although most of the woods in the settee are American, it was undoubtedly made in China. *Henry Francis du Pont Winterthur Museum.*

123

sizes, and were used on board ship or in the hongs. The trunk in the back of the shop, with the brass tacks, is undoubtedly the familiar kind made of wood which was covered with leather and then studded with tacks in a decorative pattern. The rarest of these trunks often have eagle escutcheons for the lock plates. Several have decorative swags of tacks on the front and top and written inscriptions or plates. The trunk leathers were painted maroon, blue, green, brown, dark green, black and yellow, and numerous examples had borders of flowers painted within the tack lines. The latter trunks are extremely handsome and decorative. The trunks were usually made in sets, starting from a very large one 5 feet long and diminishing in size to about 2 feet in length. Often packed one inside the other, with the smallest filled with tea, the trunks were easily transported. Many were lined originally with silver-patterned tea paper, and bore a small round label with the name of the cabinetmaker in red.

Few of the cabinetmakers are known, but the names of Ahning, Ashoe and Ashie have been found in trunks, on contemporary bills, and in reminiscences. Ahning's label is inside a trunk covered with black leather and decorative studs which was made for George Nichols of Salem in the very early nineteenth century.[6] Osmond Tiffany of Boston mentions Ahning in 1844:

> . . . we hear the sound of hammers and the grating of saws, smell camphor wood strongly, and find ourselves in the carpenters square. Three or four

123. Stack of decorated trunks, 1820–1840. Painted leather over camphorwood, trimmed with brass. Largest 36″ long, $16\frac{1}{4}$″ high. *Privately owned.*

124. Camphorwood trunk, circa 1830. Trimmed with brass, 22½″ high, 47¾″ long. *Collection of D. Roger Howlett.*

125. Dressing mirror, circa 1855. Oriental rosewood with brass fittings, 9″ high, $11\frac{3}{8}$″ wide, $22\frac{1}{4}$″ high when opened. *Lynn Historical Society, Lynn, Mass.*

126. Roll-top lap desk with fitted compartments, circa 1830. Oriental wood with brass mounts, $9\frac{3}{4}''$ high, $19\frac{1}{8}''$ long (closed). *Peabody Museum, Salem.*

> streets, joining together and forming a sort of parallelogram are wholly occupied by these artisans. Here they are making every variety of furniture, working well and cheaply. The most conspicuous articles are the camphor wood trunks, so admirably adapted for keeping woollens secure from insects. Ahning has a large establishment, comprising four or five shops filled with workmen, and when you order a big trunk, he pulls out his rule, says "Hi Yah," and sends the trunk smooth, varnished and fragrant, round to the hong, punctual to the moment.[7]

The description of the trunk ordered fits the large camphorwood trunk with brass mounts and a name plate which is shown in Illustration 124.

Benjamin Shreve bought a pair of couches from Ashie for $18 in 1817 which could have been either récamiers or cane couches used on board ship.[8] Ashoe, whose label appears in numerous trunks, also worked on Carpenter's Square. An amusing incident, related by W. C. Hunter, describes Ashoe pretending to be a translator at the trial of an Indian sailor and saying in pidgin English, which none of the Orientals present could understand, that he sold dressing cases, trunks, etc., and that his address was 9 Carpenter's Square.[9] The dressing cases could have been made in the Western manner like the
125 lacquered ones or as square or rectangular boxes which opened up to reveal drawers, a lift-up mirror and numerous compartments of all shapes and descriptions.

The large "campaign" chests of drawers, with their bail handles on the ends and handsome flush brasses, are very common in England and America. Great numbers were made by the cabinetmakers such as Ashoe and Ahning. The chests were usually made in two parts, for convenience and transporting, and the top section often had a drawer front which dropped down to a desk surface, with compartments for writing equipment inside. Some had tall drawers on the sides which were intended for bottles. The finest chests had feet to raise the bottom section off the floor. On the more ornate, sat a third section with paneled doors, behind which were shelves for books. A particularly fine example was brought to Salem in the 1840's by Captain Nathaniel Brookhouse Mansfield.

Fold-out traveling desks were purchased by almost every captain and 126
supercargo who visited Canton. Made by the furniture cabinetmakers, they generally formed rectangular boxes when closed. The front section dropped down to form a slant surface for writing, and below this surface were areas for storage of paper and supplies. At the back of the writing surface were compartments for pens, ink and wipers. On the more elaborately constructed desks, the back compartment sprang up to reveal a bank of drawers and pigeonholes, with a mirror in the center. Occasionally, the top of the compartment section was covered by a roll-top that was operated by a front drawer below the writing surface. The desks had recessed handles on the sides for carrying, or for the opening of an additional small drawer. A large collection of writing or travel desks at the Peabody Museum reveals the various kinds of construction and design used, from the end of the eighteenth century to the middle of the nineteenth.

A handsome standing desk, in the Federal style, made for Captain William Cleveland of Salem, about 1810, combines the features of the traveling desks with those of a larger piece of standing furniture. Slant-topped, 129
with drawers in the front, the desk stands on tapered legs with simple carved decoration. Two false drawer fronts on either side of the top center drawer swing out as supports for the writing surface when unfolded. When the top is opened to a full writing area, a storage section is revealed at the back which springs up to form a fully compartmentalized desk area, complete with mirror and pigeonholes. This treatment is very reminiscent of the smaller desks and forms a practical feature for a piece of furniture being used in a small space, such as a ship's cabin. The desk is unique in construction, and is thought to have been designed by Cleveland himself.

Several cane and wood settees or couches exist, similar to the one shown in the shop interior, that were undoubtedly made for ships' cabins. The best known examples to date were all used on ships which sailed from
Providence, Rhode Island. The one held by the Rhode Island Historical 127
Society was owned by Edward Carrington, who was Consul in Canton at the beginning of the nineteenth century.[10] The example at Winterthur was used on the Providence ship *Ann and Hope.* The settees have cane seats and rolled cane arms at either end, with cane back panels. The ends of the arms on the most ornate are decorated with large Adamesque rosettes, similar to those on the récamiers and sofas. All have drawers beneath the seat for storage, and the cane seat lifts up for the storage of blankets. Since the woods on two of the three of these that have been tested appear to be American, there is some question of their having been made in Providence. Though they have always been accepted as having been made in China, it is possible that they were

127. Day bed, early nineteenth century, with storage drawers and brass mounts. Cane and wood, $32\frac{1}{2}''$ high, 87″ long. Brought from China by Edward Carrington. *Rhode Island Historical Society.*

made by Chinese craftsmen from American woods. Their similarity to the récamiers and camel-back sofas supports this theory. Another example of this type of couch, much simpler in construction, with straight arms and ends and a simple back rail, extends to make a double bed. The most ambitious of these couches, undoubtedly made toward the middle of the nineteenth century, for a clipper ship of considerable size, is the width and length of a large single bed. The arms are similar to those of the Carrington couch, and the wood ends are carved with large rosettes. The ends, seat and back are caned, as is a special half-length shaped piece which fits in the front of the couch to protect the person sleeping in it. The back, which is also removable, has a large shell carved in the center. The piece is well carved and very attractive in design, but slightly heavier than its Western prototypes. There is no concern for storage as there was in the earlier couches with drawers, which were made for smaller vessels. A couch of similar design—not so wide as a single bed—at the Philadelphia Museum uses many of the same decorative motifs, such as the shell, and has short fat Empire legs very similar to those seen on Empire furniture in America. This piece of furniture could well have been made for the house of a Western trader living in the Orient. Harriet Low, who lived in Macao in the early 1830's, brought a similar one back to Salem.

Several pieces of furniture, which were undoubtedly made for the

128. Sofa, circa 1840, in the Empire style. Oriental rosewood and cane, length 79½″, height 37″. *Philadelphia Museum of Art.*

English or Dutch market but are in American collections now, provide superb examples of furniture following Western lines. One is a large slant-front desk that is bombé, with flanges down each side. The desk was made for the Dutch market and is extraordinarily well designed and constructed. The design reveals its Chinese provenance somewhat, but the overall treatment is convincing as a Western piece of furniture. Another superb item is a hall bench of Chinese wood, with a solid seat and cabriole legs ending in ball-and-claw feet, which is much in the Queen Anne mode. Both pieces probably were made in China in the 1770's.

A fine early-nineteenth century watercolor of the interior of a shop *131* making bamboo furniture provides an excellent sample of the types of bamboo furniture that were sent to America. Several shipping documents mention bamboo furniture, and it seems to have been relatively inexpensive; settees were under $20. The chairs, settees and tables made of bamboo had a tremendous vogue in the West, especially after the Prince Regent furnished Brighton Pavilion with Chinese bamboo furniture in the early nineteenth century. The pieces were very delicate in feeling and immediately imparted a Chinese look to any room in which they were placed. William Chambers, in his book on Western furniture in the Chinese style, illustrates and discusses the chairs as items to be produced by the English furniture makers.[11] Brighton

129. Desk with lift top for writing material compartments, circa 1810. Oriental woods. Brought from China by Captain William Cleveland of Salem, Mass. *Essex Institute Collections, Pierce Nichols House.*

130. Pier table, circa 1849, in the Empire/Victorian style. Ornate Chinese carving and marble inset top, 38¾″ long, 32¾″ high. Brought to America by Captain Robert Bennet Forbes in 1849. *Museum of the American China Trade.*

Pavilion holds several armchairs made in China, which are close to the English examples illustrated in Chambers. Tiffany describes the construction of the bamboo furniture in his sojourn to a shop, which may have looked very much like the one represented in the watercolor. "The furniture of the Chinese is of two kinds, the bamboo and the rosewood. The first is exceedingly light, pretty, and adapted for a warm climate, withal very cheap. The stouter parts or framework is colored dark and the ends of the stalks, tipped with ivory or horn. The young shoots of the plant are interwoven with those of stouter growth in pretty windings and book cases, tables, sofas, and chairs are thus produced at small cost."[12] The watercolor of the shop depicts all the pieces that Tiffany describes. The extension chair shown in the center of the shop is very similar to one brought back by Carrington in the early nineteenth cen-
133 tury.[13] The seat and extender are covered with bamboo slats that are painted with a Chinese decoration in black. This form of chair was very popular and was made throughout the nineteenth century for exportation to the West.

Examples of long settees in bamboo exist, and a particularly fine one,
131 close to that illustrated in the shop, is in the collection of the Museum of the American China Trade. Another similar one may be seen in the watercolor of the interior of Tingqua's studio. The chairs are known in a variety of shapes, but are usually barrel-back like those at Brighton or straight-backed with curving arms. The back supports are tipped with ivory, exactly as Tiffany reports. Several of these chairs were brought to Salem and Boston in the very beginning of the nineteenth century. Although seemingly fragile in construction, the chairs and settees have survived remarkably well, attesting to good Chinese construction. The small octagonal tables and the taller stands of bamboo are particularly attractive, and were also made throughout the nineteenth century. A small number were exhibited at the Philadelphia Centennial Exhibition and are shown in photographs of the Chinese booth.[14]
134 One small baby stroller of bamboo, made in the second quarter of the nineteenth century, is a unique example of that form of furniture.

Documented Chinese export furniture, in any of the different styles and materials in which it was made, is very difficult to locate. The Carrington pieces are the exception to the general rule, and the furniture illustrates that
135 Carrington, a typical Westerner in China, purchased furniture of all styles. Apart from his lacquerware, bamboo extension chair and ship couches, he bought hardwood furniture in the Chinese style. This furniture is generally the most difficult to date, if it is not documented, since the styles maintained a consistency throughout the nineteenth century. Generally, however, on very close examination, certain differences in the pieces made at the beginning and the end of the nineteenth century can be detected. The earlier furniture was very delicate and attenuated when used in the form of a table, whereas the later pieces diverged from the pure Chinese forms and incorporated elements of the revival styles such as gadrooned edges, ball-and-claw feet and ornate shells.

Carrington owned a pair of Chinese chairs very much in the native fashion, complete with marble insets in the seats and backs. This type of chair has always enjoyed great popularity, and is still in favor today. Robert Bennett Forbes, Benjamin Shreve and numerous other prominent merchants all purchased Chinese furniture. A watercolor of the interior of a shop which
136 manufactured furniture in Chinese styles illustrates clearly the various forms made: the large beds, desks, low benches and the ever-present small tables of

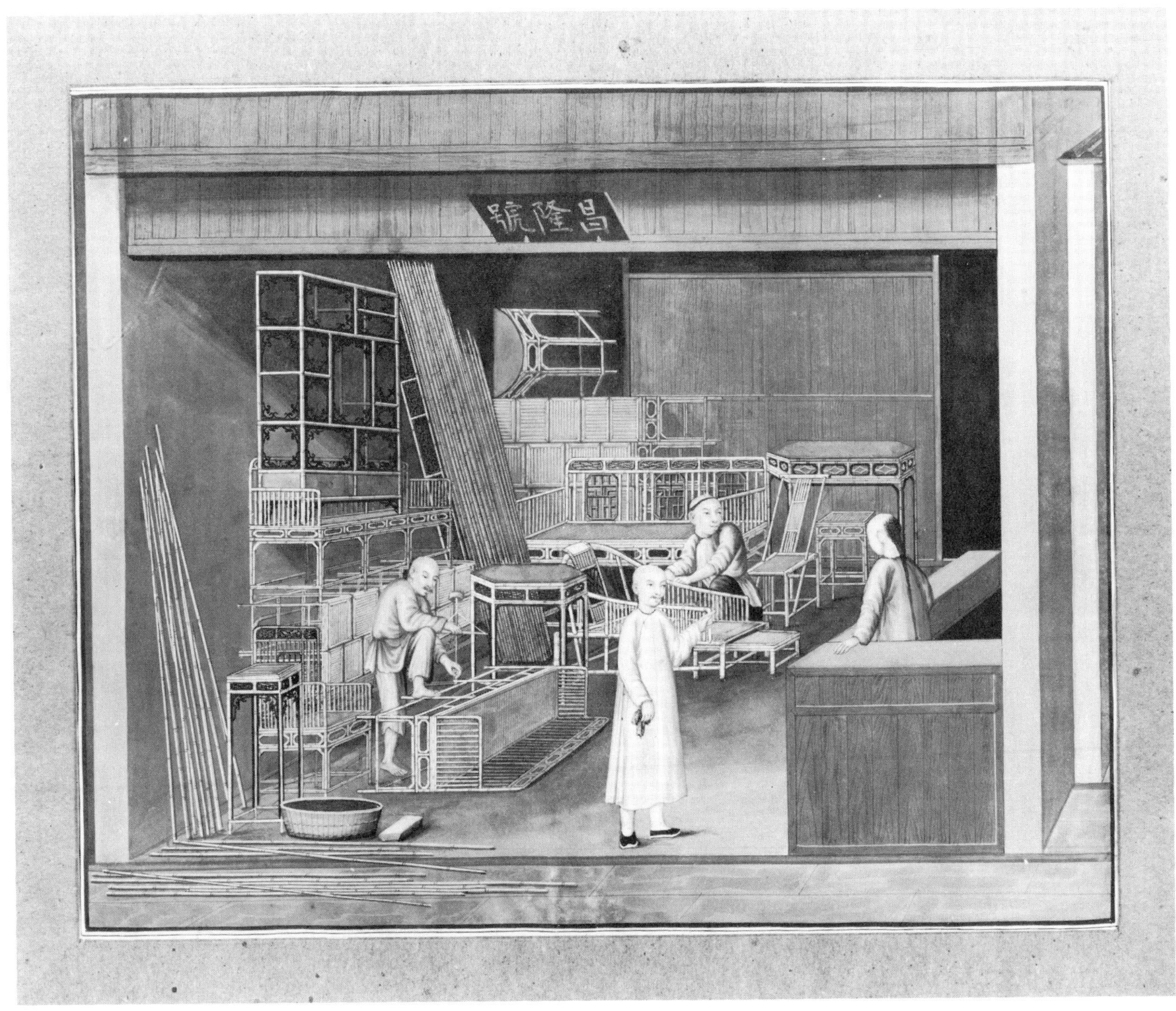

131. Interior of a bamboo furniture shop, circa 1830. Artist unknown. Watercolor on paper, 11″ × 14″. *Ginsberg and Levy, New York.*

132. Arm chair, circa 1810. Bamboo and cane, 36″ high.
Author's Collection.

133. Extension chair, circa 1810. Bamboo and cane, $40\frac{1}{2}''$ closed, 63″ long extended. Brought from China by Edward Carrington. *Rhode Island Historical Society.*

134. Child's walker, circa 1820. Bamboo and cane, 22½″ high, 19″ wide. Child's chair, circa 1840. Bamboo, 31½″ high. Both *Peabody Museum, Salem.*

all heights. Tiffany remarks of this furniture, "The other kind of furniture [rosewood] is far more costly, and is very heavy and solid. It is made of rosewood and is susceptible of high polish, and handsomely carved, looks well. . . . Some book cases are very strangely divided in accordance with whimsical taste, into shelves of unequal length and height so that volumes or curiosities do not appear in line."[15] A small example of a book case is seen on the desk to the left in the watercolor. "The tables have the sides and edges carved fancifully, and they are either entirely of wood, or set with a marble top. In these tables the stone, which is also used used [*sic*] for the seats and backs of chairs, is variegated like *verd antique* or Sienna marbles."[16] This quotation aptly describes Carrington's superb pair of side tables with their marble tops, and his set of stands of rosewood and marble of various heights. The tables, made in different heights, were found throughout America from the late eighteenth century to the present, and they seem to be the most convenient and practical pieces of furniture ever made by the Chinese for the Western market.

Few records of beds on the scale of those in the shop watercolor can be documented as having been brought back to America in the first half of the

135. Chair and table, circa 1810, in the Chinese taste. Oriental rosewood with marble insets, chair, 34½″ high; table, 41¼″ long, 33¼″ high. Brought from China by Edward Carrington. *Rhode Island Historical Society.*

nineteenth century. The heavy furniture found greater favor in the mid-Victorian period, when "Chinese rooms" had a vogue. The trunks stacked to the left in the shop are of light wood construction, possibly, covered with pigskin or other thin leather and painted. The armoires in the background are presently not known in the American trade.

Innumerable desks like the one to the left in the watercolor were made throughout the nineteenth century. Either relatively simple like the one shown, or more ambitious with more drawers down the sides and across the top, they had considerable appeal to the Western buyer for their style and practicality. Like so many of the chairs and tables for export in the Chinese vogue, it is often difficult to have an exact idea of their date of exportation. Many desks of this form are made in Hong Kong today. One desk, with a flat top and two separate side stands with two drawers each, can be dated from the third quarter of the nineteenth century. An excellent example of this form of furniture, the desk has drawer locks which are stamped IEUNUKEE, CANTON. *137*
The brass pulls are recessed like those used on the campaign chests.

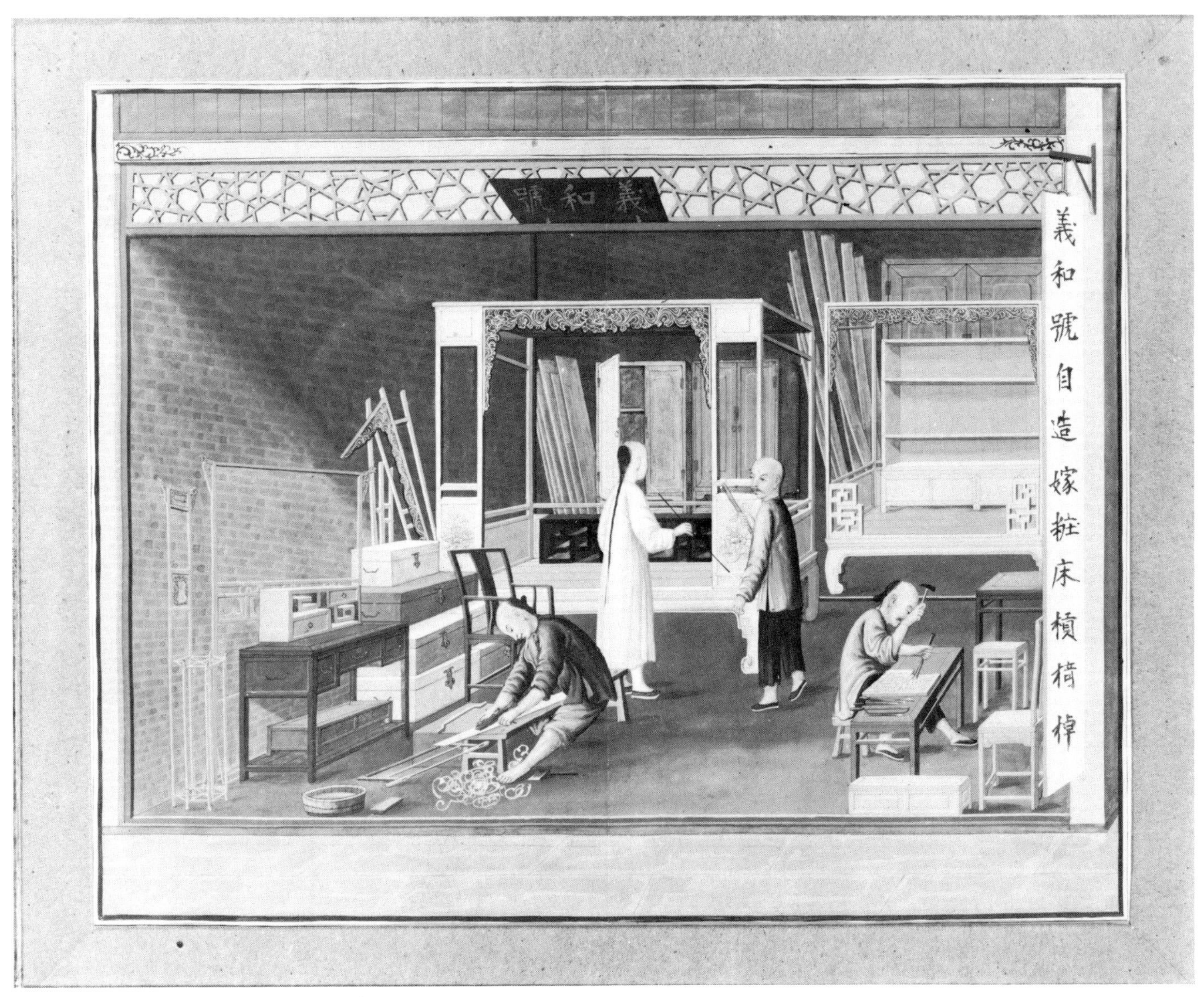

136. Interior of a shop making Chinese style furniture for the Western market, circa 1830. Artist unknown. Watercolor on paper, 11″ × 14″. *Ginsberg and Levy, New York.*

137. Desk, circa 1860. Rosewood, made in three parts; inset brasses marked "IEUNUKEE, CANTON", 55″ long, 33⅝″ high. *Courtesy Richard Mills.*

The Forbes furniture, possibly made for their houses in China, is heavily in the Chinese style, while trying to maintain some of the lines of Empire or Victorian furniture. Massive and overly decorated, the sofas and pier tables would have been perfect for the enormous rooms with high ceilings and large windows of the houses built in Hong Kong and Shanghai from 1860 to 1890. Here Chinese dragons, flowers and symbols all join together in a never-ending twist of carving reminiscent of the designs of the carved ivory and horn tusks. Enormous tables, impossible to move, with *130*
great marble insets were made for their houses in China and later shipped back to America.

A series of interior views of the rooms of the Low House at Shanghai in the 1880's shows a great quantity of furniture made by the Chinese.[17] The very late Empire style chairs, with their strange proportions and unusual design, are obviously Chinese. Several of the overly ornate pieces throughout the rooms represent the best of Victorian taste as interpreted by the Chinese. The furniture is massive, but perfect for a house on the grand scale of that period. Countless houses owned by the Westerners who lived in China in the later nineteenth century must have been filled with furniture of this style. The pure Western design of furniture had given way by this period to heavy Chinese influences, as had happened with the porcelains, silver and silks.

Notes

1. The contemporary sources describe the furniture for export as being constructed of rosewood. This is also known in England as *padouk.* The all-inclusive word *teak* is also used to describe the heavy dark woods used on the ornately carved export furniture.
2. It is difficult to select a particular term, since Adamesque, Sheraton and Hepplewhite describe English-style furniture of the late-eighteenth and early-nineteenth century, as well as American. The term "Federal," is appropriate, except it suggests American design. "Early Empire" is used for American furniture, whereas "Regency" would be used for English. Most of the terms, when applied to the export furniture, are interchangeable, and vary only because of slight stylistic traits which would relate to one style better than the other.
3. Sullivan Dorr, "Memorandum book 1801 and. . . ." Manuscript collection, Rhode Island Historical Society.
4. These chairs were exhibited at the Metropolitan Museum of Art, New York, and are illustrated in the catalogue, "The China Trade and its Influences," 1941, Figure 71.
5. *Ibid.,* p. 15.
6. Collection of the Essex Institute, Salem, Massachusetts, currently in the Pierce Nichols House. Family tradition asserts the trunk was brought home in 1801; it may possibly have been later.
7. Tiffany, *The Canton Chinese,* p. 78.
8. Shreve papers, ship *China,* 1817. Peabody Museum, Salem.
9. W. C. Hunter, *Bits of Old China.* London: Kegan Paul, Trench & Co., 1885, p. 28.
10. Three of these are known: one at Winterthur Museum; one at Metropolitan Museum of Art; and one at the Rhode Island Historical Society.
11. There is some question as to how to distinguish those made in England from those made in China; the Chinese would seem to be those with square backs or high curved backs, whereas the English may be those of barrel shape. Misidentifications of this type of furniture are common. The Chinese almost always have the small end of ivory described by Tiffany.
12. Tiffany, *The Canton Chinese,* p. 83.
13. The chair was probably brought back by Carrington when he came back to America after serving as Consul in Canton from 1802 to 1811. However, since Carrington was in the trade with his firm through the 1830's, there is a possibility that much of the Carrington material is later than his return in 1811.
14. Photographs in the scrapbook of John Robinson, Peabody Museum.
15. Tiffany, *The Canton Chinese,* p. 83.
16. *Ibid.,* p. 83.
17. In the photograph files, Peabody Museum, Salem. There is some question as to whether or not this is actually a Low house; however, family information and tradition make the identification plausible.

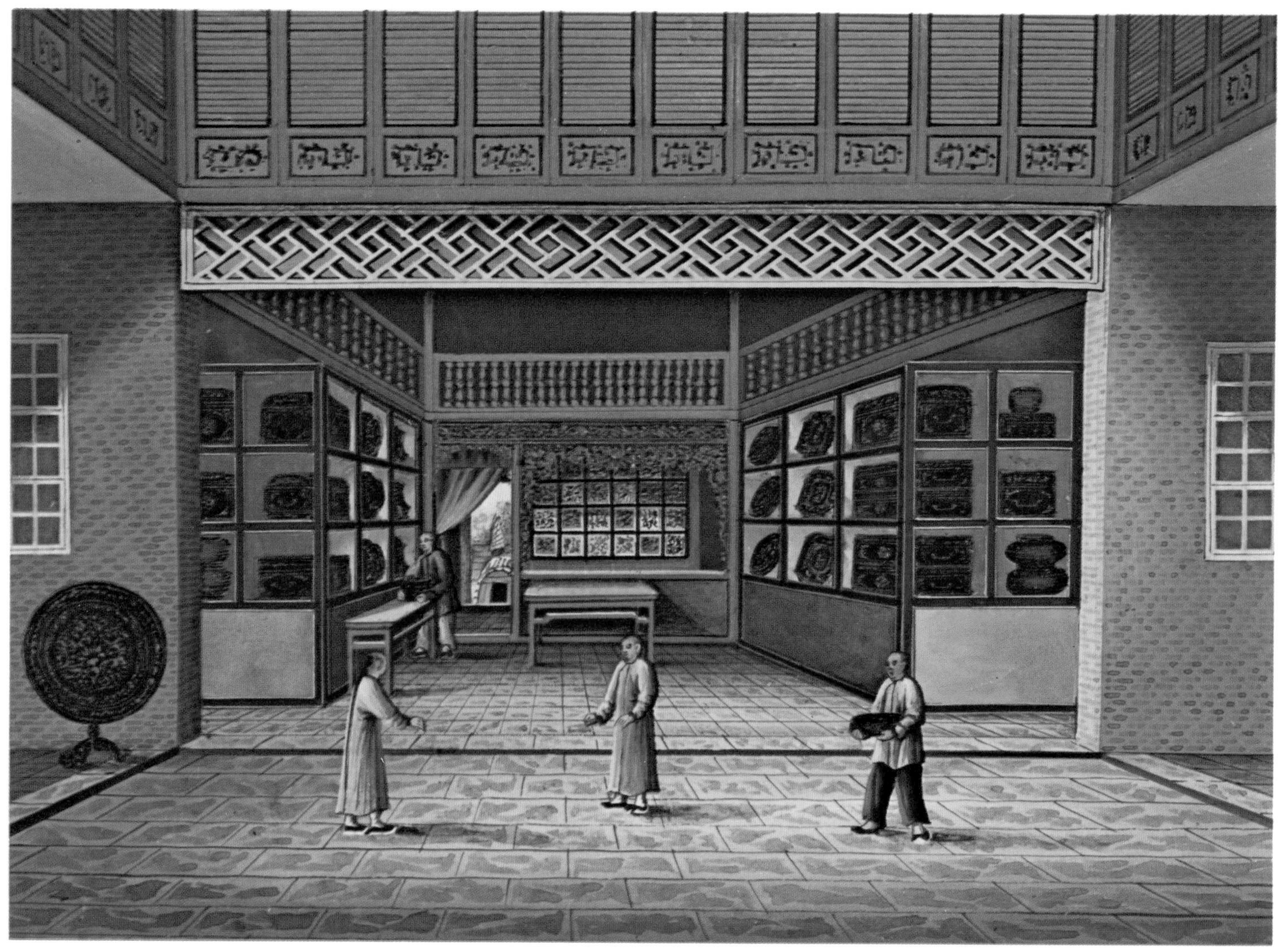

138. Interior of a lacquerware shop, circa 1840. Artist unknown. Watercolor on paper, $4\frac{1}{2}'' \times 6\frac{3}{4}''$. *Collection of William B. Osgood.*

9. Lacquerware

Westerners have been fascinated with Oriental lacquer since their first introduction to it in the seventeenth century. The hard, shiny surface and the handsome designs in gold and colors made lacquerware one of the most sought after products of the China trade. Lacquerware from China and Japan had a tremendous impact on Western decorative arts and was responsible for the custom of "japanning" Western-made furniture in the first half of the eighteenth century.

The lacquer itself comes from the sap of an Eastern form of the sumac tree (*vernix vernicia*). An 1876 account of the manufacture of lacquerware concisely defines the techniques which had been used for centuries.

> In the manufacture of lacquerware the lightest woods are used. After planing, the surface is covered with a coating of grasscloth fibre, and Broussonetia paper and a mixture of pig's or buffalo's gall and pulverized old red sandstone serves as priming. . . . The article is then placed in a dark room and a coating of the prepared lacquer laid on with a brush and allowed to dry; and according to the fineness of the ware these coatings are repeated 3 to 15 times. When the last coat is dry the articles are painted and gilded. The lacquer . . . is imported from Szechen or Kiangsi. . . . Nearly all the lacquerware is manufactured in Canton, but magnificent specimens far exceeding the Canton ware in beauty, colour and fineness are turned out at Foochow. They are made by a single family said to be of Japanese origin, who brought the secret over with them and have retained it ever since.[1]

Japanese lacquerware had always been considered more desirable than Chinese and had commanded great admiration in China. The lacquer made in Canton for export in the eighteenth century was thought to be inferior to the Nanking and Tonking products, because the Cantonese was produced hastily and decorated carelessly.[2] Osmond Tiffany described the decoration of lacquerware in Canton later, however, as painstaking: "A skillful hand

139. Card table, circa 1825, one of a pair in the Hepplewhite style. Gold and black lacquer, 28″ high. *The Vale, Waltham, Society for the Preservation of New England Antiquities.*

pricks out the designed pattern on the black surface with a sharp steel point, and the delicate preparation of gold contained in little porcelain saucers is laid on with fine brushes. This being finished, the whole is once more carefully examined, and the article is ready for sale."[3]

Furniture in Western forms in Oriental lacquer reached its greatest popularity during the second half of the eighteenth and the beginning of the nineteenth century. The furniture, of light and rather delicate construction, was most often decorated in black with gold. The forms made, gaming tables, sewing and card tables, bonheurs-du-jour, armoires, desks and poudreuses, were all copied from Western models sent to China or made from designs and plans in English and continental books and catalogues.

The furniture for the American market consisted of these pieces, as well as dressing mirrors, all types of boxes and the screens then popular in the West. "Nothing can exceed the splendor of the magnificent folding screens they make for rooms; large landscapes are represented, and scenes

140. Gaming table, between 1820 and 1822, in the Federal style. Black/brown and gold lacquer, $30\frac{1}{4}''$ high, top 35″ × 36″ open. Extremely rare, made for Nicholas and Abby Brown. Initialed "NAB" in gold in counter cups. *Loaned to Rhode Island Historical Society by Mr. John Carter Brown Washburn.*

of Chinese gardens, which are always irrigated, and in which bridges and boats are necessary as well as ornamental," as Tiffany described them.[4] Four- and six-fold screens of black lacquer with magnificent gold Chinese landscape and river scenes with delicate feather borders were made in large quantities throughout the American China trade period.

Most of the furniture is in the Hepplewhite and Sheraton styles, with several obvious Chinese changes such as dragon feet, and other minor adaptations throughout. Many of the earlier pieces are handsome in decoration and basic shape, but rather flimsy in construction. Light woods, attenuated legs, thin panels and doors, insufficient bracing and poor cabinetry led to warping, scaling and cracking in the Western climate.

Certain furniture forms in the Western manner were made in units which could be packed and shipped compactly and then screwed or fitted

141. Dressing stand, circa 1810, in the Federal taste. Lacquer, decorated with the grape-leaf design, 35½″ high. *Private Collection.*

142. Dressing glass, 1790–1800, in Federal style. Samuel McIntire, Salem. Inlaid. Made for the Derby family. *Karolik Collection, Museum of Fine Arts, Boston.*

together upon arrival in the West. Most of the bonheurs-du-jour consisted of a top section with cabinet doors and divided interior, a table bottom, and a flat section (either a portable desk or a work top), which was placed on the table in front of the cabinet. Many sewing tables had a top compartment, outfitted with ivories, that screwed to the legs which were then connected by a turned stretcher. These tables were shipped as flat rectangular packages and assembled upon arrival. A bureau cabinet at Mereworth Castle, Kent, has a separate cabinet top, bonnet top and a footed platform base upon which sits a slant-front desk with a number of drawers.[5] Mirrors on the backs of poudreuses and dressing cases were removable for easy packing and safe shipping. This type of Chinese construction in sections was extremely practical in terms of shipping costs and breakage.

Decoration of the lacquerware from 1785 to 1820 consisted of repetitive grape-leaf patterns, similar to those borders on export porcelain of the period, stripes, geometric designs, small Federal-style borders, as seen on porcelain, and Chinese scenes. Many of the pieces were in muted colors like brown and dark green, or gold and orange. The grape-leaf pattern was often slightly raised and was applied with the finest craftsmanship and the greatest intricacy. The background to the grapes and leaves in some instances is a complex network of hexagons and circles or feathery tendrils. Alternating panels of tendrils or landscapes were painted between the grapes. The application of Chinese landscape scenes and court parades, in gold, was also popular; the early versions tend to be more sparse and simple than those which

143. Dressing mirror, circa 1810. Lacquer, gold and black decoration with grape-leaf pattern and landscape designs, 32¼″ high. *Metropolitan Museum of Art, Rogers Fund 1941.*

were used after 1825. In rare examples, the landscape vignettes may appear in colors, silver, red, brown and yellow. One handsome pattern was of Japanese inspiration, a zigzag pattern with flowers and leaves.

A pair of early card tables, in the Sheraton style, possibly brought back from China by a member of the Lyman family of Boston before 1825, em- *139*
ploys this combination of the grape-leaf design and landscape vignettes.[6] The tables are excellent examples of the best lacquerware furniture coming to the West in the early nineteenth century. The striking bureau cabinet at Mereworth Castle is an example of the zigzag motif in an extensive and overall design on a large piece of cabinet furniture.

A superb card and gaming table in the Adamesque style, in the John Brown House, Providence, Rhode Island, illustrates the highest quality of *140*
lacquer furniture. Made for Nicholas and Abby Brown around 1820, the table has two gaming surfaces: a chess board with gold landscape vignettes and a plain surface decorated with gold floral designs. On the chess top, is a striking blue-green border with four recesses in brown lacquer for gaming chips, each with the initials *NAB* in gold script. Carved and gilded rosettes at the top of each tapered leg add greatly to the table's appearance. The tops are supported when opened by a pair of swing legs at the back of the table.

A small Hepplewhite style table with spade feet is of the same quality of decoration as the Lyman tables, but is covered with the grape-leaf motif. A *152*
Sheraton dressing mirror, with an oval-case base containing two drawers of fitted lacquer boxes, has the grape-leaf pattern throughout with panels of gilt *141*

144. Poudreuse, circa 1820, with lift-up mirror and inside compartments. Lacquer, 43″ wide (closed), 31″ high. *Gore Place, Waltham, Mass.*

tendrils. The most common dressing cases with mirrors of the early-nine-
143 teenth century had stepped-back serpentine front drawers, outfitted with boxes, rather than oval bases. Both styles had upright mirrors of oval or shield design. The cases and their mirrors are exact copies of English or American
142 Hepplewhite or Sheraton style wood pieces made in the late-eighteenth and early-nineteenth centuries. The stepped-back cases are decorated with either the grape-leaf pattern or random, sparsely placed Chinese vignettes. Some have fine paneled enclosures with floral motifs and delicate backgrounds of geometric patterns, circles and dots. The quality of these early dressing cases is usually high with fine construction and lacquer work.

An extraordinarily well executed and oversize desk-poudreuse at Gore Place, Waltham, Massachusetts, is an example of the larger pieces of
144 furniture brought to America in the first quarter of the nineteenth century.[7] The desk is painted with a simple gold motif of wreath and wheat sheaves in an oval on each drawer, lid and the ends, with gilt scalloped borders. The

145. Sewing table, circa 1835. Black and gold lacquer with ivory fittings, 29″ high, top 29½″ × 16½″. Inside of lid decorated with a view of the Praya Grande, Macao, in gold. Made for the Wetmore family. *Peabody Museum, Salem.*

form must have been a popular one in America, since one brought to Salem before 1800 by William Ward and another brought to Salem at approximately the same time are identical to the Gore piece, except in size.[8] Although built like eighteenth-century knee-hole desks with drawers on each side, the pieces have lift tops, inside of which are compartments outfitted as dressing tables, with mirrors that spring up in the back of the tops.

An ornate suite of furniture made for the Wetmore family of Newport, Rhode Island, who were engaged in the China trade, illustrates the various forms of the furniture in a large Western order. The suite consists of a bonheur-du-jour of fine proportions and style, a sewing (or work) table, complete with ivory fittings, three nests of small end tables, with four tables to the nest, and a large round center table. Miscellaneous lacquered boxes for varied purposes also match the suite.[9] All the furniture is completely covered with intricate Chinese scenes and designs which work together to make an extremely pleasing overall effect. Each item has a script *W* in a circle in gold on the front or top.

Although all the pieces are well conceived, the most interesting one of the group is the work table.[10] Inside the lid, painted in gold, is a complete view of the Praya Grande at Macao. Lacquered furniture with Western scenes *145* or views of the ports is extremely rare, and the Wetmore table is the finest example known to date. For that matter, only one other example is known, a set of four nested tables, each with a view of one of the four ports, Canton, Macao, Whampoa and Boca Tigris. The view of Macao in the Wetmore table is most accurate in details and in delineation of the buildings and compares well with many of the port scenes in watercolor or oil. There is the possibility that one of the port artists painted the scene in the cover for the lacquer

146. Bonheur-du-jour, circa 1825, with fold-out desk and bonnet top. Black and gold lacquer, 66⅛″ high. *Rhode Island Historical Society.*

147. Gaming table, before 1815, with gaming board. Table, black and gold lacquer, $30\frac{1}{4}''$ high, top $35\frac{1}{4}'' \times 30''$. Board, mother-of-pearl. Thought to have been brought back by the Crowninshield family of Salem, before 1815. *Author's Collection.*

dealer who had made it. A bonheur-du-jour in the Brown House is similar to the Wetmore one and is of comparable quality.[11] The Brown example, more sparsely decorated, has the same interesting carved pineapples for feet, but no round marble inset in the spreader base. *146*

A gaming table brought to Salem by the Crowninshield family before 1815 is a fine example of this type of table. The shape is based on an English or American gaming table of the Chippendale period with a tripod base, bird cage beneath the top and cabriole legs. The legs, however, have been made to look like a dragon's neck and mane, and the feet are dragons' heads with open mouths and red lacquered tongues, rather than the ball-and-claw feet characteristic of the Western prototype. The top is a particularly attractive shape with reverse-curve corners painted with a sympathetic Chinese motif of leaves and tendrils. Osmond Tiffany has described the type aptly, "The large chess tables have shifting tops, one side adorned with gilding to complete the top design, and the other, forming the board of alternating lacquer and mother of pearl."[12] *147*

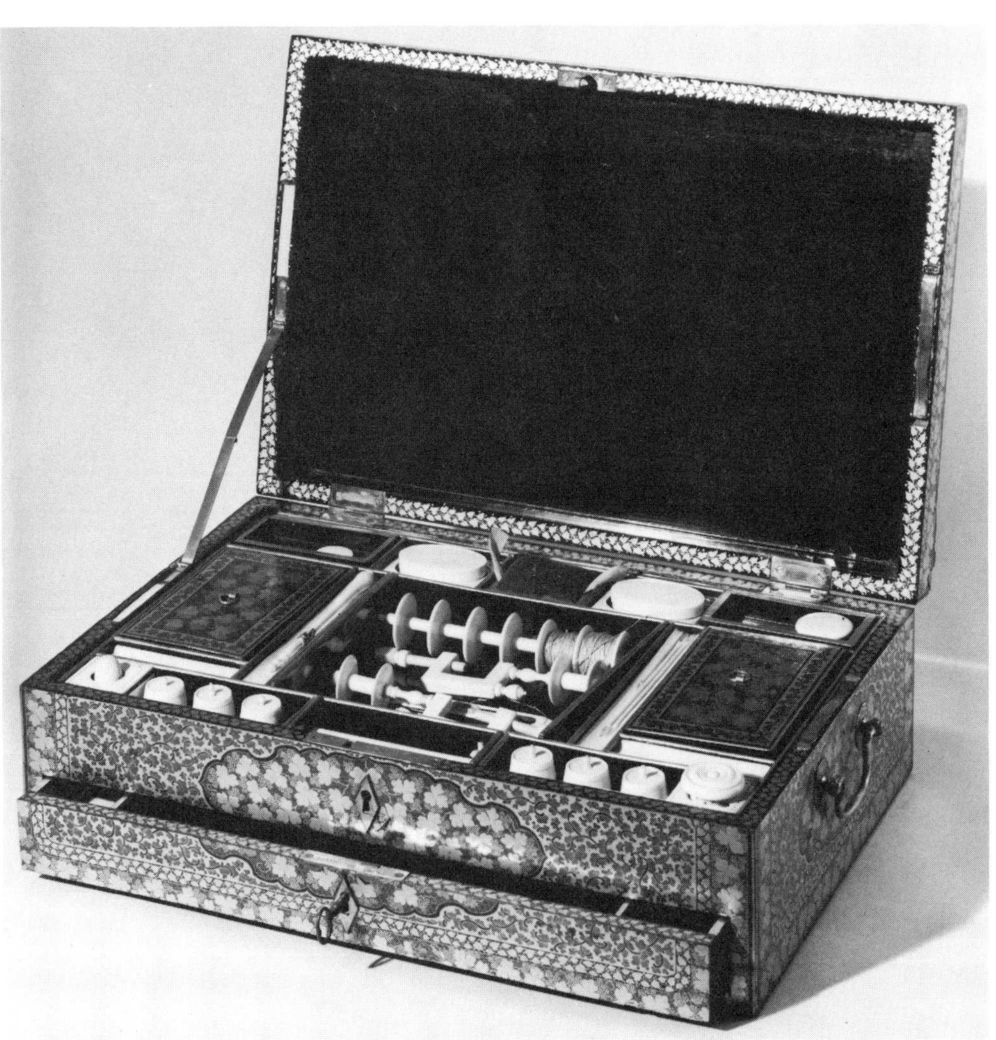

148. Sewing box, circa 1805, with handles, locks and hinges of China trade silver. Grape-leaf design and ivory fittings, 17″ × 11″ × 6″ high. *Author's Collection.*

A slant-top senatorial type desk, based on an English davenport is a most unusual furniture shape in export lacquer. Very close to the Western wood desks from which it was copied, it has scroll-front supports and banks of drawers on both sides behind pierced doors. The overall decoration is gold Chinese scenes on a black and brown background. No other example of this form in Chinese lacquer is known.

From 1785 to the mid-nineteenth century—and in some instances later—a tremendous number of lacquerware boxes of every shape and size were exported to America. Bills of lading and orders list thousands of boxes of all descriptions and for every possible purpose. Some of the most popular were sewing or work boxes, fold-out lap desks (copied from English or American prototypes), tea caddies with lead liners and glove boxes. These lacquer boxes were carefully packed in pegged wooden boxes that protected the delicate gold designs and high surface shine.[13] Tiffany describes the packing of lacquerware: "The lacquerware is packed with the greatest care in soft delicate paper chippings so that it cannot be moved or rubbed in the least. Then the whole box is varnished, to exclude air, and over the edges long strips of course [*sic*] paper are pasted. . . ."[14]

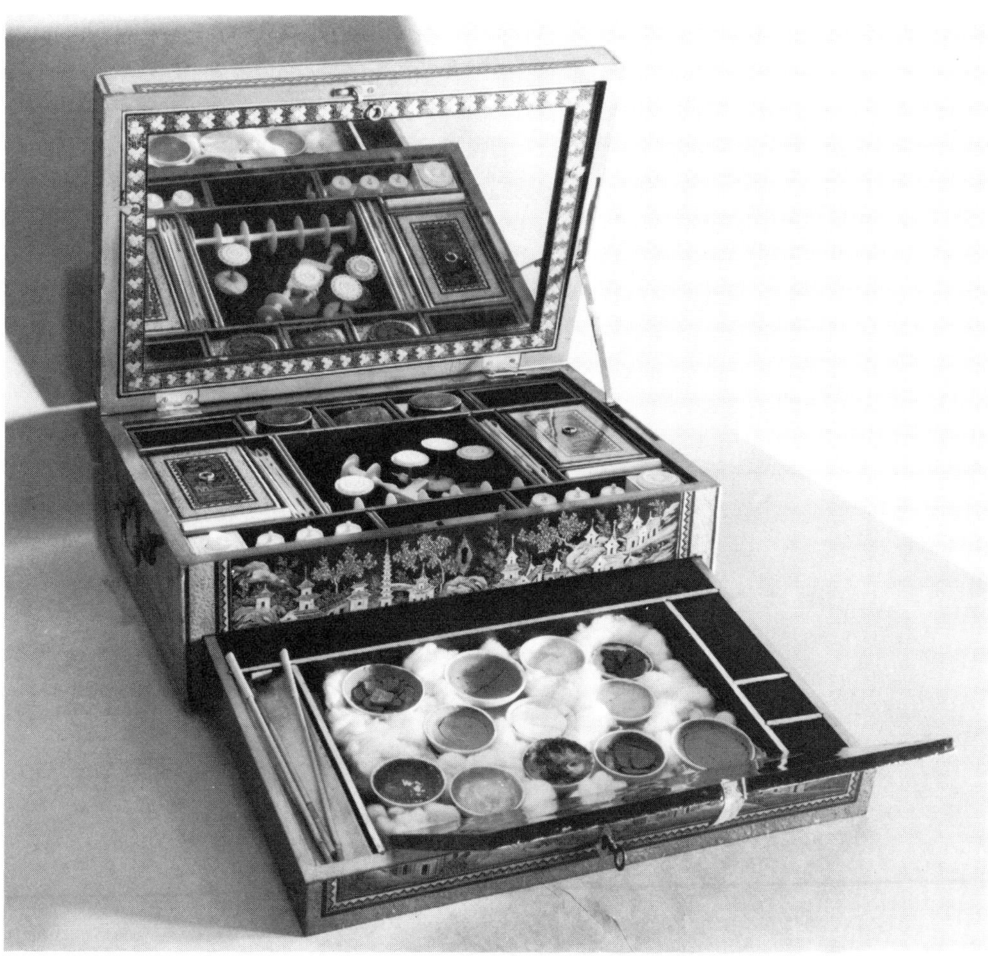

149. Work and sewing box, circa 1820. Black and gold lacquer, 17″ × 11¼″ × 6″. Bottom drawer contains original watercolors in blanc-de-chine cups. *Author's Collection.*

A fine sewing, or work, box with ivory fittings has Chinese silver handles, hinges and locks, the latter with pseudo-hallmarks of the English silversmiths Ely and Fearn, which date it around 1805.[15] The box is covered with *148*
panels of the grape-leaf pattern surrounded by tendrils and is superb in quality and execution. The initials *TKD* in gold script appear in the center of the lid. A similar box, also equipped with ivory spindles, thread-holders and boxes, possibly made around 1820, has an extensive Chinese landscape pat- *149*
tern rather than the earlier grape-leaf design. This box is singularly important, since it is the only one found to date with its original contents intact; the original watercolors in their blanc-de-chine cups, brushes, ink sticks and sealing wax in the drawer disclose another use of these boxes. Scholars had long speculated as to what the drawers of the work boxes were intended to hold, but it had never been suggested that it might have been watercolors and related paraphernalia. Watercolors would have been sensible in a schoolgirl's or lady's work box, since so many of the embroideries and memorials made from 1800 to 1840 included the use of watercolors for painting skies and faces of the figures. The colors found in this particular box are very close, upon comparison, to the colors used in many American watercolors, theorems, and memorials of the period.

150. Tea caddy, circa 1850. Black and gold lacquer, 13½″ × 9½″ × 6½″. Two lead caddies within. Scenes show making of tea. *Essex Institute.*

Tea caddies were decorated with many diverse motifs, including Chinese landscapes, the grape-leaf pattern, bamboo and some rare views showing the growing, processing, packaging and shipping of tea. The tea scenes are invariably of fine quality and are very close in composition and subject matter to the better known watercolors of tea manufacture. The tea caddies had lead liners with incised Chinese scenes and figures on the covers and lids. The liners were removable and often came in pairs, so that two varieties of tea could be stored in the same box. Some lacquered caddies had applied gilt dragons' heads at the base for feet, serpentine or curved sides and corners, and ornately shaped tops, but most caddies were rectangular boxes. One of the finest octagonal caddies with tea scenes, exceptional for its intricate painting and perfect condition, is in the Essex Institute of Salem, Massachusetts. In the second quarter of the nineteenth century, several caddies were made of black lacquer with inlaid mother-of-pearl designs of Chinese inspiration. An octagonal box of this style was sent home from China by Augustine Heard to a Mr. Kimball of Boston, and it is noteworthy for the preservation of the original letter, dated 1836, which is still kept inside the pewter liner.[16] The most extraordinary tea caddy known was made in the shape of a Western steamboat, in black and gilt lacquer.

150

Square or octagonal boxes for playing cards and gaming counters were decorated in any number of patterns and exported in great quantity. The early card boxes (1800–1825) were often covered with the grape-leaf pattern and had fine Federal enclosures for gilt script initials. Lacquer boxes were also made to hold myriad ivory puzzles so popular in the West.

Upon rare occasion, a tea caddy, work or stationery box was made in red lacquer with painted gold designs. These are especially handsome, since the rich Chinese red contrasts strikingly with the gold. An unusual slant-front stationery box in red lacquer is covered with botanical leaf motifs of indigenous Chinese plants and trees. An unusual work box, octagonal with serpentine sides and gold Chinese scenes, bears the inscription *Emily L. Smith, West Harwich, Mass.* in gold script inside the lid. This box, circa 1850, is the only piece known with the recipient's address inscribed.

Emily L. Smith.
West- Harwich.
Mass.

151

151. Octagonal sewing box, circa 1850. Red and gold lacquer, $14\frac{1}{2}'' \times 10\frac{1}{2}'' \times 5\frac{3}{4}''$. Made for Emily L. Smith of West Harwich, Mass. *Collection of Nina Fletcher Little.*

152. Octagonal table, circa 1810, in the Hepplewhite style. Black lacquer with gold grape-leaf design, 27¾″ high, top 18¾″ × 12⅝″. Possibly the base to a sewing stand. *Author's Collection.*

153

Many of the boxes were custom ordered, and had the names or initials of the intended owners inscribed on the lid or front. A Salem-owned tea caddy was a presentation gift with the initials *CS from WH* inscribed, for "Charles Sanders from William Huntington." The silk merchant Fychong sold embroidered silk shawls in square black and gold lacquered boxes with cardboard liners, the tops of which had a small cartouche in the center with the imprint *Fychong Dealer in Silk Canton.*

Apart from the furniture and the countless boxes, thousands of lacquer fans, trays, decanter stands, backgammon boards, joss dragons and miscellaneous objects were made on order or kept in stock for the Western trader. Among the more unusual lacquerware items are small steeple-top watch holders after Western models, a tray with slots, numbers and marble holes for a pinball game and small boxes lacquered to resemble closed books. The lacquer pieces were often bought singly by a supercargo or captain as gifts for members of his family or as purchases on friends' commissions. Benjamin Shreve filled numerous orders for his friends in Salem, such as Gideon

153. Steeple case to hold a watch, circa 1840. Black and gold lacquer, 10¾″ high. *Private Collection.*

Tucker and Joseph Peabody, who had invested heavily in his trip to Canton on the *New Hazard* in 1815. Peabody specifically requested a number of things, and Shreve commissioned the lacquer merchant Yinqua to have them made. Included in the order were 2 pair of oval fruit baskets ($5.50); 6 dozen fruit plates to match ($4.00); 5 tea trays from 10 to 28 inches long, costing a total of $6.50. The trays were to be, the description on the memorandum noted, "black & handsomely Gilt but not Gaudy." Also, Shreve was to buy a "Complete Work Box, if I see one that I think will answer or please." He paid the rather high price of $21.00 for such an object.[17] The box could well have been similar to the box illustrated above, which contained the drawer of watercolors and brushes.

In 1800, Nathaniel West sent home five packages of lacquerware on the ship *Minerva*.[18] He gave no further description, but the objects were unquestionably boxes and trays of various types. An invoice for the *Tartar* of Boston, in 1816, lists several lacquer pieces, among them 60 lacquered tea caddies, $51.00; 10 elegant tea caddies, $25.00; 35 sets of decanter stands, two

154. Work table, 1863, completely outfitted with ivory sewing implements. Black and gold lacquer, $29\frac{5}{8}''$ high (closed), $24\frac{3}{4}'' \times 16\frac{5}{8}''$. Made for Miss Jennie Wigglesworth. *Author's Collection.*

155. View of the lacquerware at the Chinese Booth, United States International Exhibition, Philadelphia, 1876. John Robinson scrapbook, *Peabody Museum, Salem.*

in the set, $10.00; and one "superb ladies dressing case," which may have been an oval-based one with an oval mirror or a stepped-drawer, serpentine front type with a shield or oval mirror.[19] That lacquerware, in both large and small form, was extremely popular is evident from the number of pieces listed on invoices, bills of lading and memoranda. An auction sale of the contents of the ship *Howard* from Canton, held in 1832, lists 1 round lacquered center table, 2 square lacquered card tables, 52 lacquered wash basins (to be sold in 2 lots), and 108 lacquered writing desks (lap type), 36 of which were maroon, 24 described as "light" and another 12, of which 4 each were "light," "dark" and "black," of extra quality. Unfortunately, it is not known how much these various lots of lacquer brought at the auction, which was held at the Auction Store of Mills Brothers, and Co., in New York.[20]

From the great quantities imported it is clear lacquerware's popularity continued throughout the nineteenth century, although many of the larger pieces of furniture, poudreuses and desks, were disappearing. An occasional heavy armoire was exported in the period 1820 to 1850, but, for the most part, demand for the cabinet furniture had severely diminished by the third quarter of the nineteenth century. Existing photographs of the Chinese Booth at the Philadelphia Centennial International Exhibition, held in 1876, *155* give some surprising evidence of the quality of lacquerware being made for the West, and America, at that late period in the trade.[21] The best lacquerware dealers exhibited, and their names were listed, with their show items, in the catalogue of the Exhibition. The lacquer forms are extremely diverse and include a few large tables and furniture pieces.

The Imperial Maritime Customs, organizer of the Chinese Booth, sent a number of lacquer items, undoubtedly made by artisans in Canton, although their names were not mentioned. Among the listings, complete with their

156. Gaming table, 1876. Black and gold lacquer, top 43″ diameter, 31″ high. Exhibited at the International Exhibition, and still bearing its original Yutshing label. *Courtesy Ronald Bourgeault.* *156*

Canton prices, were lacquer stationery boxes, $14.00 apiece; 9 lacquer chess and backgammon boards, various sizes, colors, kinds, $2.00 to $14.00 per piece; and 2 lacquer card boxes, various colors, $4.00 apiece.[22] Among the important exhibitors listed were Leeching (who was also a silver and jewelry dealer), Yutshing, Leen Shing and Hoaching (spelled here Ho A Ching), who was unquestionably the finest dealer in ivories, gold, silver and lacquer in Canton. Yutshing exhibited a large gaming table which still bears on it the exhibition label. Leeching and Yutshing each had work tables shown, one of which could well be the one, of superb quality and design, which appears in a photograph of the Exhibition. A similar work table, known to have been
154 given to a New Hampshire girl in 1863, was especially ornate.[23] Every surface of the table and its legs is covered with delicate feathery gold tendrils filling the spaces between the landscape panels and the river scenes.

In several photographs from the Centennial exhibit one can see octagonal lacquered work boxes, a cabinet which appears to be the top of a bonheur-du-jour, several large round tables, screens and other items of every use and description, but most of the pieces are small. The scenes which cover boxes and furniture seem to have achieved, in effect, the gaudy look that Benjamin Shreve was trying to avoid in the trays he had ordered sixty years earlier. It is typical of many designs throughout time that, the longer they are in vogue, the more ornate and less well conceived they become; and this would certainly appear to be true of the Philadelphia lacquerware, despite its splendid workmanship. The gold designs covered almost the whole surface, and little of the black background showed through. The photographs do illustrate, however, that even as late as 1876, the lacquerware being sent to the West, with its overworked decoration and design, was still of superior quality when made by the finest craftsmen.

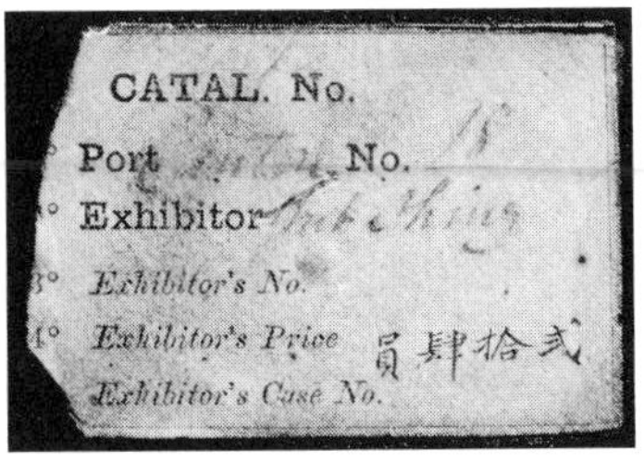

Notes

1. "A Catalogue of the Chinese Imperial Maritime Customs Collection," at the United States International Exhibition, Philadelphia, 1876. Class 289, Introduction.
2. Jenyns and Jourdain, *Chinese Export Art,* p. 19.
3. Tiffany, *The Canton Chinese,* p. 81.
4. *Ibid.,* p. 81.
5. Jenyns and Jourdain, *Chinese Export Art,* p. 85.
6. The tables are currently at The Vale, Waltham, Massachusetts, owned by the Society for the Preservation of New England Antiquities. The tables have always been in the house, the seat of the Lyman family, and were undoubtedly brought back from China by Theodore Lyman, who was active in the trade.
7. The poudreuse was given to Gore Place, Waltham, Massachusetts, but no history of the piece is available.
8. The Ward desk was exhibited at the Metropolitan Museum in 1941 and is illustrated in the catalogue of the exhibition of the China trade which took place that year (#63). At the time on loan from Mrs. William Crowninshield Endicott and George B. Dorr, it has since disappeared. Numerous other Ward items were given to the East India Marine Society in Salem before 1810.
9. The Wetmore suite was divided at the time of the sale of the contents of the Wetmore Estate in Newport, Rhode Island, in 1969. Whereabouts of pieces other than the sewing table are unknown. The bonheur-du-jour and center table were illustrated in the Parke-Bernet catalogue for the sale.
10. Now owned by the Peabody Museum, Salem.
11. There is no information connecting this particular piece with either the Brown family or the Carrington family.
12. Tiffany, *The Canton Chinese,* pp. 81–82.
13. The original boxes were simple wood constructions with a fitted lid and a cloth strap to keep the lid on.
14. Tiffany, *The Canton Chinese,* p. 86.
15. The actual hallmarks read *WE WF,* and a date letter.
16. Augustine Heard was a partner in Russell and Co. and later the owner of Heard and Co., one of the largest American firms doing business in the Orient. The box is currently owned by the Museum of the American China Trade.
17. Above references all from the manuscript papers and memorandums of Benjamin Shreve, ship *New Hazard,* to China, 1816. Peabody Museum, Salem.
18. Bill of lading of the ship *Minerva,* from Canton, 1800. Salem Customs House.
19. Account book for ship *Tartar* of Boston, David D. Hill, Master, to Canton, 1816. Peabody Museum, Salem.
20. Catalogue of the sale of the contents of the ship *Howard,* from Canton, by Mills, Brothers & Co., New York, 1832.
21. Scrapbook put together by John Robinson, Salem, of photographs and paraphernalia from the Chinese Exhibit at the United States International Exhibition, Philadelphia, 1876, and related material.
22. "A Catalogue of the Chinese Imperial Maritime Customs Collection," #4610–#4675, random selections.
23. An original letter in the table, addressed to Miss Jennie Wigglesworth of Northampton, New Hampshire, states it is a present from Miss Wigglesworth's fiance and that it was made at Canton; the letter is dated 1863, and the paper on which it is written is watermarked 1860.

157. Pagoda, before 1801. White nephrite, with carved and gilded wooden bells, 22¾″ high. Given to the East India Marine Society by Nathaniel Ingersoll in 1801. *Peabody Museum, Salem.*

10. Carvings

158. Figure of Jos, before 1800. Nephrite, $5\frac{3}{4}''$ high. Brought to Salem by Captain William Ward. *Peabody Museum, Salem.*

Of all the objects the Chinese could produce for the export market, nothing more intrigued the Westerners than the carvings of ivory, mother-of-pearl, tortoise shell, sandalwood, and hardstone. Under the hands of a skilled carver, a flat piece of ivory could convey an entire landscape scene, a fan might resemble frozen lace, or a small card case could be covered with trees and figures in three dimensions. The ivory carvings were not very expensive by Western standards, and they suited different purposes: fittings for work boxes, ribs for fans, handles for umbrellas, etc. Carvings in other materials could not serve such diverse functions because of their very nature. Tortoise shell was more brittle and could not be used for an umbrella handle; the darker, mottled color was also not so attractive when carved. Sandalwood made magnificent boxes and fans, but its grain precluded fine carving. Mother-of-pearl was used in tremendous quantities for buttons, inlay, card-counters and fan sticks, but rarely for large objects. The stones such as jadeite, nephrite and soapstone were used for pagodas, tomb models and carved Chinese gods and figures.

The Chinese had been famous for carving in jade and soapstone for centuries, but only a few documented pieces seem to have been brought to America in the first half of the nineteenth century, and stone carvings are
almost never mentioned on bills of lading or in account books. A wonderful *158*
fat figure of Jos, the Chinese god, brought back in 1800 by Captain William Ward of Salem, is one of the earliest carvings in nephrite which can be documented.[1] A superb white nephrite pagoda with carved and gilded
wooden bells is one of the finest examples of pagoda stone carvings of the *157*
early nineteenth century. It was given to the East India Marine Society in 1803. Several stone models of Chinese tombs were also brought back quite early. Three green soapstone figures on a brown soapstone base, possibly
representing three immortals, were brought back by Captain Oliver Lane of *159*

159. Three soapstone immortals, circa 1850. Soapstone base. Brought from China by Captain Oliver Lane of Annisquam, Mass. *Collection of Nina Fletcher Little.*

Annsiquam, Massachusetts, in the 1850's. Relatively crude in execution, they are in the traditional Chinese style. More examples of this kind of carving than suspected may have been sent to America as curiosities by the traders, but the pieces were probably not mentioned or listed. Westerners spoke frequently of the extremely high cost of jade, and the Chinese demand for it undoubtedly had a serious effect on its export.[2]

Benjamin Shreve bought a number of small items of ivory and tortoise shell from various dealers; most of the more ornate and expensive pieces were purchased to fill the small orders of friends or of his wife, and few were bought in quantity with the idea of resale. On his 1815 trip he bought four fans and a set of fish counters for $28.00, a price which indicates that they were of good to excellent quality.[3] In 1816 he bought a number of small objects his wife had specifically requested before he left home: an ivory screw pincushion (like those found in work tables which had a long ivory screw that allowed the cushion to be placed on a table edge) for 75 cents and 3 smaller ones for 50 cents each; 4 barrels for thread at 50 cents each and 4 smaller

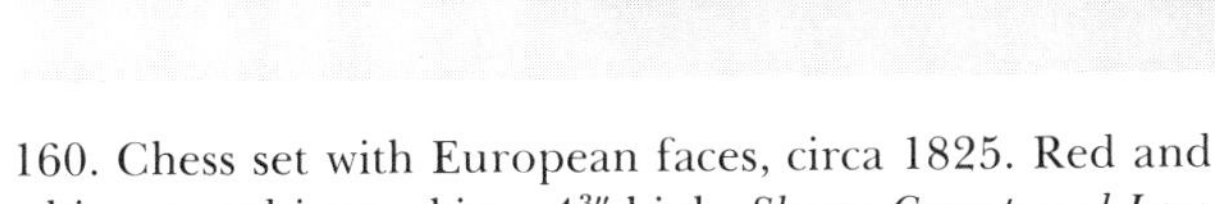

160. Chess set with European faces, circa 1825. Red and white carved ivory, king, $4\frac{3}{8}''$ high. *Shreve Crump and Low.*

161. Chess set with white king in the form of Napoleon, circa 1820. Red and white carved ivory, red king, 6″. *Shreve Crump and Low.*

for 25 cents each; and 12 pieces of ivory on which to wind silk for 75 cents the lot. He also purchased 3 ivory seals for 75 cents each. The barrels were small ivory containers that unscrewed on the top or in the middle, for putting thread in; a small hole in the side allowed the end of the thread to stick out.[4] On his 1820 trip he purchased 2 more ivory seals for $1.25 each, one Chinese puzzle for 50 cents and 33 tortoise-shell combs in paper boxes for a total of $29.80. His most expensive single purchase in ivory was a set of chessmen for $15.00.[5] Shreve's acquisitions were the typical purchases of the China trader in the nineteenth century. In his orders are listings for combs of all descriptions and prices, and random orders for fans of varied materials and prices.

Carved ivory fittings for work tables and boxes, in the first quarter of
the nineteenth century, were relatively simple, but, later in the century, they *148*
were elaborately carved with a myriad of figures and landscapes. The thread barrels in the boxes made earlier were often plain, with no carving and only one or two incised lines. The needle holders and other accessories also tended to be unadorned. A sewing table of 1863 shows how elaborate the detailing had become by mid-century: every barrel, pincushion, holder and enclosure is covered with minute figures and landscapes which are intricately carved.

In rare instances, early chess sets had figures in Western form; one
particularly valuable set has European faces on the kings and queens, while *160*
another has a figure of Napoleon for the king. The most familiar export *161*
chess sets had ornate, over-carved figures, often standing on concentrically carved balls one within another, in white and red stained ivory. The sets were popular throughout the century, and 120 sets of chessmen were auctioned in 1832 in New York, all in their original silk covered boxes.[6] Osmond Tiffany stated in 1844, "A set which brings twenty or thirty dollars in the United States, may be obtained in China for eight to ten, and from this one

162. Two concentric balls with chains. Carved ivory, to left, 5″ diameter; to right, 3⅝″ diameter. Left ball one of twenty brought back by J. P. Cushing before 1830. One on right of twelve spheres given by Francis W. Pickman before 1826. Both *Peabody Museum, Salem.*

may judge of the magnificence of the set, which was in the possession of Mouchong Gouqua, and for which he asked one hundred and fifty dollars."[7] Tiffany's description of Gouqua's set fits that of thousands exported, except for the size; "The men were as usual white and red, all clothed in the ancient dress of China, one half in position and attitude of attack, the others standing on the defensive. The largest pieces were a foot high, and every one was carved in the most wonderful manner. . . ."[8]

Tiffany's description of the ivory carvers is important, since he did not believe the ivory was carved under water or that it was softened as Westerners had assumed for centuries. He concluded it was simply carved with extreme patience and skill by craftsmen using sharp instruments. He also mentioned that the secret of their carving was just as profound as it had been five hundred years previously. On his visit to the ivory carvers, he saw card cases, completely covered with decoration, ivory boats, fans, counters, boxes, and concentrically carved balls, one within the other.[9] These concentric balls had fascinated the West for centuries, and still continue to do so. A pair of particularly fine balls, one of which had twenty inside it, was brought back to
162 ticularly fine balls, one of which had twenty inside it, was brought back to

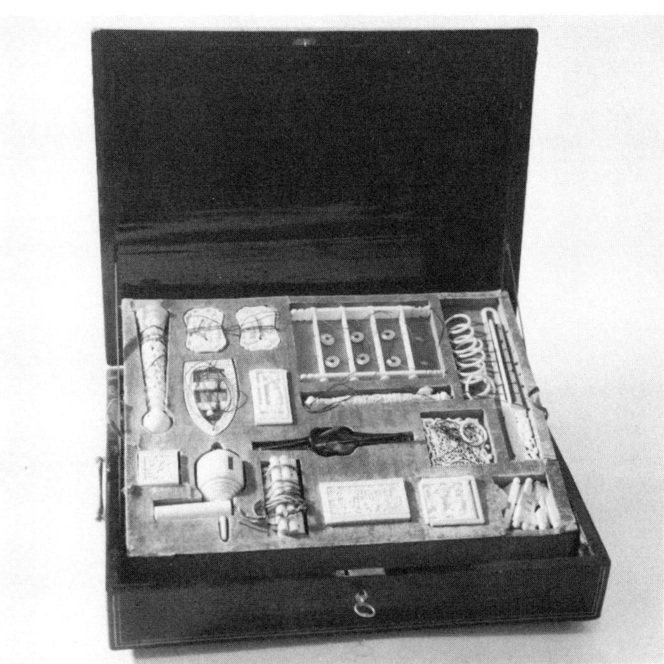

163. Box, circa 1840, with carved ivory puzzles. Lacquered, approximately 12″ square. *Good and Hutchinson and Associates, Tolland, Mass.*

Salem before the 1830's, proving this particular item was not, as often thought, a tourist attraction of the later century.[10] Backgammon sets were made complete with ivory dice and carved shakers. Dice were also sold separately, and the sale of the *Howard* cargo in 1832 listed over thirty thousand dice.[11]

The mother-of-pearl and ivory gaming counters, in all shapes and sizes, had many of the finest designs found on export objects. The counters were made in the shape of fish (such as those that Shreve bought), or round, square and rectangular. The more common designs were incised and carved Chinese scenes, with the addition of the initials or crest of the owner in the center. The lustre of the pearl and the subtlety of the carving made these pieces extremely attractive.

The sticks for fans, of sandalwood, tortoise shell, mother-of-pearl and ivory were some of the most carefully executed and most intricately carved items. The planning of the designs and the conception of the fan, both opened and closed, were particularly good. The more ornately carved and pierced ivory fans with geometric designs and shields must have taken days of work. For a complete discussion on the fan sticks and the leaves used with them, see the next chapter.

Ivory puzzles intrigued every merchant who went to China. These seemingly simple products of clever design and good craftsmanship were *163*
made in all shapes and forms and were often described in great detail by Westerners who had purchased them. Some were elaborately carved, such as the small geometric pieces that were supposed to be put together to make a cross, while others, such as the sticks to the string puzzles, were plain. The puzzles could be bought singly or in groups, either in fabric covered pasteboard boxes or very handsomely decorated lacquer boxes.

164. Seal on left of ivory and horn, circa 1830, 3″ high, with name of Thomas Perkins, Jr. Box of shell mounted with brass, before 1801, $2\frac{1}{4}$″ × $1\frac{9}{16}$″, with initials *RM* for Ruth Merritt of Salem, brought back on ship *Pallas,* 1801. Seal of mother-of-pearl in the form of a clenched fist, circa 1830, $2\frac{7}{8}$″. Seal of mother-of-pearl with fruit and leaves, mid-nineteenth century, $2\frac{5}{8}$″ high. All *Peabody Museum, Salem.*

Letter openers, personal seals, umbrella and cane handles, ornaments and jewelry made up the smaller export objects carved in ivory. The umbrella handles were often entirely carved with Chinese scenes and figures and had monograms added to the design. Letter openers had fancifully carved handles, sometimes with the addition of crests or initials. The handles or tops to
164 the stamps and seals were interesting—and occasionally amusing. Seals were topped with a carved figure of a goddess, a turned piece of ivory, a clenched fist, a landscape scene, or, in one instance, a nude figure of a woman. The bottom of this last seal has an engraved design of the *Nightingale* and the initials "DMF," for David McFarland, an officer on this ship at mid-century.[12] One of the rarest stamps known, it illustrates the Americans' penchant for objects of this nature which could be purchased readily in China.

Small ivory toys, such as English letters for spelling, jack straws (each piece a different farming implement or craftsman's tool) and small figures that whirled on stilts, were purchased for children.

The popular larger ivory objects were pierced and painted flower boats, ornate boxes, card holders to hang on the wall, lacy, delicately executed baskets and urns. The large vase of sheets of ivory with dragon handles
165 illustrated here is a first-rate example of the vases made in the mid-nineteenth century. A small cake stand on a pedestal, in its original box, was made in such a way that the entire piece could be disassembled for easy storage. The flat dish part is of pierced and carved ivory with a scalloped edge; the pedestal is

165. Large vase, mid-nineteenth century, covered with bas relief designs of Chinese scenes and flowers. Carved ivory, 20⅜″ high. *Essex Institute.*

166. Flower boat, before 1876. Possibly made by Hoaching. Carved ivory with rosewood stand. Exhibited at the United States International Exhibition in Philadelphia, 1876. *Philadelphia Maritime Museum.*

carved with a concentric ball in the center. The flower boats were some of the most ambitious projects undertaken by the carvers. The thin sheets, carefully pierced for the sides and cabins, and the painted plants and figures were all assembled to make a singularly impressive object. One that was exhibited at the 1876 Centennial International Exhibition in Philadelphia was made by either Hoaching or Yutshing and is a fine example of the most complex *166* Chinese export carving.[13] The flower boats were mounted on stands covered with fabric, or made of plain wood, and were fitted into a snug wooden box for safe transport. The makers of the boats are not generally known, but it may be assumed that most of the ivory carvers undertook these popular items.

167. Tusk, circa 1840, in elaborately carved base. Carved horn. *Henry Francis du Pont Winterthur Museum.*

168

The enormous, over-carved tusk, of horn or ivory, was the pièce de résistance of the mid-nineteenth century merchant in Canton. Varying in size from a few inches to several feet, the tusks were set into fully carved wooden bases for display. A large rhinoceros horn tusk, with its unusually ornate stand, is a prime example of this type of carving.[14] Perfectly suited for an early Victorian parlor, it is far from today's taste. One of the most spectacular of all the tusks is the ivory one brought from China around 1850 by A. A. Low of New York. Both the hardwood stand and the tusk are deeply carved with elaborate scenes of figures, trees and houses. Complex and convoluted designs wind around the tusk in a never-ending procession of Chinese life. From the superb craftsmanship and design, it may be assumed that it was carved by a major ivory carver such as Hoaching, an attribution which becomes more positive with the discovery that three soup tureens in silver, also covered with Chinese motifs, were also purchased by Low from Hoaching at approximately the same time.[15]

As in so many of the other Chinese crafts destined for export, only a few of the makers or dealers in ivories and related carvings are known by name. A marked Hoaching card case made in 1823, the Hoaching ivory carv-

168. Tusk, circa 1850, and wood base. Possibly by Hoaching. Carved ivory, 36½″ high. Brought back by A. A. Low. *Peabody Museum, Salem.*

ings exhibited at the Centennial in 1876 and the statement on his label that he dealt in carved ivory, tortoise shell, mother-of-pearl and sandalwood certainly identify this hardy veteran, and his workshop, as one of the major carvers. A label on a fine backgammon set reads: "Chongshing, Motheropearl Ivory And Silks, Tortoiseshell Carver, NEW STREET No. 5." This is the only mention of Chongshing, but his work seems to be comparable to that of Hoaching. Luenchun, of 6 New China Street, also had a label which stated he worked as a carver in all mediums. The catalogue for the Centennial Exhibition yields the names of other dealers working with carvings in that period, and several might have been working well before the 1850's, as did Hoaching. Yutshing, Leeching and Leen Shing all exhibited ivories, and Leen Shing had sent two of the cylindrical vases, which were possibly sheets of ivory carved to appear like lace. Mouchong Gouqua is known for his large chess set, which unfortunately does not appear to have survived.

It is interesting to note where the raw materials for the carvers came from, and approximately how much they cost. In 1834, elephants' teeth for ivory were $90 a *picul* (a man's load, or 132 to 140 pounds) for the largest from South Africa, Siam and Burma.[16] Mother-of-pearl was found in the

169. Eagle, circa 1815. Carved and gilt, oriental wood, 15½″ wide. *Private Collection.*

Persian Gulf, the Indian coasts and islands of the Indian Archipelago, and cost from $12 to $15 a picul in rough form.[17] Sandalwood varied in price considerably, according to its source: Malabar coast, $10 to $12 per picul; Timur, $8 to $9 per picul; and the Sandwich Islands (Hawaii), $1 to $6 per picul.[18]

Perhaps the most interesting of the export tortoise-shell boxes are those which had Western designs carved on the lids or sides. Like the porcelains and some of the paintings, the box motifs were often taken from Western prints. Several boxes exist with views of Napoleon's tomb on St. Helena, a popular subject in the early nineteenth century. Others have similar landscape designs or fine inscriptions. Names, places and crests are not uncommon on the lids of several small round or square boxes. The tortoise-shell carvers were undoubtedly the ivory carvers, and vice versa, as the labels of Chongshing and Hoaching indicate.

Tortoise-shell combs were popular from the beginning of American trade with China; they were made in all sizes and shapes, plain or decorated. The ship *Tartar* carried 10 comb sets, of cut tortoise shell, which cost $2.75 a set of three pieces. The *Tartar* also carried 200 small ones which cost only 10 cents apiece.[19] Hundreds of thousands of tortoise-shell combs were exported during the nineteenth century, and probably most of those in existence today were carved in China. A finely carved pair of combs, in its original box bearing the label of Leunchun of New China Street, Canton, is a good representation of the types of motifs used on the combs made in China.[20]

Small snuff boxes of shell (mother-of-pearl) of the eighteenth and early nineteenth centuries, with silver or gilt mounts, were often carved in China. Although the mounts may occasionally have Dutch or English hallmarks, the shell panels are mostly of Chinese derivation. The carving of the shell closely resembles the carving on the gaming counters. The silver mounts may be Chinese export silver, and, with further study, it may be established that almost all of these boxes were entirely made in China. Necessaires of shell, either plain or carved, in hexagonal or octagonal form, were made in this early period; one exemplar has Chinese silver-gilt mounts with a rare inscription. On the gilt band at the top of the base is engraved *Made at Pekin, Given to Clio, by Capt. Law of New York, 1803.* One of the earliest dated examples of silver or silver-gilt, it provides more evidence that the bandings and mounts of boxes and containers were often made in China. An early, small octagonal shell box with brass mounts, has *RM,* for "Ruth Merritt," en- *164*
graved on the lid; it was a gift from her father who sailed on the *Pallas* in 1801.[21]

The carvers worked extensively in sandalwood and native woods, making boxes and other carvings as well as fan sticks. The wooden pieces are less finely carved than those of ivory, because of the wood grains, but several magnificent examples exist. One of the most important, both for what it represents and for its quality, is an American eagle plaque. The eagle is in bas *169*
relief with a shield below and three flags above. The flags and shield and the 13 stars around the eagle are painted red, white and blue and gilt. Above the eagle runs a banner with "E. Pluribus Unum" on it. Around the eagle and insignia is a narrow rope border, beyond which is a carved frame of Chinese landscape and figure vignettes with flowers very reminiscent of the ivory vases. Although other eagles are known, this is the finest in quality and one of the earliest in date, circa 1815.

Apart from the basic materials discussed, the carvers and modelers worked with other peripheral materials and substances that could be decorated. A stick pin by Leeching is topped off with a small nut, intricately carved with an entangled group of monkeys.[22] Only half an inch long, the *208*
head is covered with more than fifteen animals of all sizes. Large, odd-shaped roots were often carved into figures or tableaux, and an especially large and fantastic one was brought to Salem as early as 1803. Stamps and seals were made of various stones such as carnelian or soapstone and were carved with foo dogs or lions on top, and incised inscriptions and initials on the bottom. One rare stamp bears the name "Gardiner" in both Chinese and English—undoubtedly it was used to stamp papers and letters in trading with the Chinese. The box for the stamp or seal has a red ink compartment at one end and is made of horn with a fitted slide top.

170. Four figures, circa 1803, all with nodding heads. Clay, each approximately 26″. Two behind given to East India Marine Society in 1803 by Captain Richard Wheatland. Priest, left foreground, given to the Society in 1803; figure on right thought to be Empress of China. *Peabody Museum, Salem.*

171. Pair of painted figures, circa 1803, of Chinese laborers, one carrying and one packing tea. Clay, each approximately 14½″ high. Given to the East India Marine Society, circa 1803. *Peabody Museum, Salem.*

A group of modelers in clay, making portrait busts and figures, worked
in Canton from the middle—possibly earlier—of the eighteenth century *172*
through the nineteenth century. The modelers doubtlessly worked only in clay or ceramic, but their craft is related to that of the carvers. The names of none of these sculptors are known, although fine examples of their craft
exist. A pair of large clay figures, a mandarin and his wife with nodding *170*
heads and handsomely painted costumes, was brought to Salem and given to the East India Marine Society in 1803.[23] A similar pair was brought back by Carrington at approximately the same date. The Salem figures, given to the Society by Richard Wheatland, were said to have been "copied from life." A
striking standing clay figure of a priest, also acquired around 1803, is embel- *170*
lished with real hair, and the careful modeling of the face would seem to indicate it was a portrait done from life. A magnificent pair of tea workers, one
carrying two boxes of tea, the other standing in a tea box, was also brought *171*
back in 1803; the two are superb small examples of the skill of the craftsmen who worked in this medium. William Hickey mentioned in his memoirs, circa

172. Three-quarter life size portrait of a Chinese merchant, circa 1805, possibly modeled from life. The head to one of a pair of figures brought to America by Edward Carrington, circa 1810. *Rhode Island Historical Society.*

1775, going with a friend to sit for a sculptor. "There was a China man who took excellent likenesses in clay which he afterward coloured."[24] Hickey and his friend were careful to wear their best and most colorful clothes, perhaps because the busts were to be painted. Not one of this type of bust figure has been located to date.

The carvings for export were generally of excellent quality, and occasionally truly magnificent pieces of art. The 5-foot pagoda of delicately carved ivory, which was brought to Boston by Samuel Shaw for his sister-in-law in 1793, is a splendid instance of the art.[25] Export carvings were extremely diversified in subject matter, materials and design. Chinese ingenuity when applied to carving led to some extraordinary artifacts, such as the large over-carved tusks, rare dioramas and landscapes in three dimensions. At the Philadelphia Exhibition in 1876, one of the visitors bought a letter opener made by Hoaching: it was carefully mounted in a scrapbook with the note, "Made by Hoaching, not the best example of his work."[26] The magnificent
166 Hoaching flower boat, perhaps one of the best carvings of its type exported to America, was also shown at Philadelphia. These carvings, then, were greatly valued in the West, and they captured the imagination of purchasers from all walks of life for generations.

Notes

1. East India Marine Society Catalogue, 1821, entry #236: "A Figure in Alabaster of the Chinese Jos or Foe, W. Ward [1803]."
2. Tiffany, *The Canton Chinese,* p. 102.
3. Shreve Mss., ship *New Hazard,* 1815. Peabody Museum, Salem.
4. *Ibid.,* ship *Canton,* 1816.
5. *Ibid.,* ship *Governor Endicott,* 1820.
6. Auction catalogue for the ship *Howard,* June 5, 1832, sale by Mills, Brothers, & Co., New York, p. 4.
7. Tiffany, *The Canton Chinese,* p. 75.
8. *Ibid.,* p. 75.
9. *Ibid.,* p. 76.
10. Peabody Museum accession records list one as being given by J. P. Cushing in 1831, the other as a gift of Francis W. Pickman in 1826.
11. Auction catalogue for ship *Howard,* 1832.
12. Seal collection of Nina Fletcher Little. McFarland was an officer on the *Nightingale* in 1854, when it went to China, and possibly got it then. However, the ship made a previous and successive journeys to China, and since McFarland was a friend of the Captain, it could have been a gift.
13. Two flower boats are listed in the "Catalogue of the Chinese Imperial Maritime Customs Collection," at the United States International Exhibition, Philadelphia, 1876, one by Hoaching and one by Yutshing. The one currently in the possession of the Philadelphia Maritime Museum, which was purchased at the Centennial Exhibition, may well be by Hoaching.
14. Henry Francis du Pont Winterthur Museum, Winterthur, Delaware.
15. Hoaching's label states that he worked in "Sandalwood, Ivory, Mother o'pearl silver." Since the tureens were by Hoaching, it would seem that the tusk must be also, since Hoaching was considered the finest ivory carver in Canton.
16. *Chinese Repository,* Vol. IX, February, 1834, #7, p. 462.
17. *Ibid.,* p. 464.
18. *Ibid.,* p. 469.
19. Account book for the ship *Tartar,* bound for Boston, 1816. Peabody Museum, Salem.
20. Finely carved with low-relief floral designs. Collection Peabody Museum.
21. The information comes from an old card placed in the box by the donor to the Peabody Museum.
22. Leeching was a noted silversmith of the third quarter of the nineteenth century who also dealt in other articles, according to the entries under his name in the "Catalogue of the Imperial Maritime Customs Collection." His advertisement in a *Ladies' Redbook* in Shanghai, 1878, stated he worked in gold.
23. East India Marine Society Catalogue listing #233: "A Chinese mandarin modelled in clay and painted"; and #234: "His wife, both copied from the life and brought from Canton in 1803"; both given by Richard Wheatland.
24. *Memoirs of William Hickey,* ed. by Alfred Spencer, 8th ed. London: Hurst and Blackett, Vol. 1, p. 227.
25. The pagoda was purchased by the Metropolitan Museum from a descendant of Mrs. Josiah Quincy, Jr., Shaw's sister-in-law. It was originally thought to have been brought back on the *Empress of China,* but the dating confirms that the ship would have to have been the *Massachusetts,* which Shaw sailed on in 1793.
26. Penciled inscription under the Hoaching letter opener, mounted in the John Robinson scrapbook. Peabody Museum, Salem.

173. (Top) Fan with the *Empress of China* at anchor at Whampoa Reach, 1784. Watercolor on paper, mother-of-pearl sticks. *Historical Society of Pennsylvania.*

174. Fan with a view of the Anchorage at Whampoa Reach, circa 1850. Gouache on paper, lacquer sticks, 11″. *Peabody Museum, Salem.*

175. (Opposite) Fan with a view of the hongs at Canton, circa 1855. Gouache on paper, sandalwood sticks, $10\frac{1}{2}$″. *Peabody Museum, Salem.*

11. Fans

Hundreds of thousands of fans found their way to America between the time the *Empress of China* brought the first ones in 1785 and the end of the nineteenth century.[1] Proof of the numbers exported is in the bills of lading, auction records and account books of the period. The prices for the simplest were less than a penny; but those of the finest quality and rarest materials and workmanship could cost well over twenty dollars. The fans had a tremendous vogue in nineteenth-century America, and there were few women on the East coast who did not open a Chinese fan on a hot summer evening or at a dress ball.

There were three categories of fans: (1) a fan composed of sticks which fold together, called *brisé;* (2) a stationary fan with a shaped frame over which fabric or paper was stretched, known as a *screen fan;* and (3) a fan with a paper or silk *leaf* mounted on short sticks which opened and closed. A fan with more than one leaf, arranged one above the other on the sticks, was a *cabriolet.* The fans for export were made of every conceivable material and combination thereof—sandalwood, ivory, tortoise shell, mother-of-pearl and painted silk. Silver and gold filigree were used on the rarest fans, as were cloisonné, kingfisher feathers and semi-precious jewels. Round and shaped screen fans with carved ivory handles were often elaborately embroidered with plain stitch or the noted Peking stitch. Some of the least expensive were fans of imitation sandalwood or paper on thin bamboo sticks. After a visit to Canton, Osmond Tiffany remarked, "The most common kind are of blackened oil

176. Fan with European vignettes, copied from engravings, circa 1800. Watercolor on silk, ivory sticks, 10¾″. *Peabody Museum, Salem.*

paper stretched on the fibers of bamboo, split where the handle joins the paper; costing about half a cent apiece, and packed in boxes containing five hundred, they are sent away thicker than the leaves in Valombrosa."[2]

The ship *Tartar,* out of Boston, had 1000 Chinese fans on board in 1816; 500 were green silk with lacquered sticks which cost $60 for the lot; 250 of green silk with ebony sticks cost $32.50; and 250 of black silk with ebony sticks cost $32.50.[3] An 1832 auction in New York of "Canton Fans" listed hundreds of all possible descriptions, including 500 palm leaf fans; 500 painted silk fans; 500 rice fans [pith paper?]; 600 cut and painted bone fans [undoubtedly ivory]; 400 imitation sandalwood fans; 144 palm-leaf fans, ivory handles and tassels; and 100 white feather fans.[4] Unfortunately, the prices these fans brought are not recorded.

Two of the earliest fans were brought to the United States on the *Empress of China.* The rarer of the two has carved mother-of-pearl sticks and a paper leaf, which is decorated with an extraordinarily rare and early view
173 of Whampoa Reach, complete with the *Empress of China* at anchor. The fan was presented to Captain John Green by Chinese officials in Canton in 1784. The view of Whampoa is in the Chinese style, redolent of the early port of the period in its handling and execution. The second fan is a fine small black lacquer brisé fan with no decoration other than the gold design on the two end sticks. The fan is in a small pasteboard box with a geometric-patterned fabric covering.[5]

Unquestionably the finest group of Chinese export fans in America available for study is in the Oldham Collection at the Peabody Museum. Here are the greatest and rarest of all the export fans, made of dazzling combinations of materials and fashioned with exquisite craftsmanship. When this collection is placed with the Peabody's own collection of fans accumulated since its founding in 1799, the entire spectrum of the Chinese export fan industry is covered. At the Peabody is another view of the Anchorage on a

177. Fan with mythological scene, based on a European engraving, circa 1800. Gouache on paper, ivory sticks, 12½″. *Private Collection.*

fan, possibly painted around 1850, and closely related to the idea and conception of the *Empress of China* Whampoa Reach fan. The fan has lacquered sticks decorated in gold, and the semi-circular leaf on which the view is 174
painted is trimmed around the edge with painted flowers. The view of Whampoa shows several ships of different countries at anchor, and is accurate in its depiction of the port. It is close in style to the work of many of the watercolorists of the mid-nineteenth century.

The Peabody owns two of the prized fans with views of the hongs at Canton. One has carved sandalwood sticks, the other carved tortoise shell. 175
The leaves on which the vignettes of Canton are painted are also decorated with flowers, birds and butterflies. The views show the Canton of 1855, with a Western sidewheeler and small river cutter in the harbor. The depiction of the hongs is accurate, and each building and flag can be readily identified. Like the view of Whampoa above, the fans could have been decorated by one of the recognized watercolorists, since they are of excellent craftsmanship and quality.

The fans of the late eighteenth and early nineteenth century often used designs based on European prints, like those motifs used for the decoration of other objects. One early example, circa 1800, has handsomely carved and pierced ivory sticks and a paper leaf decorated with a small vignette and floral sprigs. The vignette consists of an Italian landscape with castles in very delicate colors. This is the same sort of subject which was used on porcelain. A second fan, of a similar type, has the ivory carved sticks and a silk leaf painted with three vignettes on one side and flowers on the reverse. The 176
sticks are intricately carved, and when the fan is open, a shield design appears in the center. Each of the three vignettes is of European inspiration. The one to the far left is composed of a castle and a Western ship; the one in the center, a pagoda with Western-style buildings, each with a cross on the roof; and the one on the right, of a British frigate off a lighthouse. This last view is very

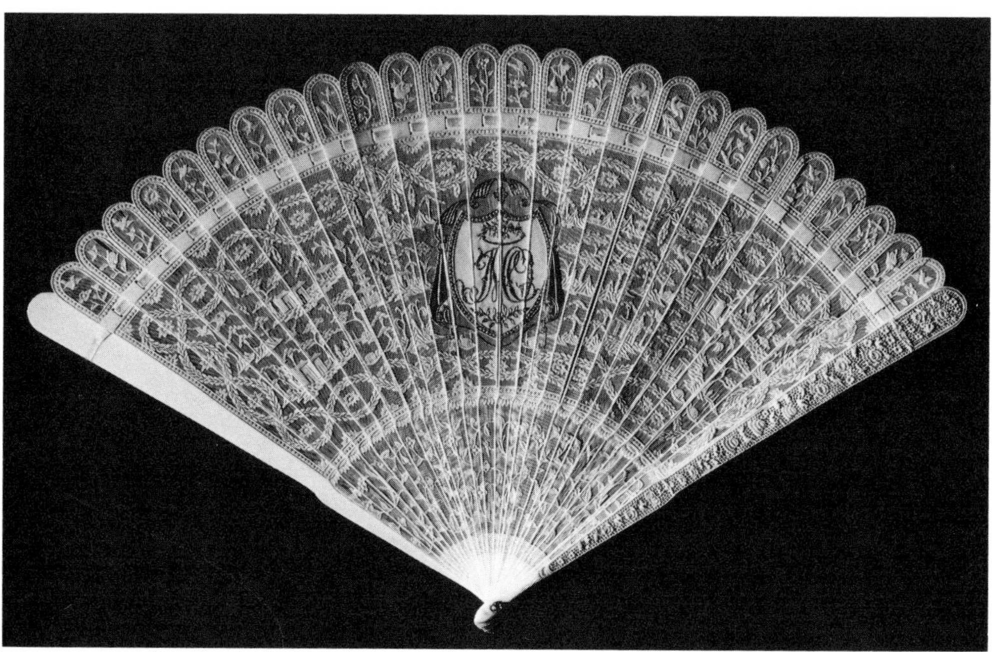

178. Carved and pierced ivory fan with gold initials *TMC* within shield enclosure, circa 1810. $10\frac{1}{2}''$ sticks. *Peabody Museum, Salem.*

similar in all respects to many of the ship designs on export porcelain bowls and tea services. The fan was made at the turn of the eighteenth century or a little earlier.

Landscape views and ships were not the only subjects for the early fan leaves based on Western prints. One of the finest fans ever executed for
177 export has a mythological theme with figures representing Minerva and Cupid. Painted in the best European tradition, the scene is done in bright colors and in a style which does not belie its Chinese background. The reverse is decorated with a large Chinese bird and flowers. The sticks for this fan, like so many of those with views copied from Western prints, are carved and pierced ivory of the most competent workmanship. A similar fan of approximately the same period, first quarter of the nineteenth century, carries a French garden scene based on a print after a painting by either Fragonard or Boucher.

The carved ivory sticks were used not only to support the paper and silk fan leaves, but were also made for brisé fans. They are of splendid quality when executed by the best carvers, and the minute ribbons of ivory defy the imagination as to how they were carved. Osmond Tiffany made this note after his visit to an ivory shop, "From what I have seen of Chinese skill, I do not believe that the material is softened at all, but that it is cut into with sharp instruments and the art handed down from father to son has become perfect."[6] This would seem to dispel the notion that the ornate and delicate ivory sticks were carved under water, an idea prevalent in the West for centuries.

178 Many of the ivory brisé fans have a shield design carved in the center within which are the owner's initials. The shield motif is very similar to that found as an enclosure for initials on export porcelain, lacquerware, or, on rare occasions, engraved on a piece of Chinese export silver.

One magnificent fan has ivory sticks pierced with geometric patterns

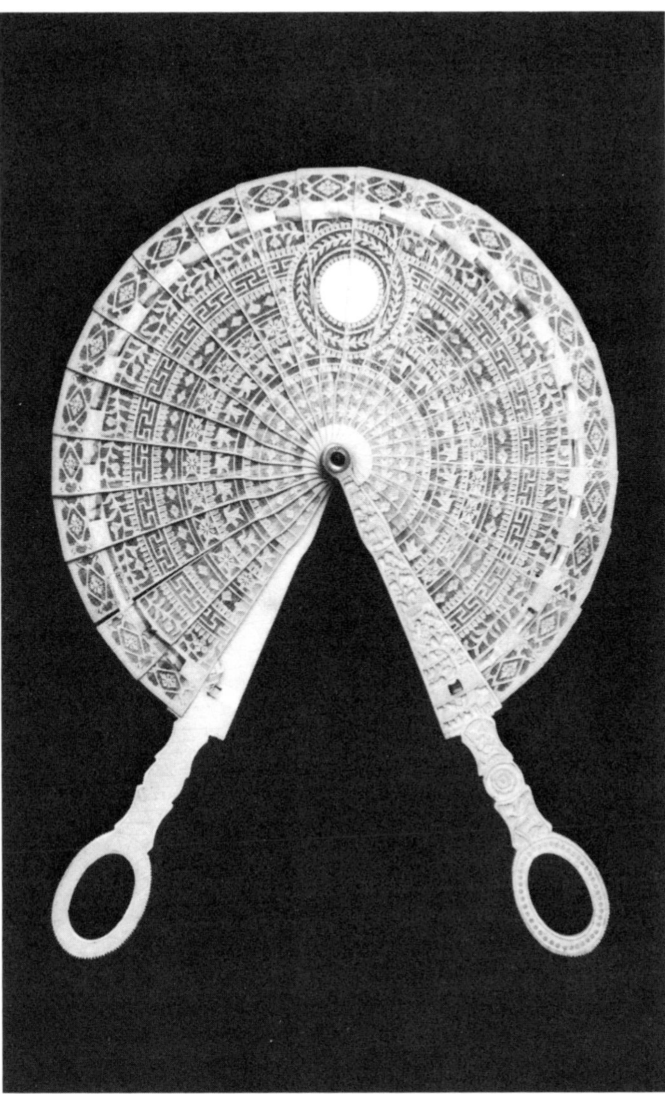

179. Carved and pierced ivory "scissor" fan, circa 1815. $6\frac{3}{4}''$ diameter, opened. *Peabody Museum, Salem.*

around and in three vignettes. The center vignette contains the initials *ETC;* the other two repeat the background decoration. The end sticks are deeply carved with flowers and scrollwork, a characteristic of many end sticks of the early nineteenth century. The silk leaf is decorated with a superb painting of a nosegay of bluettes; such quality suggests that it may well have been worked on the undecorated silk by a Western painter.

The handsome shield enclosure on one unusual fan has a "mantle" carved around it which is heightened with gold. Another fan of this type for the French market bears the carved inscription, *"gage d'amour et fraternel."* A brisé fan of carved and pierced ivory has genre scenes painted on the center of the sticks which show when opened. Called a puzzle fan, the small scenes on each side change completely when the fan is opened from right to left rather than from left to right. A "scissor" fan of carved ivory has handles like
those of a small pair of scissors, and opens into a full circle rather than the *179*
traditional half-circle or wedge shape. The finest pierced and carved ivory

180. Carved tortoise-shell fan, circa 1830. 9⅛″ sticks. *Peabody Museum, Salem.*

fans with shield enclosures and painted motifs were made at the end of the eighteenth and in the early part of the nineteenth century. By the mid-nineteenth century, the quality of the craftsmanship of ivory fans (except when done by the best carvers such as those of the Hoaching studio) had seriously diminished, and the fans became crude and unattractive.

Fans of tortoise shell were made both as brisés and with silk and paper leaves. The tortoise shell was carved in much the same manner as the ivory,
180 but the design does not show up so well because of the dark color and mottling of the shell. Tortoise was used uncarved, and, on some occasions, designs were painted in gold on the sticks of brisé fans like the decoration on the lacquer fans. Mother-of-pearl was carved as was the ivory and tortoise, and used in a variety of ways as fan sticks. On some fans, all of these materials were used together, with each stick of a different material. For even more variety, the ivory was dyed red or green. A fan in the Oldham Collection has
181 sticks of carved and pierced ivory, sandalwood, tortoise shell, mother-of-pearl, stained green and red ivory and silver-gilt. The paper leaf of this fan has a Chinese court scene, with the figures covered in small pieces of silk and painted faces on oval pieces of ivory. Sandalwood was popular for fan sticks and was usually ornately carved. (Sandalwood was brought from Hawaii by American merchants as trade goods.) For less expensive fans, a mock sandalwood was used.

181. Fan with sticks of carved and pierced and stained ivory, sandalwood, tortoise shell, mother-of-pearl and silver gilt. Paper decorated in gouache, figures with fabric costumes and painted ivory heads. Circa 1850. 10⅝" sticks. *Peabody Museum, Salem.*

Some of the most common leaves on fans of the second quarter of the nineteenth century and later were those decorated with Chinese landscape or court scenes with dozens of figures. Many of the fans carried figures decorated with small swatches of silk which has been cut out and pasted on as clothing. Small oval pieces of ivory were then painted with a simple face and glued on the body. Some fifteen examples in the Peabody collection, with all types of sticks, are treated in this manner. The quality varies with the period of manufacture, and a late fan, circa 1860, by Hoaching, undoubtedly one of the best craftsmen in Canton, is a disappointment with its awkward figures and unattractively painted landscape background. Tiffany remarks on this type of leaf, after a trip to a fan shop, "Others, again, are made of silk stretched upon a frame inscribed on one side with Chinese characters and on the other with groups of figures, their dresses formed of various pieces of colored silk, and their hands and faces of ivory."[7] He is undoubtedly describing the screen fans, which did not open; the technique for the figures, however, was the same for all types of fans. *182*

Feather fans, of all colors and in many shapes, were brought from China in great quantities. The 1832 New York auction advertised "72 slate colored feather fans, carved handles and tassels, as well as 100 white feather fans."[8] These would seem to have had stationary feathers, because of the ivory handle, but others were mounted on sticks that opened and closed. Feather fans were exhibited at the Centennial International Exhibition in Philadelphia in 1876 and cost from $1.20 to $13.00 apiece, Canton prices.[9] The folding feather fans, like so many of the other folding fans, came in

182. Fan with paper decorated with painted gouache landscape, figures with silk bodies and painted ivory heads. Carved ivory sticks, 11½″. Circa 1840. *Private Collection.*

183. Black and gold lacquer fan in the grape-leaf motif. Shield encloses initials *LAB*. Circa 1810. 6″ sticks. *Peabody Museum, Salem.*

beautifully made silk and lacquered boxes. Some of the feather fans were painted with flowers, birds and scenes, but this type of decoration often wore off rapidly with the opening and closing of the sticks.

The lacquer fans were some of the most handsome of all the export wares. The designs followed very closely the decoration of the lacquer furniture and boxes. In the early period, from 1790 to 1820, the grape-leaf motif was used extensively, as were fine designs of Chinese scenes and landscapes.[10] A fine brisé fan of about 1810 has the grape-leaf pattern on the sticks surrounding three vignettes, two oval and one in the shape of a shield. The shield
183 encloses the initials *LAB* and two ovals have a leaf pattern which matches the borders. The grape-leaf pattern is similar to that on the dressing mirrors and boxes and the fan was probably made by one of the lacquerware dealers who dealt in all type of objects. The ends of the sticks have the fine hexagonal pattern with circles so characteristic of backgrounds in the first quarter of the nineteenth century. The fan may well have come in a box decorated in the same pattern. Several lacquer fans of the grape-leaf pattern do exist, and all would seem to have been made before 1825.

Most of the lacquer fans seen today were made during the second and third quarters of the nineteenth century. Most of them have leaves of silk and paper, and many fold. Two fans at the Peabody are highly unusual in construction and decoration; because of their similarity in design and their
184 being sheathed in identical boxes they must have come from the same dealer, possibly as a pair. Both have lacquer sticks and paper leaves. The end sticks are shaped like elongated vases (a not uncommon stick shape in this period), and the center sticks are of varying lengths, so that when the fans are opened, the pivot upon which the sticks are attached is far to the right of the oval formed. The sticks are decorated with a relatively simple series of Chinese vignettes. One of the fans is in the traditional black and gold lacquer, with a leaf of black paper decorated with birds, flowers and bamboo in gold heightened with red. The second, however, has silver decoration on the black lacquer background, and the black paper is decorated in silver. Although both

184. Fan with black and silver painted papers, sticks of rare black and silver lacquer, circa 1860. 16$\frac{1}{8}$" sticks. *Peabody Museum, Salem.*

were undoubtedly made after 1850, they are of interesting construction and unusual decoration. Their extraordinary length of 16 inches classes them among the largest fans made for the export market.

Many later fans, which had leaves covered with Chinese figures with applied silk costumes and ivory faces, had lacquer sticks, and lacquer boxes lined with silk to match. The typical decoration for the lacquer is simple landscape or figure vignettes with groups of flowers and birds.

The lacquer fans are some of the few whose makers are identified. *185*
Hoaching's name has appeared stamped in red in the lids of two boxes containing fans with lacquer sticks. An extremely unusual lacquer brisé fan with the Chinese scenes in the colors of gold, silver-blue and pink is in its original silk box with a label "OLD HIP Lacquerd Ware." Another label reads, "Hipqua, Lacquerd Ware New China Street No. 17." Since *Qua* freely translated means "*Mister,*" it would seem that the two labels were from the same merchant. Tiffany mentions a visit to Hipqua's lacquer shop where, he said, the tradesman had about forty persons working for him, ranging in age from

185. Fan of pink, blue, black and gold lacquer, with original box. Label for lacquer merchant *HIPQUA,* circa 1840. 9¼″ sticks. *Author's Collection.*

little boys to old men, who did the finest work. Tiffany was impressed with the work: "so fine is some of the work that a man engaged for six entire weeks in painting a fan which I bought."[11] The quality and workmanship of the colored lacquer OLD HIP fan is so superb, that it may well have been one of the fans on which so much time was expended.

186 Some of the finest fans were made by the gold- and silversmiths, or fan merchants working in these materials. The sticks were in filigree while the leaves were of fabric or paper. A fan in the Oldham Collection has silver-gilt filigree end sticks with applied silver filigree, and alternating center sticks of ivory, tortoise shell, and silver-gilt. The leaf for this fan is decorated with a court scene of figures with applied silk and ivory. Another fan of silver-gilt filigree sticks has inlaid kingfisher feathers in an imitation of cloisonné; a cabriolet fan with sticks of silver-gilt filigree has actual blue and green cloisonné inserts and applied silver dragons on the end sticks.

The screen fans are equally diverse in their decoration and use of materials. Usually of a round, octagonal or free symmetrical form, they have an outer frame within which is taut fabric or paper, and an ivory handle

186. Fan of silver filigree, circa 1840. 8″ sticks. *Peabody Museum, Salem.*

which projects up to the top of the fan for support. Some of the finest are embroidered with landscapes and figures done in the Peking stitch, or the more ordinary stitches seen on clothing and robes. Others have painted designs of birds, flowers, and Chinese landscapes, and occasionally fine applied designs of figures with padded silk clothing and ivory faces. One of the most unusual screen fans, on an octagonal frame, has an ornate flower and bird *187*
design inlaid with kingfisher and other feathers to create a rich textured surface.

Very fragile ribbed screen fans were made by taking a series of thin pieces of bamboo or leaf ribs and tying them together. Over this framework was stretched a thin sheet of Chinese paper which was painted with a small scene or design. Fans made of plaited palm leaves often had the same appearance and shape as the more complex constructions.

Cases for fans were made in several ways and from many materials. The most familiar in the mid-nineteenth century were pasteboard boxes covered with geometric fabrics, and lacquered boxes with gold decoration and fitted silk interiors. Fan cases of painted or embroidered fabric were also made. Some of these are extremely fine works of embroidery with the designs entirely worked out in the knotted Peking stitch. The motifs for the *188*
cases were usually flowers and birds. An occasional case is made of fine straw with applied embroidered designs worked in. The boxes and cases for the fans were often as beautiful and well executed in design and decoration as the fans they were made to contain and complement.

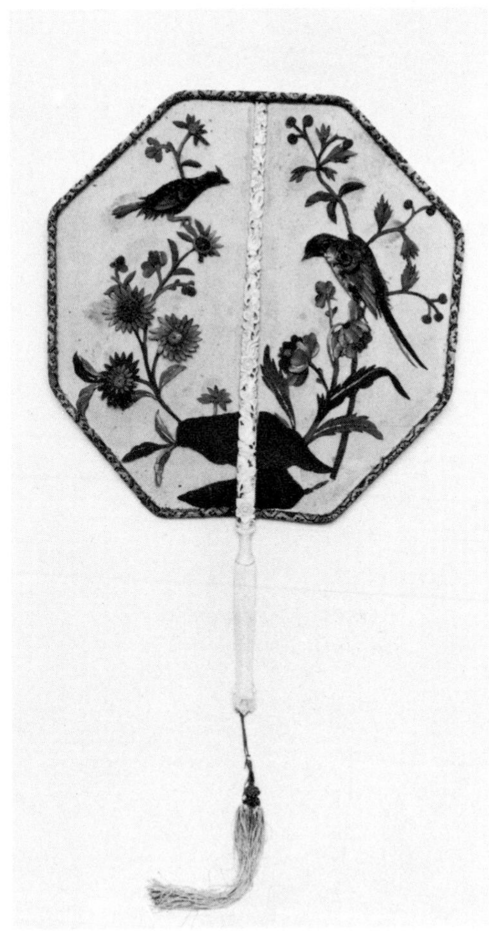

187. Screen fan with designs of metal outline and feather inlay. Carved ivory rib and handle. Circa 1850. Overall length, $15\frac{1}{4}$″. *Peabody Museum, Salem.*

188. Three fan cases, mid-nineteenth century. Left: embroidered silk, $13\frac{7}{8}$″. Center: embroidered Peking stitch, $11\frac{7}{8}$″. Right: Peking stitch embroidered on plaited straw, $12\frac{3}{8}$″. All *Peabody Museum, Salem.*

Notes

1. The fan with the *Empress of China* at Whampoa Reach painted on the leaf was brought to America in 1785 on that vessel.
2. Tiffany, *The Canton Chinese,* p. 77.
3. Account book for the ship *Tartar,* 1816. Peabody Museum, Salem.
4. "Catalogue of Canton Fans . . .," ship *Howard* sale, New York, 1832.
5. In the collection of the Peabody Museum, Salem, Family tradition claims the fan was brought over on the *Empress of China.* The style, design and workmanship all are congruent with that period.
6. Tiffany, *The Canton Chinese,* p. 75.
7. *Ibid.,* p. 77.
8. "Catalogue of Canton Fans . . .," 1832.
9. "A Catalogue of the Chinese Imperial Maritime Customs Collection," at the United States International Exhibition, Philadelphia, 1876, Dept. II, Class 254, p. 38.
10. See Chapter 9 for discussion of the periods of motifs on lacquerware.
11. Tiffany, *The Canton Chinese,* p. 80.

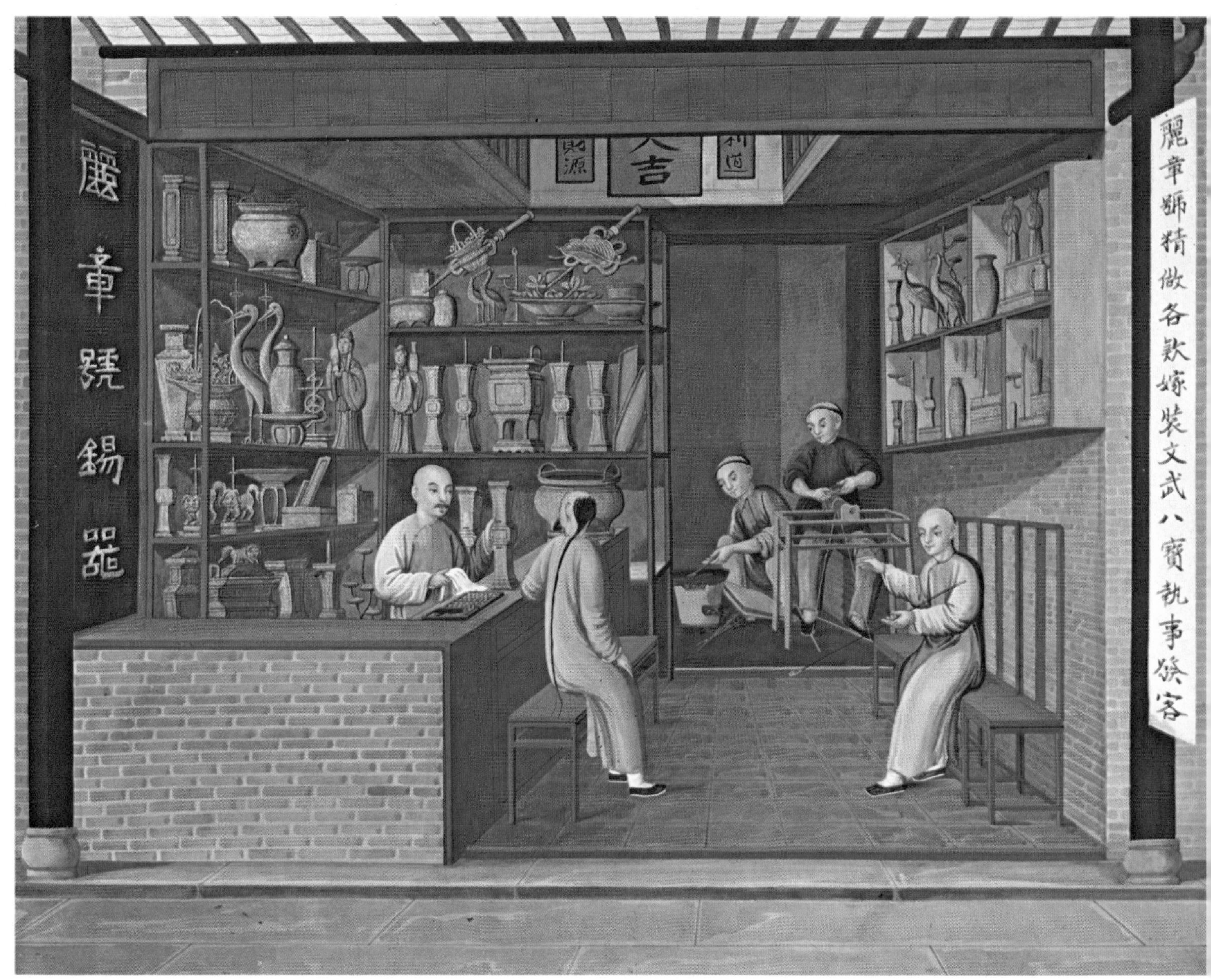

189. Interior of a pewter shop, artist unidentified, circa 1830. Gouache on paper, 11″ × 14½″. *Peabody Museum, Salem.*

12. Silver and Pewter

Silver for the export market is one of the most recently discovered objects in the China trade; it was not until 1965 that its existence was generally acknowledged.[1] Since then, thanks to the industrious work of a number of scholars in the field, a great deal of information has been brought to light. In no other area, other than export furniture in the Western style, has there been so much controversy over what is Chinese and what is not. Pseudo-hallmarks, the presence of Western marks and the lack of documentation have left many aspects of the subject still unclear, but time and study will reduce the areas of uncertainty. The names of some of the silversmiths appear throughout this chapter, but the list is a preliminary one.

Silver with Chinese decoration and Chinese ideograms is, of course, the most readily identifiable. Silver in completely Western form, based on known English or American silver patterns, is more difficult to identify, and many examples of it have passed unnoticed for years. Through contemporary references to the manufacture of silver and letters and bills of sales by merchants in the China trade, definite documentation is available for this group. Tiffany described his visit to a silversmith on Old China Street in 1844.

> He can manufacture any article, from a salt spoon to a service of plate in the most elegant manner. He will line a pitcher with its coating of gold, or produce a favorite pattern of forks at a very short notice. The silver is remarkably fine and cost of working it a mere song. Its intrinsic value is of course the same as it is in Europe, but the poor creatures who perspire over it are paid only about enough to keep the breath in their bodies. Filigree baskets, or card cases seem to be favorites with these silversmiths. It is much cheaper to have a splendid service of plate in China than in any other country, and many Europeans send out orders through supercargoes.[2]

One of the earliest references to the purchase of China trade silver is made by Sullivan Dorr of Providence in his letters. Dorr, at the age of twenty-

190. Sugar bowl with gadrooned base, marked *CS,* circa 1815. *Yale University Art Gallery.*

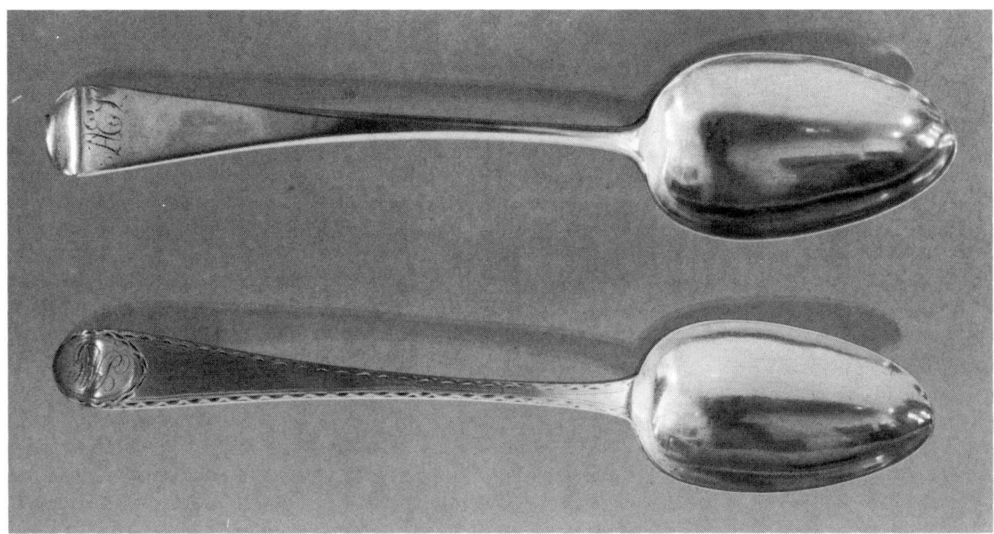

191. Silver spoon (top) by Pao Yin, initialed *AEL,* another from the set is dated 1808. $8\frac{9}{16}$". *Author's Collection.* Bright-cut spoon marked *SS,* initialed *LMG,* circa 1810. *Privately owned.*

three, was the Vice-Consul in Canton. In a letter to his brothers of February 5, 1800, Dorr wrote, "You will see hereafter I have procurred about one hundred dollars worth of silver plate for my table, which when done shall Credit you with due proportion taking to home with me for my familys use, they are necessarys that must be procurred."[3] Robert Bennet Forbes mentions a teapot which is still in existence, in a letter to his wife in 1839, and, in another reference, he speaks of buying spoons from Cutshing. Many of the regatta mugs for the Canton Regatta Club were also purchased from Cutshing.[4]

Another early reference to silver manufacture in Canton states, "The 10th of January I accompanied some gentleman to visit the warehouses for China ware, ivory manufactures, silk mercers, and silversmiths. . . ." This account continues, "The articles in silver were well executed many with English cyphers and coats of arms upon them. The engravers have books of heraldry, which they consult and copy with great exactness."[5] These books were undoubtedly the same ones used by the porcelain decorators for the cyphers and arms on dinner and tea services.

Early silver in various patterns exists, but it is difficult to correlate original bills of sale with actual silver brought back in the early-nineteenth century. Benjamin Shreve bought an extensive amount of silver from Synshing and Lunshong, but none of his flatware exists today.[6] One of the earliest makers is Pao Yin, whose mark is a Chinese character. The mark appears on an early set of spoons with plain backs and rounded ends. The spoons are engraved *AEL* on the handles, and one is marked *1808,* also, a date close to the style and period of the spoon.[7] Another important early piece, a cruet stand with bright-cut design, circa 1810, also has the Pao Yin character. This stand is one of the most striking pieces of export silver, with its fine ball-and-claw feet and beautiful bright-cut swags and initials. A fine marrow spoon has a Chinese character for its only mark, as does an octagonal tray with ball feet and a Chinese border, but it is not the mark of Pao Yin.

191

192

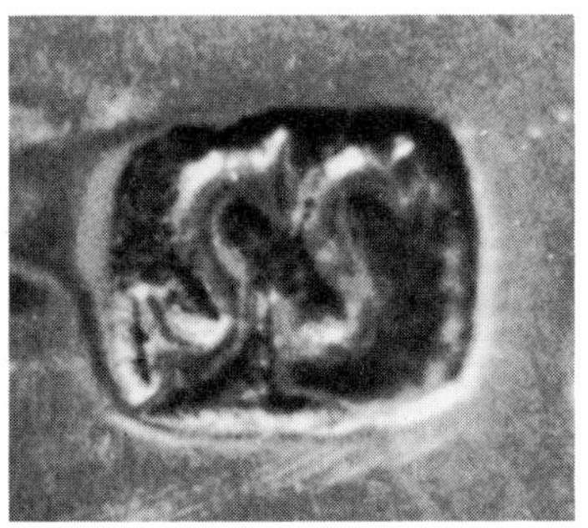

Among Shreve's purchases were six silver tumblers, a fish knife, soup ladle, cream pot and sugar dish, and much flatware. A pair of silver-gilt spectacles and case illustrate the use of this finish on Chinese export silver. These were purchased from Synshing, who could well be the early maker whose stamp is *SS*.[8] Several early pieces of silver in the Federal style have the *SS* mark; this would suggest the maker was working about the time Shreve was in China. It is unfortunate that no piece of the Shreve silver has been discovered. A handsome early Federal mustard pot with bright-cut crest and engraving, which has been attributed to an American maker, has the mark *SS* and appears to have been made in the early nineteenth century.[9] A strikingly American or English sugar bowl, with cover and gadrooned base and fine handles, bears the mark *SS* and may well be very similar to the one Shreve had purchased. A complete tea service in the early Empire style, with gadrooned base to each piece, but more complex in design, also bears the same mark with pseudo-hallmarks. Another tea service in a very simple style, which would have been popular in American silver in the 1820's, is stamped *SS* with pseudo-hallmarks, as is a soup tureen of completely Western appearance.[10] An early bright-cut spoon also bears this mark. The *SS* pieces in no
way indicate their country of origin, since they adhere so strictly in design and *191*
decoration to their Western prototypes. The silver is of a remarkable purity, as high as 985 parts in a 1000. There are also several pieces of the mid-century and later which are clearly marked *SS,* but these are by a different and later smith. The mark is distinguished from the earlier one by a small dot between the two *S*'s.

The most readily identifiable pieces of the early flatware for the Western trade are those with Chinese ideograms used alone or with letters and Western marks. A group of spoons with plain pointed handles decorated in bright-cut are stamped *WF* with a Chinese character. (These characters, upon translation, are generally meaningless.) *WF* might be a copy of the
mark of William Fearn of London. The spoons are particularly rare, since *193*
the originals from which they were copied are still in existence. Made for the Gilchrist family of Baltimore, the Chinese spoons are exact copies—except for the marks—of the originals made by Standish Barry of Baltimore. The Chinese spoons undoubtedly were made to expand or fill in a set, and probably they were made not long after the original spoons.

A handsome lacquer sewing box, decorated in the early grape-leaf *148*
pattern, has silver mounts for handles, locks and hinges. The locks to the top and the drawer are both stamped with *WE WF* pseudo-hallmarks and the date letter *F*. The mark in English would date the box as 1803, but the *WE WF* are obviously Chinese copies of the English marks for William Ely and William Fearn of London. Several spoons of the fiddle-thread and shell pattern are all marked with *WE WF WC* and pseudo-hallmarks, and are found among the flatware services bearing other makers' marks.

The letter *W* is also found on export silver, and several pieces by this maker are known. A partial set of flatware in the fiddle-thread and shell pattern, brought back by Captain Cunningham of Boston in the second quarter of the nineteenth century, bears a single *W* with pseudo-hallmarks. On this particular set, a very distinctive Chinese characteristic is readily observed. The Chinese must have cast the shells for this pattern separately, for just below the shell on the handle is a *V* mark, which would indicate the shell had been applied and then burnished to join the rest of the piece. This does not

192. Base to a cruet set, decorated in bright-cut with later initials, and dates. By Pao Yin, circa 1810. $7\frac{3}{4}''$ long. *Gebelein Collection.*

appear in English or American silver of the same pattern. Other pieces bearing the *W* with pseudo-hallmarks are the teapot mentioned by Robert Bennet Forbes, which he sent to his wife in 1839 after he had won it in a race, flatware in the fiddle pattern and various small pieces. A set of twelve knives with silver blades and mother-of-pearl handles are stamped *W* with pseudo-hallmarks. The knife handles are very similar to another set with Western plate blades and Chinese ivory handles. An ornate ewer, standing 12 inches high, is made of Chinese silver and marked *W* with a lion and other pseudo-hallmarks. Covered with an allover grape-leaf design, it has a large clump of grapes as a knob on the lid. On the front is engraved, *This jug is made from Sycee silver, taken from the Chinese at the Storming and Capture of the Taku Forts Aug 1860—Presented to T. B. Lenon Esq. by his affectionate son E. H. Lenon—Lieut. 67 Reg*^{t}.

The mark *W* may be Wong Shing's, since a label in a box owned by Robert Bennet Forbes reads, "Wong Shing, Gold and Silver Smith No. 15, China Street." Wong Shing may be the merchant whom Tiffany visited, since the address is close to the other shops he visited at the same time. The *W* on pieces of the period of the ewer could stand for "Wohing," whose name appears on a label with that of Hoaching. A tea kettle and stand are marked *Wo Shing,* a third possibility for the mark *W*. Other pieces which are engraved or dated seem to suggest that *W* was working in the second and third quarters of the nineteenth century.

From the forms and shapes of the silver marked *CS,* this unidentified
maker would appear to be one of the earliest silversmiths. *CS* may well be *190*
Cunshing.[11] Several distinguished pieces with his mark exist, and most are *195*
relatively plain with little ornamentation, a characteristic of the American and English silver of that period. A four-footed tea tray marked *CS* is engraved *H* on the top with the Higginson crest, and inscribed on the bottom

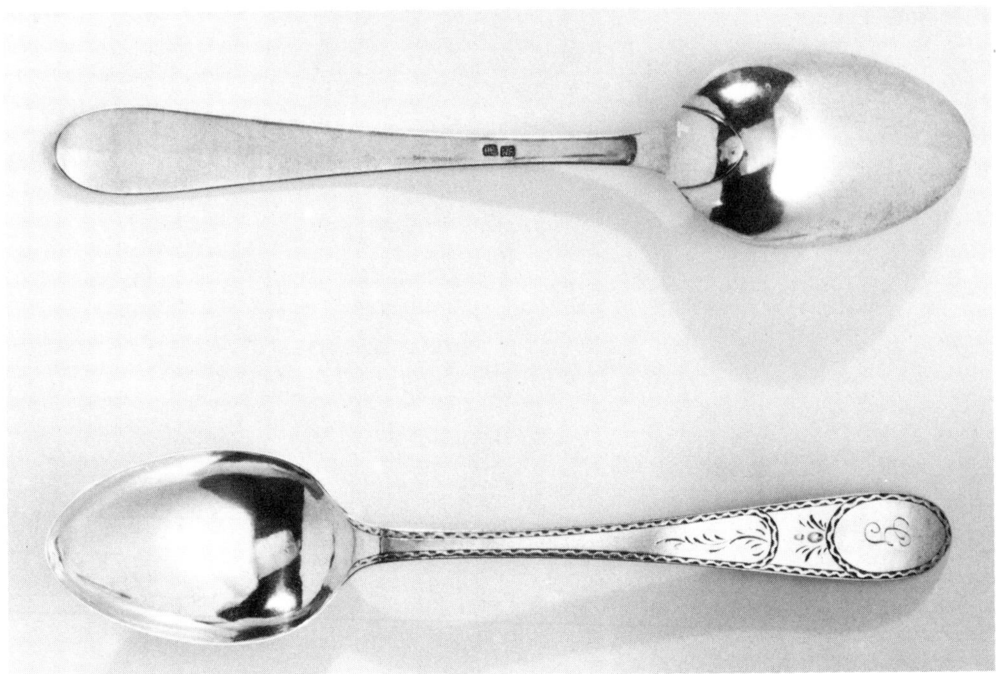

193. Two bright-cut spoons by *WF* after the originals by Standish Barry of Baltimore, circa 1820. Initialed *G* for Gilchrist family. *Author's Collection.*

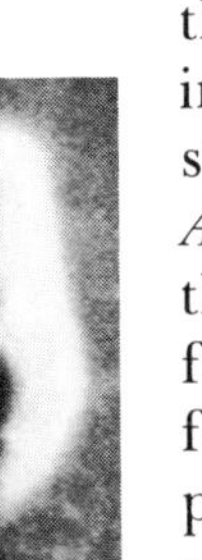

Barbara Higginson–Samuel G. Perkins, 1795.[12] With this date, it is one of the earliest documented pieces of silver for the American market. The Perkins family of Boston was engaged in the China trade, and it would be natural for them to be among the first people to own export silver. An important pitcher, in a Paul Revere form, also bears the *H* and the Higginson crest, and is stamped *CS*. A fine small ladle, with rounded turn-down handle is engraved *AP* and marked *CS*. A magnificent gadrooned teapot with horn handle of
the 1820's is stamped *CS* with leopard's face and the letter *I*. It is doubtful, 194
from the early design of most of these pieces of silver, that *CS* could stand for "Cutshing," who seems to have been working later. A repoussé silver box, possibly made for Elizabeth Hunt, who lived in China in the mid-1850's, is stamped *CS,* but the mark does not resemble that of the earlier maker.

Cutshing was a most prolific silver maker, whose mark would appear to be *CUT*. *CU* was also used as a mark, but it is not certain if this was another mark for Cutshing or for a completely different maker. Cutshing is known to have made some of the mugs for the Canton Regatta Club;[13] those mugs
undoubtedly looked very much like the ornate repoussé mug marked *CUT,* 197
which has a wash gold lining like the one Tiffany described.[14] Several pieces of flatware, in varied patterns, are by Cutshing, and they all seem to date from the 1840's to the 1880's.

A set of Chinese flatware in the olive-leaf pattern, which was introduced into American silver in Boston around 1845, bears the mark *CUT*. A
silver filigree hand flower holder, similar to the filigree card cases of the 196
period, still in its original silk covered box, has a label inside the lid that reads, "CUTSHING Gold and Silversmith, New Street No. 8." A large heavy creamer with acanthus leaves around the base, and a moulded handle of the

194. Teapot with gadrooned base in the early Empire style, by *CS*. Horn handle, 10½″ long. Engraved *JF*, circa 1820. *Gebelein Collection.*

195. Silver teapot and footed sugar, sugar by *CS;* pot marked with pseudo-hallmarks and *AL*. Circa 1800-1810. Pot initialed *PL;* sugar, *JLS*. *Rhode Island Historical Society.*

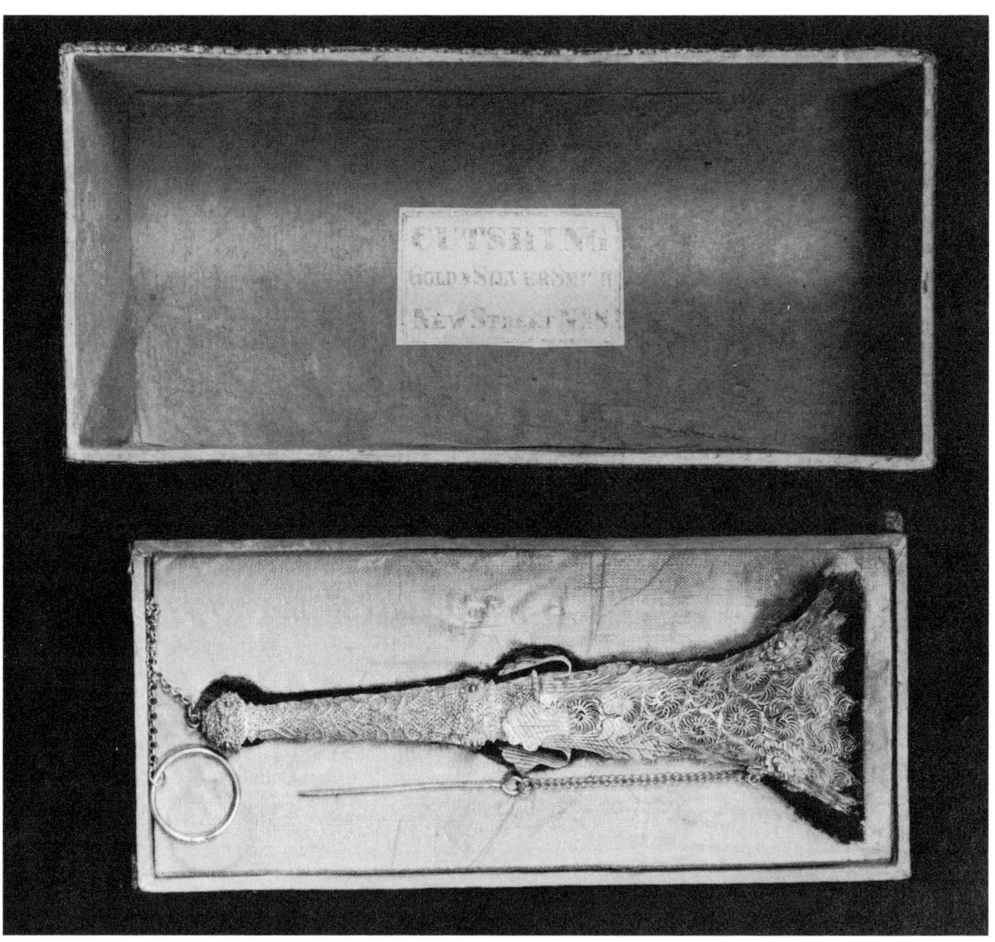

196. Silver filigree hand flower holder by Cutshing, circa 1850. In original fitted box. 7″ long. *Peabody Museum, Salem.*

197. Three mugs, all circa 1850. Left, repoussé with dragon handle marked *S.S.* Center, repoussé with dragon handle marked *CUT* (Cutshing). Right, repoussé with bamboo handle with mark for Hoaching. Left and center, *Privately owned;* right, *Collection of Jon F. Vining.*

mid-nineteenth century style strongly resembles a number of *KHC* pieces, but is stamped *CUT*. Cutshing seems to have been fond of the heavy raised designs and overall repoussé popular at mid-century, since so much of his ware is distinguished by these motifs. Small boxes, holloware and the flat- *198*
ware—all are Victorian in feeling and reflect the tastes prevalent in this later period of the China trade. A bowl with ornate side panels of Chinese motifs, engraved *CL 1854,* exhibits this characteristic of Cutshing's work, as does an over-decorated ewer completely covered with a Chinese landscape fantasy and a handle in the form of a branch.[15]

The most prolific of the Chinese silversmiths, judging from the quantities of his silver in existence today, would seem to be *KHC*. The identity of this maker is presently unknown, as are his street address and his precise working dates. From the style of his silver, both in hollow- and flatware, it would appear that he was working in the second and third quarters of the nineteenth century. His silver is excellently crafted, and was made in most of the patterns popular in the export market. Many examples of the fiddle-thread and shell pattern of flatware made by him are extant, including a large service for twelve made for Abigail Edwards Cook of Salem, whose husband was a partner of Thomas Hunt in the ship chandlery business at Whampoa Reach around 1850. The Cook fish slice, with its engraved and reticulated
blade, is identical to the *KHC* slice made for a member of the Shillaber family *199*
from Salem, who also had members living in China. Elizabeth Hunt, Thomas's
wife, had a small nutmeg grater in the form of a classic urn made by *KHC*. *200*
Similar nutmeg graters, varying only slightly in size and shape, include a

198. Cream pitcher marked *CUT* for Cutshing, circa 1850. $5\frac{1}{2}''$ high. *Author's Collection.*

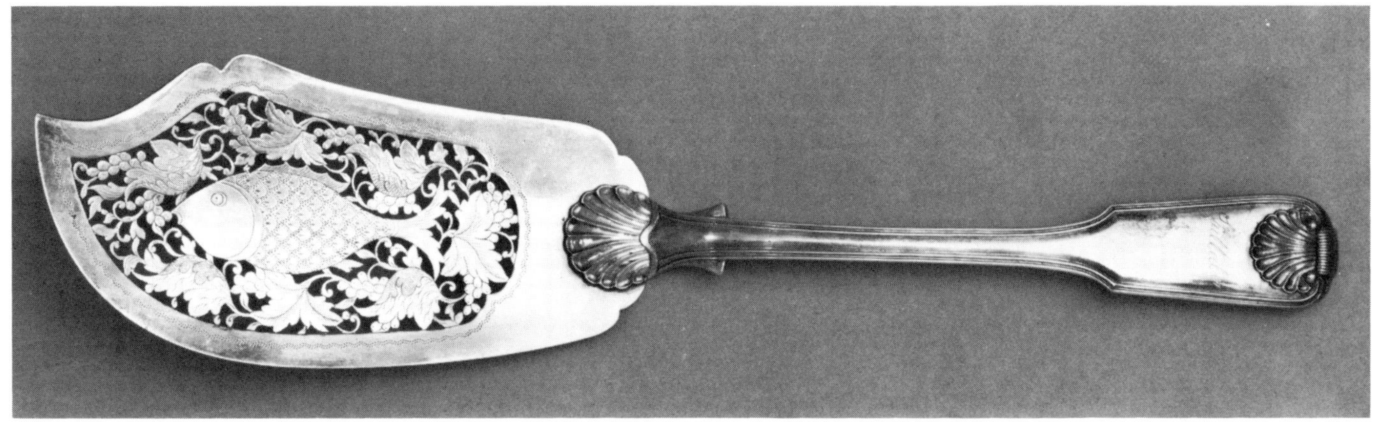

199. Fish slice in fiddle-thread and shell pattern, marked *KHC,* circa 1840. Handle engraved *Shillaber* for Salem family. 12½″ long. *Privately owned.*

pair made for Robert Bennet Forbes, and one in the Metropolitan Museum
collection, all bearing the mark *KHC.* A simple and handsome beaker with a
bamboo edge at lip and base is marked *KHC* and engraved *HGH to FAH,*
Canton, Feb. 1st, 1844.[16] Possibly the most impressive pieces of silver by *KHC*
are his enormous tea sets. One set, made for Elizabeth Hunt, included a tray
completely covered with an engraved floral design, with *Elizabeth Hunt Canton*
China 1854 engraved in an oval space in the center. The other pieces have
borders which match that of the tray. One wonders how anyone was able to
lift the entire set on the tray, because of its tremendous weight. A similar tea *201*
service, consisting of six heavy, over-decorated pieces of the same nature, is
marked *KHC* on each piece. Several repoussé boxes of various shapes also reflect *KHC*'s strong use of the overall patterns with Chinese motifs. A pair of
KHC footed salvers, with repoussé borders and engraved centers, bears the
initials *RBF* for "Robert Bennet Forbes," and is dated 1845. A nutmeg grater
of another shape, in the form of a tear, is more simply engraved with restrained geometric motifs.

A simple and extremely attractive platter by *KHC* is more in the refined style of the nutmeg graters resembling classic urns. Oval in shape with slightly scalloped outer edge, the platter has a delicate gadrooned border with a shell design at either end and in the middle of each side. A pair of casters, with gadrooned rims and center bases, again reflects this more restrained style in *KHC*'s silver.[17]

The maker *YS* is similar to *KHC* and *CUT* in some of his manufactures and probably worked at approximately the same dates. *YS* could be Yutshing,

200. Nutmeg grater in the form of a classical urn, circa 1850. Marked *KHC*. Engraved *EH* for Elizabeth Hunt who lived at Whampoa Reach. $3\frac{1}{4}''$ high. *Peabody Museum, Salem.*

201. Large ornate tray marked *KHC,* engraved *Elizabeth Hunt, Canon, China 1854.* Overall length, including handles, 31½″. *Privately owned.*

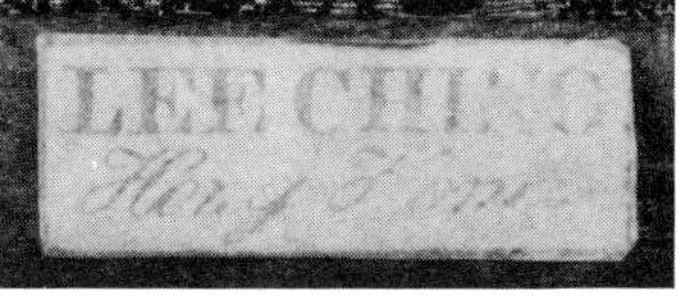

203

a dealer in metals and carvings, who exhibited at the Philadelphia Centennial Exhibition of 1876.[18] A set of fiddle-thread and shell spoons, with the initials *FH*—possibly for "Frederic Hunt"—includes five stamped *YS* and one stamped *WE WF WC,* and all have pseudo-hallmarks. The spoons are of superb quality and craftsmanship. *YS* also made a handsome undecorated mug of fine quality and a simplicity which appears to represent an early form. A magnificent pair of vegetable tureens with covers and ornate borders like those on the Hunt tea service, with reeded ball feet, bears an engraved *F* for "Forbes."[19] The marks on these are *YS* with pseudo-hallmarks. The two were probably purchased in the second quarter of the nineteenth century. The Chinese could make magnificent silver, either in the Western or Chinese manner, and, if the silver were not marked in some way, it would be extremely difficult to distinguish from Continental or American silver. It is puzzling to find different makers' marks on pieces of silver in the same set, and the questions thus raised have not been answered as yet.

A later smith of the third—and possibly the fourth—quarter of the nineteenth century is Leeching, whose mark is *LC.* An advertisement that he dealt in gold and silver, as well as ivory, appeared in the *Lady's Red Book* for Shanghai in 1878.[20] Several ornate and over-decorated pieces of silver by this craftsman exist, and most of it is very Oriental in feeling, with overall repoussé and Chinese scenes. The later silver departs from the restrained Federal and classical forms of the early periods and becomes more Chinese in concept and design.

Most of the silversmiths dealt in many other materials. Hoaching's label stated he worked in silver, tortoise shell, mother-of-pearl, ivory and sandalwood.[21] Hoaching's work covers a long span of time, since an ivory card

202. Child's knife, fork and spoon in the Kings pattern. Marked *KHC*, circa 1855. Made for a member of the Hunt family. *Peabody Museum, Salem.*

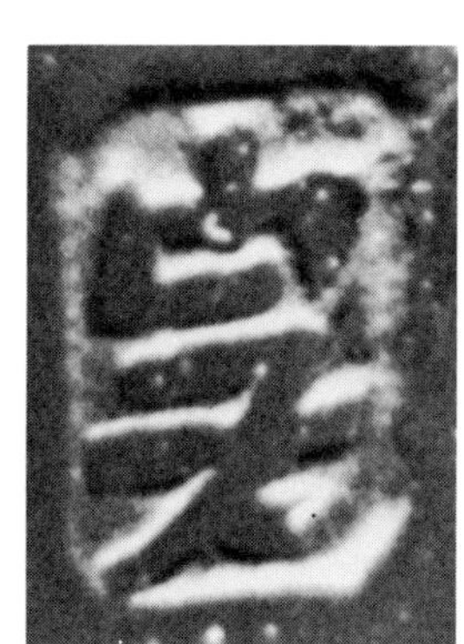

case by him in its original box carries the date 1823; he was also one of the
craftsmen shown at the Philadelphia Exhibition (*see Chap. 10*). Several pieces
of silver and gold by him are known. A set of extremely ornate soup tureens
with dragon-heads for handle terminals and lid knobs, is completely covered
with repoussé designs of Chinese scenes. The tureens were brought back by
A. A. Low in mid-nineteenth century; with them was an enormous carved
elephant tusk on its stand which was also by Hoaching. The Peabody Museum
owns a standing cup, with twisted dragons for a support, that has a cover with
204 a finial exactly like that on the Low tureens, and Hoaching's mark on the
205 base. The cup is still in its original wood box with fitted silk interior, which
bears the original Hoaching label on the cover. A small snuff box, a mug and
various other pieces are known to have been made by this prolific craftsman,
197 whose shop was considered one of the most expensive in Canton.[22] The mug
described by Tiffany had its washed lining of gold on the inside. A very rare
set of evening studs with cuff links, in solid gold, is stamped with the Hoaching
H and remains in the original box with *HOACHING* stamped inside the
207 cover. Hoaching's mark is this *H,* in a Victorian script form, with a Chinese
character beside it. Unrecognized quantities of silver and gold by this smith
must exist today, since he was so prolific.

Other marks of silversmiths, working in the Western style for an export market at the mid-century were *Kemki, CWG., WC, E* and others. These makers are for the most part unidentified.

Although the silver was inexpensive by Western standards, it was not cheap, and so it remained a commodity that was purchased for the most part

203. Pair of spoons in the fiddle-thread and shell pattern, with the mark of *YS*, circa 1850. Engraved *FH*, possibly for Frederick Hunt. *Privately owned.*

by Westerners who were living in China. Benjamin Shreve's six tumblers cost him $53.10 and his fish knife, which was probably very much like those made for Elizabeth Hunt and Shillaber, cost $9.95. The twelve tablespoons cost $41.33, while the cream pot and sugar dish were $49 for the pair.[23] Sullivan Dorr purchased considerable silver in 1801 and listed it in his memorandum book for May 2, 1801:[24]

1 ladle, 1 Table 6 Tea & desert spoons	$38.00
One Castor stand 6 Bottles	21.00
One pair Salts spoons &c	7.50
Sugar and Cream pot with d°	11.00
Mustard & Spoon 5. 1 Cheese Knife 3.	8.00
One fish Knife 7.25 1 butter d° 3.	10.25
12 desert. 6 Table & 6 Tea spoons	46.25
One Coffee & 1 Tea pot and stand	129.50
One Grater	3.00

The total is $274.50, a goodly amount in those days, but Dorr had also bought a large and very varied quantity of silver, which retains its intrinsic value. The castor stand might have resembled the one by Pao Yin, since the period and design would be congruent. The grater was probably a small nutmeg grater in the form of a classic urn, while the coffee and teapots may have been in the form of the American silver of the period with bright-cut decoration. For all this silver, Dorr bought one silverware case for $4.50, which he listed under furniture. A service of the size and weight of Elizabeth Hunt's tea service, which was purchased in 1856, must have cost a large sum of

192

204. Ornately decorated soup tureen with dragon head handles. Stamped with the mark of Hoaching. Made for A.A. Low. 10″ high with cover, 16$\frac{3}{4}$″ long. *Metropolitan Museum of Art, Purchase, Robert C. Goelet Fund.*

206

money, because of its weight and designs; however, it was undoubtedly much less expensive than a heavy early-Victorian silver tea service made in New York or Philadelphia.

A number of the silversmiths and jewelers continued to make silverware and small decorative objects into the twentieth century. Popular items were the silver filigree card cases and the open baskets, which both Leeching and Yutshing exhibited at the Philadelphia Centennial Exhibition in 1876. A number of silver salt and peppers, in the form of Chinese shoes, have the mark *SF* and "90" for the weight of the silver, a requirement at the end of the nineteenth century for objects being sent to this country. A small silver shoe, in European style, had a lift-lid so it could be used as a box, and was stamped on the inside *Wang Hing.* A photograph of a sign with his name outside a shop in the 50's, Queens Road, Hong Kong, shows him listed as a jeweler. The silver shoe is of fine quality. Another gold- and silversmith, the jeweler *Wah Loong,* was located at No. 88 Queens Road Central, in the 1870's, according to his label. Other small pieces of silver in the form of place-card holders and ornate figure groups for salts and condiments have been marked *WH*

205. Chalice with dragon support and knob. Stamped with the mark of Hoaching. With original box bearing the Hoaching label. Circa 1860. *Peabody Museum, Salem.*

with the "90" mark. Many of the dealers working in silver made gold jewelry, often incorporating carvings of tortoise shell and ivory.

The Chinese metalsmiths worked in metals other than silver and gold. Paktong, an alloy made of copper, nickel and zinc, was used extensively in China for export objects, and candlesticks and other small items made in the Western style were bought in the eighteenth and nineteenth centuries.[25]

An important watercolor of the interior of a pewter shop clearly illustrates the types and forms of pewter articles being made for the Western market. Many of the tall vases and the ibis figures are familiar to the collector

206. Silver filigree card case, circa 1860. Marked unidentified, possibly Leeching. 4¾″ high. With original box. *Author's Collection.*

today. A pair of pewter ibises, painted black and probably made for the
210 Dutch market in the eighteenth century, is a superb example of Chinese craftsmanship. The figures are important for the addition of the flat, incised figures of Dutchmen holding vases, which arise out of the backs of the ibises. This blend of Western and Eastern design elements is unique in pewter.

Very possibly there was a great deal of pewter exported to America in the nineteenth century. The Philadelphia Exhibition listed a number of

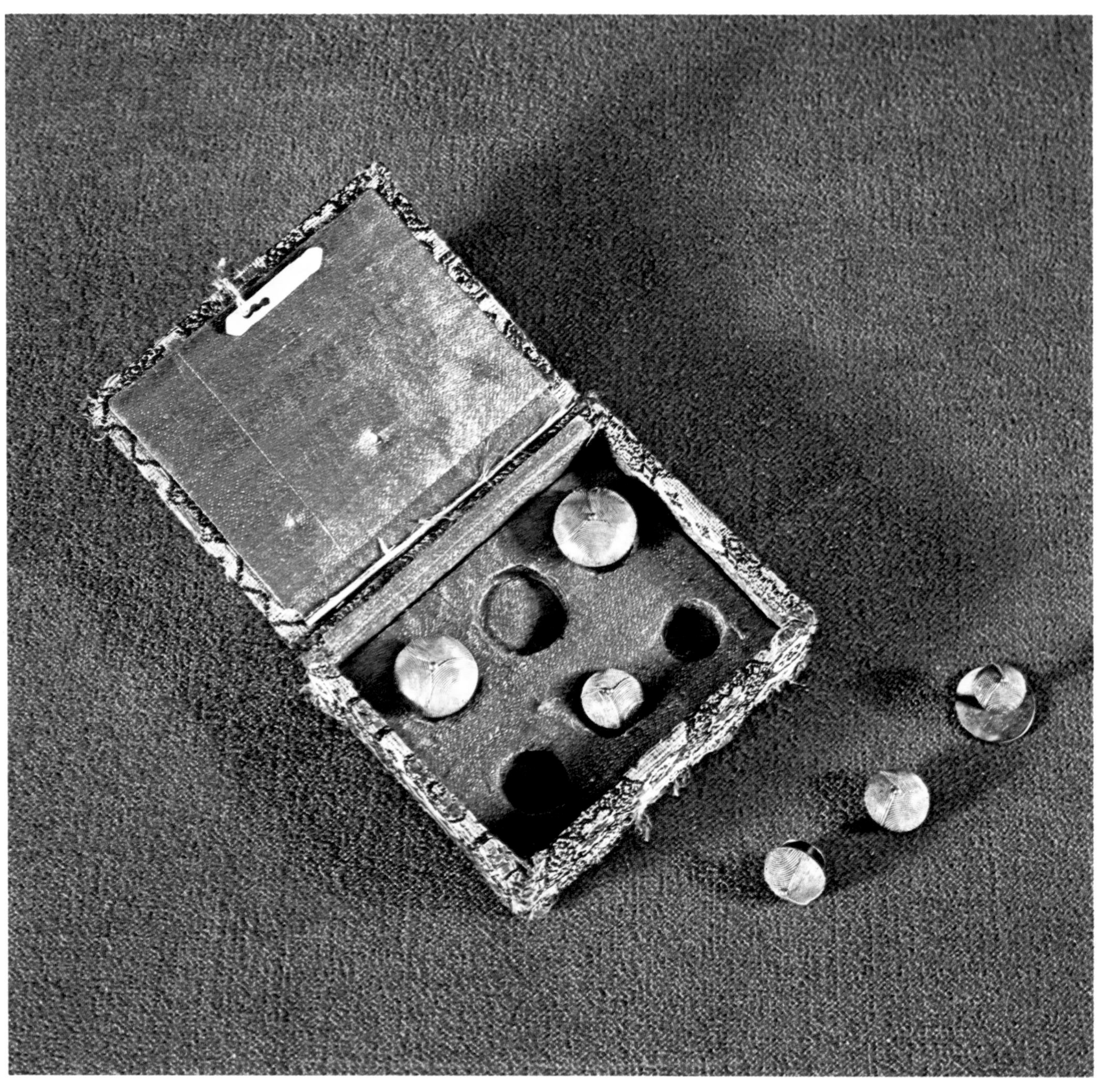

207. Set of evening studs and links in gold, by Hoaching, circa 1860. With original box. *Privately owned.*

208. Stick pin with gold shaft and head decorated with carved monkeys, by Leeching, circa 1870, 3″ long. With original box and label. *Privately owned.*

209. Pewter inkwell, copy of an American or English model. Stamped with Chinese character. Circa 1840, $2\frac{1}{2}''$ high, $3\frac{3}{4}''$ diameter. *Peabody Museum, Salem.*

pieces of pewter from China which were in the "Foreign shape," that is, Western.[26] Unless the pewter were marked, it would be next to impossible to distinguish a piece of Chinese pewter in the Western form from a piece of American or Continental pewter. An inkwell, so characteristic of thousands
209 made in England and America, bears a Chinese character for a mark and, hence, suggests that this type of copying was not unusual. Some serving and condiment dishes and tureens, teapots and sugar bowls with jadeite decorations and handles were sent to this country in the second half of the nineteenth century. These employed Chinese shapes and decorations and are easily identified.

The work in brass made in the Western form is equally difficult to distinguish. A folding brass candlestick is close to its Dutch prototype, but again bears the stamp of a Chinese maker. Brass hinges, locks, lock plates and keys were made for the countless sewing, tea and work boxes, and many are stamped with an English crown and the word *Patent,* directly copying the English models. The brass escutcheons on the leather trunks were distinctive, and one of the finest designs is that of an American eagle.

Pewter or lead was used for the liners of tea caddies, and the tops were often decorated with Chinese figures and landscapes. A tremendous amount of research is necessary to discover exactly how many metalsmiths there were in Canton in the nineteenth century, and what each one was making. It appears that the smiths could and would make anything for the Western market, and many metal objects held in America, which have always been readily accepted as Western manufactures, may indeed have been of Chinese crafting in the long period of the China trade.

Notes

1. "China Trade Silver: Checklists for Collectors," by John Devereux Kernan, in *Connoisseur,* Nov., 1965, p. 198. Earliest reference was an ad in *Antiques,* July, 1954, p. 8, for Gebelein Silversmiths which illustrated the Shillaber fish slice and silver from the Derby-West-Landers family.
2. Tiffany, *The Canton Chinese,* p. 73.
3. "Letters of Sullivan Dorr," ed. by Howard Corning, *Proceedings of the Massachusetts Historical Society,* Vol. LXVII, 1945. Letter of S. Dorr to Joseph and John Dorr, Canton, Feb. 5, 1800.
4. R. B. Forbes "wastebook," August 6, 1831–August 1, 1834, mentions buying from Cutshing half-dozen teaspoons, curry spoons, tablespoons. Forbes papers, Massachusetts Historical Society.
5. James Wathen, *Journal of a Voyage in 1811 & 1812 to Madras and China.* London, 1814, pp. 188–189.
6. Shreve Mss., papers for the voyages of 1815 and 1819–1821. Peabody Museum, Salem.
7. The spoon engraved *1808* is in the collection of the Yale University Art Gallery.
8. Bill for Shreve's purchases from Synshing is with the papers for his trip on the *Governor Endicott,* 1819–1821. Peabody Museum, Salem.
9. Kathryn C. Buhler and Graham Hood, *American Silver, Garvan and Other Collections in the Yale University Art Gallery.* Yale University Press: New Haven, 1970, Vol. II, p. 268, #1015.
10. Both illustrated in *Connoisseur,* Nov., 1965, fig. 17, p. 206, and fig. 15, p. 205.
11. John Devereux Kernan, "Further Notes on China Trade Silver," in *Connoisseur,* July, 1972, Vol. 180, No. 725, p. 212.
12. Illustrated in *Antiques,* "China Trade Silver," by John Devereux Kernan, Nov., 1966, fig. 8, p. 197.
13. W. C. Hunter, *Bits of Old China,* p. 279.
14. Tiffany, *The Canton Chinese,* p. 73.
15. Illustrated in *Antiques,* Nov., 1966, fig. 5, p. 196.
16. Collection of the Marblehead Historical Society.
17. Illustrated in *Antiques,* Nov., 1966, fig. 6, p. 197.
18. "A Catalogue of the Imperial Maritime Customs Collection," at the United States International Exhibition, Philadelphia, 1876.
19. Illustrated in *Connoisseur,* 1965, fig. 9, p. 202. In the collection of the Museum of the American China Trade.
20. *The Ladies' Directory or Red Book,* for the year 1878. Shanghai: Broadhurst Tootal, p. 63.
21. Label on Hoaching chalice box.
22. John Henry Gray, *Walks in the Streets of Canton.* Victoria, Hong Kong, 1875, p. 292.
23. "Inventory of the personal purchases of B. Shreve," Shreve papers, ship *Governor Endicott,* 1819–1821. Peabody Museum, Salem.
24. Sullivan Dorr's Memorandum book for 1801, Mss. collection of the Rhode Island Historical Society.

210. One of a pair of pewter Ibises, circa 1800, with Dutch figures painted black. Approximately 12″ high. *Photograph courtesy Childs Gallery.*

25. The problem of eighteenth-century candlesticks of paktong is a perplexing one. Few scholars have resolved the conflict as to how many were made in China. Some sticks do exist with pseudo-hallmarks, like the silver, while others bear legitimate English hallmarks. It would seem a natural product for the Chinese to make, since they were familiar with metals and were very adept at using European forms, as shown in the thousands of Western porcelain and silver shapes made in Chinese export porcelain.
26. "A Catalogue of the Imperial Maritime Customs Collection," Class 283, p. 84.

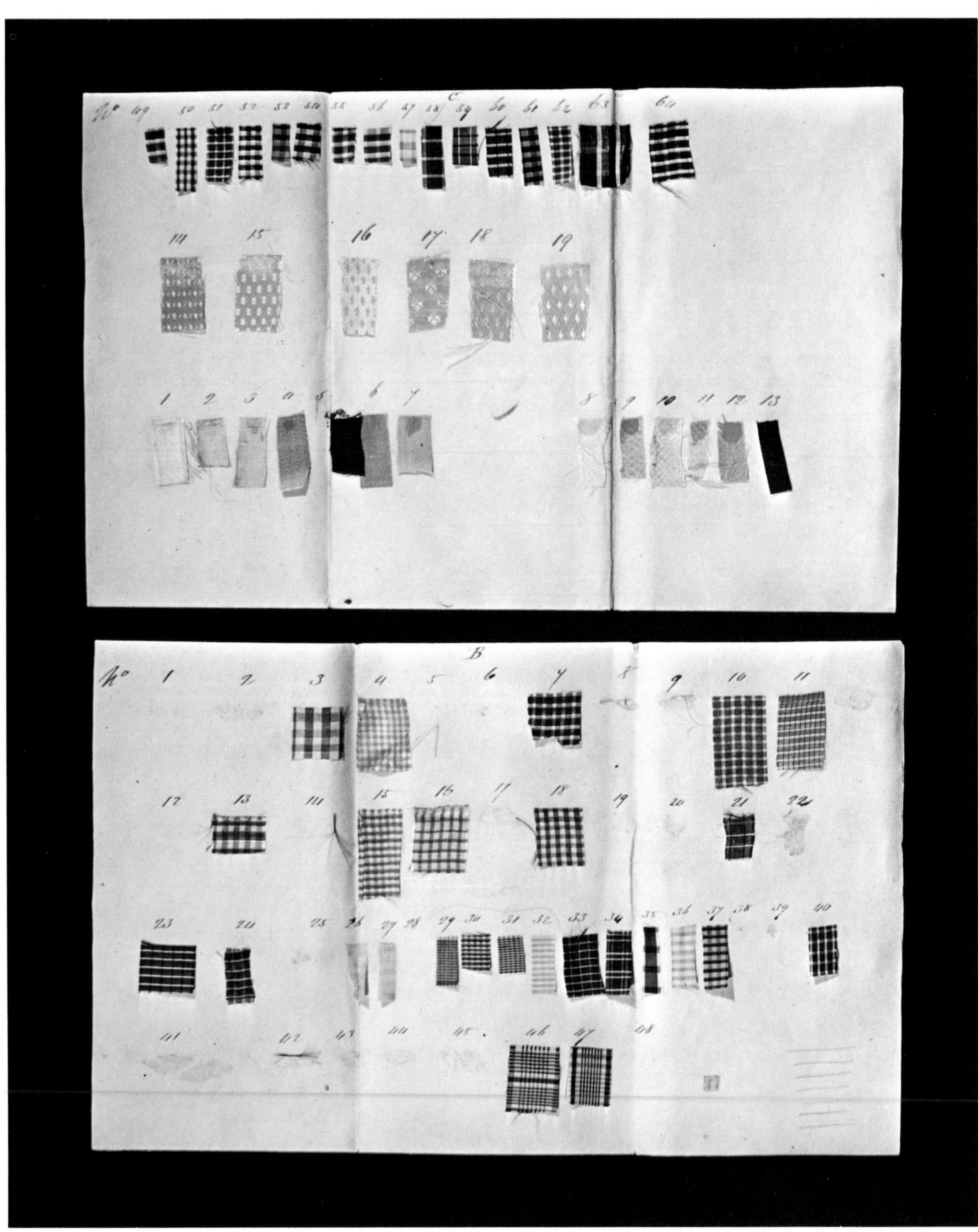

211. Silk samples from Eshing given by Pickering Dodge of Salem to Benjamin Shreve in 1819 as buying guide. *Peabody Museum, Salem.*

13. Household Goods, Silks and Wallpapers

212. Silk bolts belonging to Mrs. Edward Carrington of Providence, Rhode Island, with original box bearing her name and that of the silk dealer Washing. Circa 1815. *Rhode Island Historical Society.*

Many, many commodities and products were brought from China which do not fall into the established boundaries of the decorative arts as generally defined in the study of the China trade. Many of the more "disposable" and practical of the products have long since disappeared. The household goods and small items used in kitchens and stores, such as feather dusters and horn apothecary scoops, are not to be found today.

Two "household" commodities which seem to defy detection are window blinds and straw floor carpeting. Although the carpeting is known to have been brought in during the Victorian period, examples which can be dated before 1820 simply do not exist. Because of its very nature, one can reasonably assume that as soon as the carpeting wore out, it was completely replaced.

One of the first references to straw carpeting from China came from George Washington. In a letter dated January 15, 1789, he wrote from Mount Vernon to Robert Morris in Washington, "I pray you to receive my

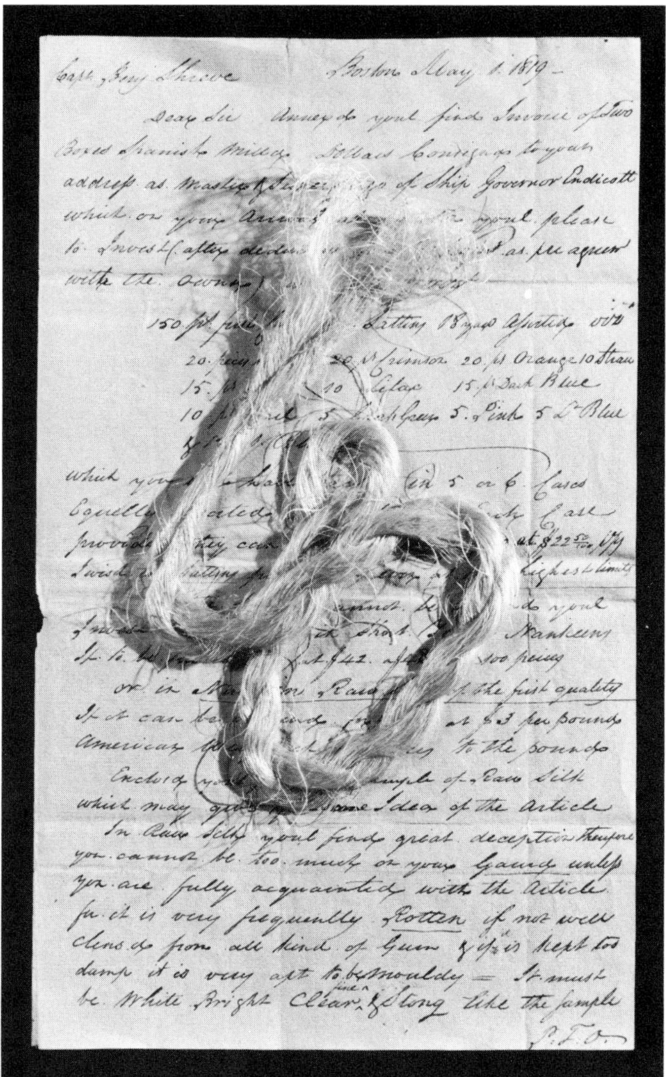

Capt. Benj. Shreve Boston May 1. 1819 –

Dear Sir Annexed you'l find Invoice of Two Boxes Spanish Milled Dollars Consigned to your address as Master & Super[illegible] of Ship Governor Endicott which on your arrival [illegible] you'l please to Invest (after deduc[illegible]) as per agreem with the owners [illegible]

150 [illegible] 18 yards [illegible]

20 [illegible] 20 [illegible] Crimson 20 [illegible] Orange 10 Straw

15 [illegible] 10 Lilac 15 [illegible] Dark Blue

10 [illegible] 5 [illegible] 5 [illegible] Pink 5 [illegible] Blue

[illegible]

which you [illegible] in 5 or 6 Cases [illegible] [illegible] Case provided they can [illegible] at $22 50/100 [illegible]

[illegible]

[illegible] $42 [illegible] 100 pieces

or in [illegible] Raw [illegible] of the first quality If it can be [illegible] at $3 per pound American [illegible] to the pound

Enclosed you'l [illegible] sample of Raw Silk which may give [illegible] some Idea of the Article

In Raw Silk you'l find great deception therefore you cannot be too much on your Guard unless you are fully acquainted with the Article for it is very frequently Rotten if not well cleaned from all kind of Gum & if it is kept too damp it is very apt to be mouldy = It must be White Bright Clear fine & Strong like the sample

P. T. O.

213. Letter to Benjamin Shreve of Salem from Dudley Pickman with a sample of raw silk, 1819. *Peabody Museum, Salem.*

thanks for your favor of the 5th, and for the obliging attention which you have given to the Floor matting from China. . . ."[1] Thomas Jefferson also discussed the use of grass cloth or straw floor covering with Thomas Claxton, his assistant. Claxton wrote and enclosed a sample of the cloth "used by the genteelest people" and stated it could be made in a variegated red and white. Jefferson, however, declined it by saying that it was beautiful, but not what he had in mind, since he wanted to use it in the dining room and needed something which could be easily cleaned and would not wear with the rolling and unrolling.[2]

One of the first records of a large amount being brought in on a Boston ship is contained in the account book of the ship *Tartar.* In this book is listed: "158 Matts [sic]" of varying widths (36, 41, 51, 56), of Nankin Straw carpeting, "208 Matts of figured carpeting," same widths, and "75 Matts of Canton quality," the latter being each in lengths of 40 yards. The first two types varied in yardage from 15 to 40 yards per mat. The price for the entire quan-

214. Silk samples brought from China by Mrs. Thomas Hunt who lived at Whampoa Reach. Circa 1850. *Peabody Museum, Salem.*

tity, which totaled some 16,500 yards, was $2,144.[3] That is a tremendous amount of carpeting, and surely quite a few Boston households must have made use of it in many of their rooms. A large number of merchants in the first quarter of the nineteenth century mention buying the carpeting, either plain or decorated. It would be interesting to speculate whether some of the floor coverings seen in paintings of American room interiors of the first half of the nineteenth century were, indeed, China trade. The practice of using straw matting for summer in large houses was a common one throughout the nineteenth century, and this kind of carpeting is still found in some homes today.

Although several early American window blinds or shades still exist, few can be thought or proven to be China trade. Several have many elements of Chinoiserie in the design, but they reveal more the hand of a Western painter executing Chinese scenes than that of an Oriental. It is possible that some of the European-styled window shades were made in China from prints, such as those used for the porcelain decoration and the paintings on glass of Western subjects. The 1832 auction of the ship *Howard* from Canton listed a roll of 25 green window blinds, 5 silk painted window blinds 4 by 4 feet, 6 silk painted window blinds 6 by 4 feet; $6\frac{1}{2}$ by $3\frac{1}{2}$ feet and $12\frac{1}{2}$ by $3\frac{1}{2}$ feet.[4] These could well be the type often accepted as Continental, English or American, since the silk would be ideal for making them translucent, as so many of the Western shades were. Also in the *Howard* group was a surprising item, "1 piece painted window blind 30 yds by 4 feet wide." In toto, the auction had 156 of the green blinds.[5]

The list of the *Howard* auction is extraordinary, since so many of the items recorded are not generally thought of as made in China; 500 feather dusters, 50 dozen horn scoops for apothecaries' drawers, 500 chowries or fly dusters, 600 black shoe horns, and 73 sinew fish lines make up a partial list.[6] Some of these objects are unfortunately not known today, and there is no way of knowing what their actual appearance may have been. Clearly, the Chinese were making every type of household product needed in America and exporting them in tremendous quantities.

The major staples of the trade, other than tea, were silk and nankeens. It was for these magnificent fabrics that the traders haunted the shops of the silk merchants and the hongs of Canton. The yardage exported to America ran into the millions every year, and silk was sold in every pattern, quality and size. The silk market fluctuated tremendously with demand, and a trader of the period of Benjamin Shreve had to be extremely careful to pick the patterns which would meet the fashion needs of Europe and America. As the Italian and French silks came into demand, many of the Chinese silks became poor investments. Thousands of costumes found in historical museums on the Eastern seaboard are made of China trade silks—the most frequently used fabric for fine garments in the first half of the nineteenth century.

211 Superbly documenting the Chinese silks of 1815 to 1820 is the folder of silk samples from the merchant Eshing given to Benjamin Shreve to use as a buying guide by Pickering Dodge of Salem. It was a standard practice for merchants investing in a cargo of silks to give the supercargo samples of the silks they wished to buy. These samples were obtained from merchants returning from China to America, who brought them from the various silk merchants they had traded with. The Eshing silk samples are extremely varied, and show several of the patterns and colors that were available. The

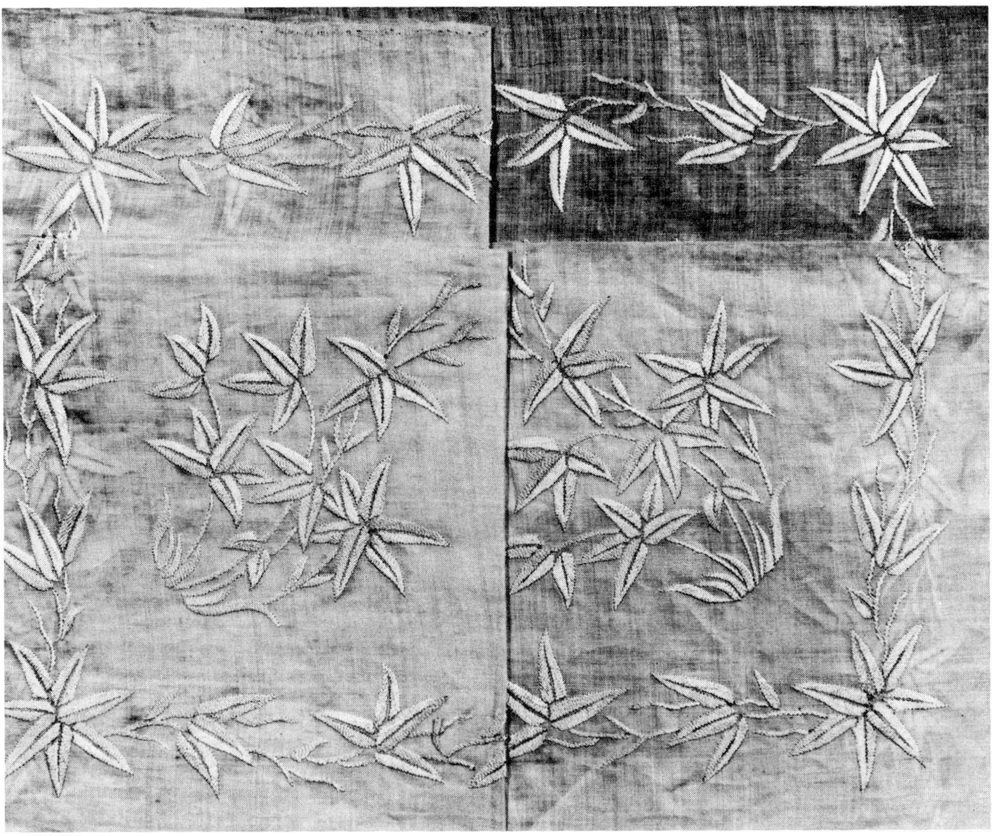

215. Grasscloth handkerchief brought from China by John Robinson, Sr., in 1836. Robinson notebook, *Peabody Museum, Salem.*

colors range from very light to black, and the patterns are small geometric designs or small and large plaids. Many of these samples are very contemporary in feeling.

Dodge sent an extensive note with the samples, explaining the problems of buying in Canton. This was Shreve's first voyage to that port. Along with the descriptions of the silks, Dodge posed several important questions to the trader:

> Besides the caprice of taste and fashion, the following queries present themselves with more than a common force, and require more than common sagacity to answer satisfactorily, viz/ Will there be any an if any, how great a demand for Teas, Nankin,s Silks of any description for exportation, from this country? Will the peace in Europe enable France and Italy to supply silks at a much lower rate than usual and thus in a great measure supercede Canton silks to which, they are unquestionably superior?

Dodge's strongest recommendation was to buy the fabrics that were least like the European. His instructions for packing silks are important. "Silks shoud be pack'd in clear dry weather, other wise they are apt to be spotted and mouldy. As a general rule, would advise putting twenty five ps Silks or Crapes in a case."[7] With his instructions Dodge included sample cards with a note, "The object of these is soley to furnish you with colors and figures not samples of fabric, tho in this respect some of them are worth imitating for sarsnets." The silks listed and described below were "Synchaws, Lustrings, Sarsnets, Bonnet silks, Ponges, Crapes, Sewings, Satins, Levantines or twilled silks, Florentines, Camblets, Pelong Satins, Black and Check'd Hkfs [handkerchiefs] and Nankins." In the sarcenets he recommended fewest of the smallest figures, such as 29 to 32 (bottom group of samples) and the largest 41 to 48. "It may be well to make up some cases of the large plaids and other figures of high and bright colors by themselves for the Havana market, but few however."

A sample card sent to Shreve from Dudley Pickman in 1819 was stamped with the name of Washing, and bore two samples of Levantines in black. The samples are of a particularly handsome ribbed fabric, similar to that seen in clothing of the period, and very much like that used on the back-
213 grounds of some American silhouettes. With the Shreve papers was a hank of raw silk and a letter from the merchant who wished to place an order for several pounds, "In Raw Silk youl find great deception, therefore you cannot be too much on your *Guard* unless you are full acquainted with the article for it is very frequently *Rotten* if not well clensd from all kinds of Gum & if is kept too long damp it is very apt to be mouldy—it must be White, Bright Clear fine & Strong like the sample."

All the merchants brought back large quantities of sewing silks in all the colors of the rainbow; they were quite bright, if not gaudy. These silks were used for embroidery also and were considered to be of the best quality.

The largest number of merchants investing in the Shreve voyage wanted silks, crêpes and nankeens and they were extremely particular in what they ordered. Most of the men wrote long letters describing exactly the quality, size, colors and types of silks they had in mind. For their wives, they often bought smaller yard goods of the highest quality, or specified a particular expensive and unusual pattern, which could be used either for an evening gown or possibly for window draperies. A box of silks, stamped with
212 the name of the merchant Washing, was sent to Edward Carrington of Providence, Rhode Island, in the early years of the nineteenth century, and it contains many of the original silks, still rolled up. Among them is a superb bolt of a heavy silk, similar to a peau de soie finish, in a silvery buff with cherry red end bands, a rich brown and a blue damask, a coarse ribbon-blue silk and a heavy blue silk embroidered with white designs; all popular silks in this particular period, and all expensive.

Mrs. Thomas Hunt of Salem gave John Robinson of Salem several
214 samples of silk which she herself had obtained in China in the 1840's and early 50's. These silks, as bright today as they were then, are mostly damasks and brocades, and resemble quite closely one or two of the Carrington silks. Several dresses still extant in Salem today are made of fabrics very much like the darker samples seen in the Robinson scrapbook.

Grasscloth, a form of linen, was another popular fabric, especially for
215 handkerchiefs. A particularly fine example, carefully embroidered with a leaf design, was brought back by John Robinson's father and is in his scrapbook. The cloth is in remarkable condition, and its fine quality indicates how desirable it was in the nineteenth century. Grasscloth of this type made up a large part of the orders, although it never rivaled the silks and nankeens, nor was it so versatile a cloth.

The quantities of silk and fabrics brought back on a voyage such as Shreve made in 1819 are tremendous. Fabrics made up the major part of the cargo, and it is difficult to imagine a market for so much material in Salem and Boston. However, since the fabrics were used for furniture, draperies

216. Paper samples brought from the Chinese Booth of the United States International Exhibition, Philadelphia, 1876, possibly by Mrs. James Hammond of Salem. Robinson notebook, *Peabody Museum, Salem.*

and clothing, such a cargo probably turned a considerable profit. Shreve contracted with Namshong for silks on September 13, 1820, and bought $28,988.24 worth; this was in addition to the $86,513.66 worth of silks he had bought from the same dealer on August 28. Shreve kept account of his purchases for each man investing by drawing out a large graph on which was carefully recorded the yardage, color and size of the silk for each purchaser.

Throughout the nineteenth century, the merchants brought home examples of Chinese clothing, both as curiosities and for wearing apparel. John P. Cushing of Boston, early hit by the China mania, often wore Chinese clothing at home. In 1801 Benjamin Hodges presented to the East India Marine Society a full-size figure of the merchant Yamqua dressed in *2*
his original robes. Edward Carrington also brought home a figure of a mandarin and his wife in their original clothing. How many of these costumes and clothes were actually worn in the first half of the century is not known, but by the mid-century, Salem ladies were wearing mandarin robes and skirts to Hamilton Hall balls. Another equally popular commodity was the large silk shawls, most often white but also in pastels or blacks, plain or heavily embroidered, with long fringes. Packed in fancifully decorated pasteboard boxes and lacquered boxes, they were brought back for wives and sweethearts throughout the century.

Several types of papers, either decorated or plain, were sent from China to America, and those shown at the Philadelphia Centennial Exhibi- *216*
tion in 1876 are particularly interesting examples of this product. The ship

Howard also auctioned 1600 sheets of rose, light blue, orange, pea green, yellow and buff paper in 1832. The merchants in the trade often bought these colored papers for themselves or their families, but they were not a large trade product.

Chinese export wallpaper was popular in England during the second half of the eighteenth century, and limited quantities of it did find their way to America in the late-eighteenth and early-nineteenth centuries. However, there are few examples of this paper in existence today in America. The designs were usually repetitive and basically simple; there was little pattern variation. The designs were most often of Chinese foliage, birds, fantasies, and figures engaged in Chinese industries or trades. The papers were usually painted in a type of gouache upon either silk or paper. The wallpapers were probably backed with a canvas or linen before being hung in a room.

A magnificent set of wallpaper was ordered by Robert Morris, circa 1790, but was never used. It was found in its original boxes in Marblehead, Massachusetts, and is now installed at both "Beauport" in Gloucester, Massachusetts, and "Winterthur," Delaware. The design is a continuous fanciful Chinese scene and is painted on paper. In the Edward Carrington House in Providence, Rhode Island, a drawing room is hung with a paper whose design repeats every strip. The bottom of each panel has large fantastic peacocks, while the background and area above is of flowering shrubs and foliage. *frontis* The paper was probably brought from China between 1810 and 1815 by Edward Carrington, or it may have been ordered by him after his return to this country.

Only a few private houses and public museums show rooms with Chinese wallpaper. The Metropolitan Museum has examples, and the ball room of the Governor's Palace at Williamsburg is papered in a Chinese wallpaper with a floral design on a blue ground. The Robert Bennet Forbes House in Milton, Massachusetts, has a copy of a period Chinese wallpaper on one of its drawing rooms.

Another Robert Bennet Forbes wallpaper, currently owned by the Peabody Museum, was painted on silk and is one of the most ambitious of all the Chinese papers for the American market. The design consists of a series of panels, possibly originally as many as 24, each with a different step in the raising, gathering, drying and processing of tea illustrated in the bottom third of the panel. The panels join together to form a continuous panorama around the room. Above the scenes of the tea trade are large flowering trees, a different variety on each panel. The papers are extraordinarily fine in quality and color, and probably were brought from China by Forbes in the second quarter of the nineteenth century.

Wallpaper was occasionally used on folding screens which were made in China for the export market. Other screens with Chinese designs were painted with motifs appropriate to the size of the screen. The motifs were generally like those of the wallpapers, and the backs of the screen panels were often covered with a plain paper. A three- or four-fold screen seems to have been the standard size. These screens were convenient for disguising doors or dividing rooms, but did not enjoy a great vogue. Magnificent screens of all heights and sizes were made in black and gold lacquer, and several of these products of the nineteenth century exist today.

Notes

1. Rodris Roth, *Floor Covering in 18th Century America,* United States National Museum Bulletin 250. Smithsonian Press: Washington, D. C., 1967, p. 27.
2. *Ibid.,* pp. 27, 28.
3. Account book for the ship *Tartar,* 1816. Peabody Museum, Salem.
4. "Catalogue of Canton Fans . . .," auction of the ship *Howard,* New York, 1832.
5. *Ibid.*
6. *Ibid.*
7. Shreve papers, for the ship *Governor Endicott,* 1819–1821. Peabody Museum, Salem.

Appendices

A. List of Chinese Painters Working for the Western Market

Name	*Working Dates*	*City*	*Medium and Subject Matter*
Spoilum	1785–1810	C	Portraits, ship paintings, port scenes, Court of Inquiry
Pu Qua	1800	C	Original watercolors for London stipple engravings
Fatqua	1805–1835	C	Paintings on glass, watercolors, ships
Carwick painter	1810–1830	C	Portraits, other?
Mayhing	1810–1820	C	Port scenes
Lucqua	1820's	C	Portraits
Greyhound painter	1825–1840?	C or W	Ships
Henry Tuke painter	1830's	C?	Ships
Master of 1822	1810–1830	C	Ports
Yin Qua	1830's	C	?
Lam Qua	1825–1860	C	Portraits, landscapes, port scenes, figure studies; watercolors and pith papers by studio
Sunqua	1830–1870	C & M	Ships, port views, landscapes, watercolors on pith
Protin Qua	1835–1850	C	?
Tingqua	1840–1870	C	Watercolors, pith papers, portrait miniatures
Youqua	1840–1870	C & HK	Port views, landscapes, copies after prints, pith papers, watercolors
Namcheong	1845–1875	W & HK?	Port views, ships, pagoda scenes, shipping
Yeuqua	1850–1885	HK	Portraits, ships, miniatures, port views
Taicheong	1850–1875	HK	Port views, ships, copies
W. E. Chung	1850–?	HK	Ships
Chow Kwa	1850–1880	S	Houses, miniatures, portraits, port views
Lai Sung	1850–1885	HK	Ships, photographs
Chongqua	1850's	C	Pith papers
Cheungqua	1860's	?	Pith papers
Lee Heng	1850's–1870's	HK	Ships
Hing Qua	1850–1880	HK	Ships, portraits, charts
Chincqua	1850's	C?	Pith papers
Woo Cheong	1860–1880	HK	Ships, portraits
Chang Qua	1860's	HK	Ships
Wing Chong	1860–1880	HK	Ships
Hung Qua	1860–1890	HK	Portraits, ships, charts
King Kee	1860's	S	Watercolor of Heard House
K. C. Chan	1860's?	?	Junks
Qua Sees	1880's	HK	Ships
Pun Woo	1880's	HK	Ships
Yat On	1880's	HK	Ships, portraits
Chou Pai Chuen	1890's?	P	Pith papers
Lai Fong	1870–1900	Calcutta	Ships

Abbreviations in the third column represent: C–Canton, W–Whampoa, S–Shanghai, M–Macao, HK–Hong Kong, P–Peking.

B. Identifying the Chinese Ports

1. Macao, oil on canvas, attributed to Captain Elliot, R.N., circa 1825–1830, 25″ × 35½″. Looking from the south to the north. The long sweeping curve of the harbor is known as the Praya Grande. The fort on the hill in the center is Fort Monte; the fort on the hill at the right, Fort Guia. Below Guia is the Monastery and Fort of San Francisco. The churches in the center are St. Lorenzo and St. Dominico. *Photograph courtesy Childs Gallery.*

2. Macao, gouache on paper, by Tingqua, circa 1850, 8¼″ × 10½″. From the north, looking south. A fine, detailed view of the Praya Grande and the Western buildings there. The hill to the far left in the background is Penha with its church. *Peabody Museum, Salem.*

3. Macao, oil on canvas, by Youqua, circa 1855, 31¾″ × 57¾″. From the harbor, looking directly to the center of the Praya Grande curve. The hill on the far left is the Penha. The two large buildings in the very center, above the bow of the sidewheeler, are the Palacio on the left and the East India Company to the right; to the right of the latter is the Governor's Residence, in front of which is the small Fort St. Peter. The fort on the hill to the right of center is Fort Monte, and that to the far right, on the hill, Fort Guia. The fort below is San Francisco, and the Monastery. *Peabody Museum, Salem.*

4. Bark *Monsoon* off Lin Tin, oil on canvas, by Sunqua, circa 1835. $17\frac{3}{4}'' \times 23''$. View of Lin Tin Island in the background. Lin Tin was the anchorage for the opium hulks, 60 miles from Canton. *Privately owned.*

5. Boca Tigris, oil on canvas, artist unknown, circa 1815, $18'' \times 23\frac{1}{2}''$. The forts 40 miles below Canton protected the Pearl River. *Photograph courtesy Childs Gallery.*

6. Whampoa Reach, oil on canvas, artist unknown, before 1800, $18'' \times 23\frac{1}{2}''$. Early view of the Whampoa Anchorage and Customs House, from an unusual angle. Western vessels are seen at anchor, and partially dismasted, to the far left. *Photograph courtesy Childs Gallery.*

7. Whampoa Anchorage, oil on canvas, artist unknown, circa 1815, $17\frac{1}{2}'' \times 23''$. The town of Whampoa is on the island beyond; the famed nine-stage pagoda is in the background at the far end of the island. The island in the foreground is Dane's; that to the left, French Island. Whampoa was 10 miles downriver from Canton. The river continues to the left of the pagoda to Canton. *Photograph courtesy Childs Gallery.*

8. Whampoa Anchorage, oil on canvas, attributed to Youqua, circa 1850, measurements unknown. Junk Island is seen to the right, and the Junk River separates the island from Whampoa. Note the addition in this later view of the cemetery in the foreground on Dane's Island. *Mystic Seaport.*

9. Hunt fleet at Whampoa, oil on canvas, by Namcheong, circa 1855, $19\frac{3}{4}'' \times 41''$. Thomas Hunt was part-owner of a ships' chandlery at Whampoa at mid-century; his family lived on a houseboat there. *Peabody Museum, Salem.*

10. Pagoda at Whampoa Reach, oil on canvas, by Namcheong, circa 1850, 20″ × 15″. View is toward Canton. *Childs Gallery.*

11. French Folly Fort, oil on canvas, artist unknown, circa 1810, $18\frac{1}{2}$″ × $29\frac{5}{8}$″. A river fort just below Canton. *Photograph courtesy Childs Gallery.*

12. Dutch Folly Fort, oil on canvas, by Sunqua, circa 1856, $17\frac{1}{4}$″ × $29\frac{1}{2}$″. The fort was across from and below the Western quarter of Canton. *Peabody Museum, Salem.*

13. Hong Kong, gouache on paper, by Tingqua, circa 1850, $8\frac{1}{4}'' \times 10\frac{1}{2}''$. Kowloon and the mainland are to the far left. *Peabody Museum, Salem.*

14. Hong Kong, oil on canvas, artist unknown, circa 1850, measurements unknown. The view is from Kowloon (or the mainland). *Photograph courtesy Childs Gallery.*

15. U. S. supply ship at Hong Kong, oil on canvas, by Yeuqua, 1868, $13'' \times 18\frac{1}{4}''$. View of the center of Hong Kong to the left. The island mountain looms behind. *Privately owned.*

16. The Bund at Shanghai, oil on canvas, artist unknown, circa 1865, measurements unknown. The houses and trading emporiums of the Western merchants in Shanghai were located in this quarter. The large tall house of Augustine Heard of Ipswich, Massachusetts, can be seen at mid-left. The two buildings of Russell and Co. are just to the right of the foremast of the vessel in the left foreground with the painted ports. *Photograph courtesy Childs Gallery.*

C. Dating of the Views of Canton

There are in existence today thousands of views of the hongs at Canton, the site of most trade with the West before the opening of the Treaty ports in the 1840's. No convenient set of guidelines, however, has been established for dating these views. Below is a description of the changes at Canton from 1760 to 1856 with a general outline for dating the scenes. The Western area of Canton was in a constant state of flux, and even the most minute changes were carefully recorded by the Chinese artists painting the area for Western clients. An excellent chronology was established in James Orange's book, *The Chater Collection;* this collection was located in Hong Kong before World War II. However, there are minor errors and certain gaps which can now be filled in, through documentation and study of additional paintings.

Most of the dating comes from contemporary accounts, known dates of execution and exportation of the paintings. Much additional information can be gleamed from examination of the moving of fences in the front of the hongs, the progress of reclamation along the waterfront, and such structural changes in the hongs as were necessitated by fires as well as expansion.

1. Canton, view of the hongs, circa 1760. Artist unknown. Gouache on silk, $18\frac{3}{4}''$ × 29″. Similar to a scroll of the same scene of approximately the same date, illustrated in *Chater* and now in the possession of the British Museum. The only hongs architecturally in the Western style are those occupied by the foreign countries. The Danish hong is to the far left, Old China Street is to the left of center, and the French, Imperial (Austrian), Swedish, British and Dutch hongs, each behind their respective flag, follow to the right. It is necessary to note here that the first-floor porch supports of the British and Dutch hongs are poles or columns, lacking the more enclosed arches of the 1780's. *Peabody Museum, Salem.*

2. Canton, "The European Factories of Canton in China," 1805. William Daniell. Large folio engraving. The importance of this print lies in the fact that the drawing for it was done by Daniell on his stop at Canton on the way to India in 1784, 1785. Thus, it is an invaluable document of the hongs in the year of the arrival of the Americans. The most obvious change since the 1760's is the arches with supports on the first floor of the British and Dutch hongs. *Peabody Museum, Salem.* This can also be seen in Illus. 3. An early engraving, circa 1789, published in *Chater,* depicts the fences and gates in front of the hongs which must have gone up sometime after Daniell's trip. The land area behind the fences is somewhat foreshortened and gives a distorted view of the actual space.

3. Canton, view of the hongs, 1785–1790. Possibly by Spoilum. Oil on canvas, approximately 28″ × 40″. Note the similarity between this painting and Illus. 2. *Photograph courtesy Peabody Museum, Salem.*

4. Canton, view of the factories, circa 1795. Michel Felice Corné. Oil on panel, $33\frac{1}{2}$″ × $53\frac{1}{4}$″. This American fireboard is a highly important painting in the dating sequence. Painted for the East India Marine Hall (now the Peabody Museum), it was obviously based on a Chinese export view of the factories which Corné had seen in Salem. Here are the fences, and a very stylized treatment of the arches and columns of the British hong. The American flag has moved over in front of the hong to the left of Old China Street, a hong later owned by Chung Qua and referred to as such throughout this dating sequence. Whether the moving of the flag from the building to the right of Old China Street, always considered the American hong, to the lefthand side is artistic license on Corné's part or actual fact is not known. The center group of hongs between Old China Street and Hog Lane (to the left of the British hong, in the Corné) is similar to those in Illus. 2, althought the hong to the right of Old China Street has been remodeled. The fences are very similar to those seen in the 1789 *Chater* print. *Peabody Museum, Salem.*

5. Canton, circa 1790 to 1800. Artist unknown. Reverse painting on glass, $17\frac{1}{2}'' \times 25\frac{1}{2}''$. This view shows fences similar to both the 1789 *Chater* print and Illus. 4. Here the American flag flies to the right of Old China Street, and the placement of the hongs is very much as it was in Illus. 2. There are, however, more buildings than in the earlier views. A new building in the Western style has been added to the left of the group of four Western buildings in the block between Old China Street and Hog Lane. *Peabody Museum, Salem.*

6. Canton, before 1803. Artist unknown. Oil on canvas, $18'' \times 23\frac{1}{4}''$. Five hongs in the Western style in the center block between Old China Street and Hog Lane. By 1800, a number of changes had been made in the area of the hongs and to the waterfront fences. The fences at the water's edge in front of the central groups of hongs had been removed, but the fences in front of the Danish and French hongs to the left, and the British and Dutch hongs to the right, remain to the water. The French flag flying here was to be removed in 1803 and not flown again until the return of the French in 1832. Thus, this painting must have been done before 1803, but after Illus. 5. The waterfront itself is changed in this view, with more land reclamation in front of the American hong. *Peabody Museum, Salem.*

7. Canton, circa 1810. Artist unknown. Oil on canvas, $18'' \times 23\frac{1}{2}''$. Additional changes to both the hongs and fences are shown here. By 1810, the fences to the left are gone, and the heavy fences in front of the hongs between Old China Street and Hog Lane have been erected. Several other small but important changes have taken place: Chung Qua's hong, to the left of Old China Street, has a first-floor addition with a porch roof on the second floor, and the old English hong (second to the left from Hog Lane) has been given a new front with Palladian windows and a pediment. *Photograph courtesy Childs Gallery.*

8. Canton, after 1810. Artist unknown. Oil on canvas, 18″ × 23½″. Small but subtle differences show in the period between 1810 and 1820. Chung Qua's hong has lost its second-floor porch roof, and all three windows on the second floor are full length. The building between the British East India Company and the Dutch hong is shown clearly remodeled to a Palladian facade with a pediment. This was done sometime after 1810, when the East India Company bought the land and remodeled the building. *Peabody Museum, Salem.*

9. Canton, night of the fire, November, 1822. Master of Fire of 1822. Oil on canvas, 7″ × 11½″. By this time still another subtle change had taken place: the American hong has been remodeled and the extensive porches removed. The painting also clearly represents the earlier renovation of the building between the British East India Company and the Dutch hong, where the fire began. The fences in front of the center block of hongs burned in this fire, never to be rebuilt. An interesting note to observe in Illus. 4–9 is that the paintings are compositionally similar, with the same arrangement of vessels in the foreground, but minute changes in architecture recorded in detail. This is an insight into the compositional repetition of port views, but it also illustrates the detailed recording within the compositions of small changes which took place along the waterfront. *Photograph courtesy Childs Gallery.*

10. Canton, before 1832. Artist unknown. Oil on canvas, 18″ × 23½″. The period after the rebuilding of the hongs until 1832 is more confusing, since few significant changes were made. The return of the French took place in 1832, hence their flag becomes a convenient dating device. By 1828 there was still no enclosure in front of the American hong, other than a small fence close to the front of the building. The East India Company was rebuilt with heavy first-floor arches (squared off at the top for the first few years and then rounded) and a square pediment was put on the Old English hong, second from the left of Hog Lane. Chung Qua's hong, to the left of Old China Street, was totally rebuilt, and a pagoda was added to the roof. *Photograph courtesy Childs Gallery.*

11. Canton, after 1832. Artist unknown. Gouache on paper, 7″ × 11″. The French flag flying confirms the painting's date is after 1832. Few changes other than the removal of Chung Qua's pagoda are seen between 1828 and 1833. Shortly after this, the area in front of the central hongs was landscaped with parklike plantings and fenced nearer the water. Another notable addition is a higher roof with a balustrade behind the East India Company hong, no longer occupied by the official company after 1834. *Private Collection.*

12., 13. Two views of the area in front of the hongs, circa 1835. Artist unknown. Oil on canvas, 18½″ × 28½″ each. *Peabody Museum, Salem.*

14. Canton, circa 1841. Artist unknown. Sepia ink on paper, 12½″ × 21″. Canton was evacuated by the Westerners in 1841, and was soon to be looted and burned by the Chinese. The elaborate staircase and balcony on the East India Company hong are very much in evidence. The flags have been removed in this painting, confirming the fact the area is unoccupied. *Peabody Museum, Salem.*

15. Canton, circa 1844. Lam Qua studio. Oil on canvas, 11½″ × 22″. The British, Dutch and Creek hongs (the latter so called for its relationship to the creek which ran through the area), all to the right of Hog Lane, were looted and gutted in May of 1841. The area, minus the factories after the fire, is seen clearly in this rare painting. *Museum of the American China Trade.*

16., 17. Two views of Canton, 1847–1856. Artist unknown. Oil on canvas, 17″ × 30$\frac{1}{2}$″ each. Both these views show Canton with the addition of the church and the new buildings on the now-crowded waterfront. Shortly after the fire, two imposing edifices were erected on the site of the old factories, similar in style to the architecture of Western buildings at Shanghai and Hong Kong. The land for a church in front of these buildings at the end of Hog Lane was purchased in May, 1847, and the church was built shortly thereafter. Jardine Matheson and Augustine Heard occupied the building on the site of the old Dutch and Creek factories and flew a Danish flag, since a member of Matheson's firm was the Danish consul. 16. *Photograph courtesy Childs Gallery.* 17. *Private Collection.*

18. Canton, before 1856. Tingqua. Gouache on paper, 10$\frac{1}{2}$″ × 13$\frac{7}{8}$″. An interesting side view of the church, undoubtedly executed from the veranda of a projecting building, shows the fully developed park in front of the hongs that was started with the Canton Indemnity Fund in the mid-1840's. *Peabody Museum, Salem.*

19. Canton, 1856. Sunqua. Oil on canvas, 17″ × 29$\frac{1}{2}$″. By 1856 all this area was to be levelled – and never rebuilt – by the incredible fire shown in the Sunqua painting. Few architectural or landscape changes of any significance took place after the erection of the church and before the disastrous fire. *Peabody Museum, Salem.*

Bibliographical Note

There are many, many sources of information about the China trade, some more readily accessible than others. This is a selective list of the sources that proved most valuable in the author's research; they may prove helpful to others working in the field.

The China Trade

Chinese Repository, Volumes I–XX, 1833–1851.

The Chinese Traveller, Containing a Geographical, Commercial, and Political History of China. London: Braddon and Brodderice, c. 1800.

Davis, John Francis, *The Chinese: A General Description of the Empire of China and Its Inhabitants,* 2 volumes. New York: Harper & Brothers, 1836.

"The Letters of Sullivan Dorr," ed. by Howard Corning, in the *Proceedings of the Massachusetts Historical Society,* Vol. LXVII, 1945.

Forbes, Robert Bennet, *Personal Reminiscences,* 2nd. ed., revised. Boston: Little, Brown, 1882.

Gray, James, *Walks in the Streets of Canton.* London: 1875.

Hickey, William, *Memoirs 1745–1809,* 4 volumes. London: Hurst and Blackett, 1925.

Hunter, William C., *The Fan Kwae in Canton before the Treaty Days.* London: Kegan Paul, Trench & Co., 1882.

———., *Bits of Old China.* London: Kegan Paul, Trench & Co., 1885.

Orange, James, *The Chater Collection.* London: Thornton Butterworth, 1924.

Rhode Island Historical Society, manuscript collection, for Sullivan Dorr, Edward Carrington and William Townsend.

Shreve, Benjamin, papers, for the voyages to China from 1815 to 1822. Peabody Museum, Salem, Massachusetts.

Tiffany, Osmond, Jr., *The Canton Chinese, or the American's Sojourn in the Celestial Empire.* Boston and Cambridge: James Monroe and Co., 1849.

Tilden, Bryant, papers, concerning living in China. Peabody Museum, Salem, Massachusetts.

The Paintings

Brewington, M. V. and Dorothy, "Marine Paintings and Drawings in the Peabody Museum." Salem, Mass., 1968.

Hong Kong City Art Gallery: "Catalogue of Chinnery Exhibition," 1965.
"Chinnery & Other Artists of the Chinese Scene." Peabody Museum, Salem, Mass., 1967.
Exhibition records of the Boston Athenaeum, Pennsylvania Academy of Fine Arts, Philadelphia, The Apollo Association, New York, and the American Art Union, New York.
"Old Nick" [Paul Émile Daurand Forgues], *La Chine Ouverte.* Paris: H. Fournier, 1845.
Gardiner, Albert Ten Eyck, "Cantonese Chinnerys: Portraits of How-Qua and Other China Trade Painters," *The Art Quarterly,* Winter, 1953.
Photograph files of the Peabody Museum, Salem, Massachusetts.
Salis, William Fane de, *Reminiscences of Travel in China and India in 1848.* London: Waterlow and Sons, 1892.
Vollée, M. La, in *L'Artiste: Revue de Paris,* 1849. In translation in *The Bulletin of the American Art Union,* 1850.

The Objects

Antiques Magazine, 1926–1972.
"Catalogue of Canton Fans, Grass Cloths . . . from the Ship *Howard,* from Canton . . . at auction . . . June 5th, 1832." By Mills Brothers, & Co., New York.
"The China Trade and Its Influences," catalogue of the exhibition held at the Metropolitan Museum of Art, New York, 1941.
Connoisseur Magazine, selected articles, particularly those on silver, November, 1965, and July, 1972.
Crossman, Carl L., "A Catalogue of China Trade Paintings and Objects." Peabody Museum, Salem, Massachusetts, 1970.
Records of the East India Marine Society, and the catalogue of the collections in the Peabody Museum, Salem, Massachusetts.
Jenyns, Soame, and Jourdain, Margaret, *Chinese Export Art of the 18th Century.* Middlesex, England: Spring Books, 1967.
Los Angeles County Museum, "American Ships in the China Trade," *Art Bulletin,* Vol. 7, No. 1, 1955.
Accession records of the Metropolitan Museum of Art, New York.
Collections of the Museum of the American China Trade, Milton, Massachusetts.
John Robinson scrapbook, Peabody Museum, Salem, Massachusetts.
Accession records of the Henry Francis du Pont Winterthur Museum, Winterthur, Delaware.
"A Catalogue of the Imperial Maritime Customs Collection," at the United States International Exhibition, Philadelphia, 1876. Shanghai, 1876.

Sources and Acknowledgments

Every author is indebted to a great number of people for cooperation in research and the putting together of a book, but I feel particularly indebted to those people who have presented so many new ideas, patiently helped to find sources and new material and have listened to my theories over the past few years.

Ernest Dodge, the Director of the Peabody Museum, has continually encouraged me in my research and he sponsored the exhibitions of China Trade Porcelains and China Trade Paintings and Objects—the catalogues for which were the inspiration for this book. The entire staff of the Peabody Museum has worked with me on this project, and I particularly wish to thank Mr. Markham W. Sexton for his fine photographs of the museum objects; Mrs. Margene Bishop for her overseeing of the orders; and Mr. Anthony A. Winfisky and Mrs. Lucy B. Batchelder for the hours they spent taking things out of storage and off exhibition for photography. Mrs. Barbara B. Edkins spent a great deal of her valuable time helping me find books and manuscript sources in the museum's Phillips Library.

Francis B. Lothrop, a trustee of the Peabody Museum and an expert on George Chinnery, helped me immensely on the Chinnery-Lam Qua chapter and found paintings and sources hitherto unpublished. He has generously turned over to me all his notes on the Chinese painters; it was he who found the all-important Meares reference to Spoilum, which conclusively identified that painter. Philip C. F. Smith of the Peabody Museum staff sat with me for days and diligently drew upon the files and his own knowledge of voyages, Salem traders, and the China trade in Salem, an invaluable aid to the historical background of the trade.

The final identification of Spoilum could not have been made without the initial discoveries of Miss Helen Sanger of the Frick Art Reference Library, who, like me, had been fascinated with this painter for several years.

She was very kind in sharing with me so much of her original research. Frank Goodyear, formerly of the Rhode Island Historical Society, provided a tremendous amount of information on that institution's collections and allowed me to reproduce his recent discovery of the China trade paintings of the Providence Marine certificate.

My especial thanks to Mr. Richard Nylander, of the Society for the Preservation of New England Antiquities, for making it possible for me to visit the Society's houses to study the furnishings and collections. Miss Sherry Fowbler, of the Henry Francis du Pont Winterthur Museum, provided excellent information on the China trade material in that museum, and Mr. Gordon Saltar patiently did the wood analysis on all those questionable pieces of Federal furniture which we had thought to be Chinese. Mr. H. A. Crosby Forbes, of the Museum of the American China Trade, and Mr. Herbert Gebelein both gave me valuable information on China trade silver. The forthcoming book from the China Trade Museum should be the definitive book on this subject for years.

I particularly wish to thank my close friend, Mr. Richard Mills of Exeter, New Hampshire, for having ferreted out so many wonderful objects of the China trade over the past few years, and for finding books and historical references that were impossible to locate under other circumstances. Miss Alice Winchester is to be thanked, and congratulated, for having thought of distinguishing between the styles of the different port artists, and for encouraging me to undertake this endeavor years ago.

I am deeply indebted to my staff at the Childs Gallery for so patiently working with me, and running the gallery while I researched and worked on the manuscript. Ms. Angela Noel arranged for permissions, appointments and photographs, and took care of overwhelming details. My business partner, D. Roger Howlett, receives my undying gratitude for photographing over a hundred illustrations for the book, reading and proofing the manuscript at every draft, reading and correcting the galleys, and providing brilliant insights into the relationships of the paintings and the artists. Without his aid this book could not have been finished.

The following institutions and individuals also provided invaluable assistance:

Abby Aldrich Rockefeller Collection, Williamsburg, Virginia; The British Museum, London, England; Childs Gallery, Boston, Massachusetts; Essex Institute, Salem, Massachusetts; Frick Art Reference Library, New York City; Gebelein Silversmiths, Boston, Massachusetts; Gore Place, Waltham, Massachusetts; Henry Francis du Pont Winterthur Museum, Winterthur, Delaware; Historical Society of Pennsylvania, Philadelphia, Pennsylvania; Lynn Historical Society, Lynn, Massachusetts; Manchester Historical Society, Manchester, Massachusetts; Maryland Historical Society, Baltimore, Maryland; Metropolitan Museum of Art, New York City; Museum of the American China Trade, Milton, Massachusetts; Museum of Fine Arts, Boston, Massachusetts; Mystic Seaport, Mystic, Connecticut; New Haven Colony Historical Society, New Haven, Connecticut; New-York Historical Society, New York City; Philadelphia Maritime Museum, Philadelphia, Pennsylvania; Philadelphia Museum of Art, Philadelphia, Pennsylvania; Rhode Island Historical Society, Providence, Rhode Island; Society for the Preservation of New England Antiquities, Boston, Massachusetts; Yale University Art Gallery, New Haven, Connecticut; Yale University Medical Library, New Haven, Connecticut.

J. Sanger Atwill; Edgar M. Bingham, Jr., Shreve Crump and Low; Ronald Bourgeault; David Brubaker; Philip Budlong, Mystic Seaport; Mrs. John M. Bullard; Joseph T. Butler; Miss Marie Kalat; Frank Carpenter; Mrs. H. Vose Carr; Charles D. Childs; Mrs. Lester F. Crossman; Richard Faber; Jonathan Fairbanks; Henry Fearon; Mrs. Stephen Ferguson, Rhode Island Historical Society; Mrs. H. H. Gibson, Pierce Nichols House, Salem; Mr. Benjamin Ginsberg; Miss Mary Glaze, Metropolitan Museum; David Good; Roland D. Grimm; Ferenc Gyorgyey, Yale University Medical Library; J. Welles Henderson; Mrs. Judith Coolidge Hughes; Julius Jensen III; Miss Devorah Kanter, *American Heritage;* George Lewis, Jr.; Mr. and Mrs. Bertram K. Little; David B. Little, Essex Institute; Mrs. Ronald T. Lyman, Jr.; Mrs. Jean Y. Mills; Paul Molitor; Mrs. Richard Nylander; Miss Esther Oldham; Mr. and Mrs. Andrew Oliver; William B. Osgood; Mrs. Laurence Polson, Gore Place; Sir Lindsay Ride, Hong Kong; John Ricketson; Miss Caroline Rollins, Yale University Art Gallery; the late Mrs. E. J. L. Ropes; Edward J. L. Ropes; Miss Beatrix Rumford; Mrs. William H. Shreve; Samuel Sokobin; Theodore M. Stebbins, Jr.; Samuel Stokes; Henry S. Streeter; Dr. William E. Strole; Miss Juliette Tomlinson; S. Morton Vose.

Index

Names of ships appear in italics; titles of paintings are indicated by quotation marks.
Page numbers in italics refer to illustrations.